*Let Them Speak for Themselves*

WOMEN IN THE AMERICAN WEST

*1849-1900*

# Let Them Speak for Themselves

## WOMEN IN THE AMERICAN WEST

### 1849-1900

Edited and with an introduction by

CHRISTIANE FISCHER

*Archon Books    1977*

*Library of Congress Cataloging in Publication Data*

Main entry under title:

Let them speak for themselves

    Bibliography: p.
    Includes index.
    CONTENTS: Life in mining camps and mining towns:
Behrins, H. F. Reminiscences of California in 1861. Ballou, M.
"I hear the hogs in my kitchen." Mansur, A. Ms. letters to her
sister, 1852-1854. Haskell, R. "A literate woman in the mines."
[etc.]
    1. Women—The West—Biography. 2. The West—His-
tory—Addresses, essays, lectures. I. Fischer, Christiane, 1947-
HQ1410.L39 1977     301.41'2'0978     77-5094
ISBN 0-208-01645-7

*Second printing 1977*

© The Shoe String Press Inc 1977
First published 1977 as an Archon Book,
an imprint of The Shoe String Press Inc,
Hamden, Connecticut 06514

*Printed in the United States of America*

# Contents

ACKNOWLEDGEMENTS                                                9

INTRODUCTION                                                    11

TIMES AND PLACES DESCRIBED IN THE EXCERPTS                      23


PART 1: LIFE IN MINING CAMPS AND MINING TOWNS

Harriet F. Behrins. *Reminiscences of California in 1851.*     27
    (n.p., 1900 ?)
Mary Ballou. *"I Hear the Hogs in My Kitchen": A*             42
    *Woman's View of the Gold Rush.* ed. Archi-
    bald Hanna. (New Haven. Yale University
    Press, printed for Frederick W. Beinecke),
    1962.
Abby Mansur. *MS Letters Written to Her Sister, 1852-*        48
    *1854,* Horseshoe Bar, Miner's Ravine, Califor-
    nia. Beinecke Library, Yale University.
Rachell Haskell. "A Literate Woman in the Mines: the          58
    Diary of Rachel Haskell." ed. Richard G.
    Lillard, *The Mississippi Valley Historical Re-*
    *view,* vol. xxi, n° 1 (June 1944), 81-98.

*Let Them Speak for Themselves*

PART 2: LIFE ON FARMS AND RANCHES

Virginia Wilcox Ivins. *Pen Pictures of Early Western*     75
*Days.* (Keokuk? 1905)
Henria Packer Compton. *Mary Murdock Compton.*     83
(Privately Published)
Mrs. C.A. Teeples. "The First Pioneers of the Gila     94
Valley," *Arizona Historical Review*, vol. 1, n°
4 (January 1929), 74-78.
Mary Ann Hafen. *Memories of a Handcart Pioneer,*     101
with some account of frontier life in Utah and
Nevada. (Denver, Colorado: privately
printed for her descendants), 1938.

PART 3: ARMY WIVES

Mrs. Orsemus Bronson Boyd. *Cavalry Life in Tent and*     111
*Field.* (New York: J. Selwin Tait & Sons),
1894.
Ellen McGowan Biddle. *Reminiscences of a Soldier's*     124
*Wife.* (Philadelphia: J.B. Lippincott Co.),
1907.
Martha Summerhayes. *Vanished Arizona.* (Phila-     137
delphia: J.B. Lippincott Co.), 1908.

PART 4: WORKING WOMEN

Luzena Stanley Wilson. *Luzena Stanley Wilson, '49er.*     151
Memories recalled years later for her daugh-
ter Correnah Wilson Wright. (Mills College,
California: The Eucalyptus Press), 1937.
Mrs. Caroline N. Churchill. *Active Footsteps.* (Color-     166
ado Springs: Mrs. C.N. Churchill Printer),
1909.

## Contents

Mary McNair Mathews. *Ten Years in Nevada, or, Life*     177
*on the Pacific Coast.* (Buffalo: Baker, Jones &
Co.), 1880.

Helen Doyle. *A Child Went Forth: the Autobiography*     193
*of Dr. Helen MacKnight.* (New York: Gotham
House), 1934.


PART 5: LIFE IN THE GROWING CITIES

Mrs. Nina Churchman Larowe. *An Account of My*     207
*Life's Journey so far: its Prosperity, its Adver-*
*sity, its Sunshine and its Clouds.* (Portland:
Kilham Stationery and Printing Co.), 1917?

Mrs. Mary E. Ackley. *Crossing the Plains and Early*     229
*Days in California: Memories of Girlhood in*
*California's Golden Age.* (Privately Printed
for the Author), 1928.

Isabelle Saxon. *Five Years within the Golden Gate.*     237
(London: Chapman & Hall), 1868.


PART 6: CHILDHOOD AND ADOLESCENCE IN THE WEST

Sarah Bixby-Smith. *Adobe Days.* (Cedar Rapids, Iowa:     247
The Torch Press), 1925.

Sarah Winnemucca Hopkins. *Life among the Piutes,*     260
*their wrongs and claims.* ed. Mrs. Horace
Mann (Boston: for sale by Cupples, Upham &
Co., G.P. Putnam's Sons, New York, and by
the author), 1883.

Edith White. *Memories of Pioneer Childhood and*     271
*Youth in French Corral and North San Juan,*
*Nevada County, California.* With a brief
narrative of later life, told by Edith White,
emigrant of 1859, to Linnie Marsh Wolfe, 1936.

[7]

*Let Them Speak for Themselves*

Edith Stratton Kitt. *Pioneering in Arizona: the Reminis-*      283
*cences of Emerson Oliver Stratton and Edith*
*Stratton Kitt.* ed. John Carroll Alexander
(Tucson: Arizona Pioneers' Historical Society), 1964.


PART 7: LIFE IN THE WEST AS SEEN THROUGH
THE EYES OF TRAVELLERS


Mrs. D.B. Bates. *Incidents on Land and Water; or, Four*      301
*Years on the Pacific Coast.* (Boston: E.O.
Libbey & Co.), 1858.
Myriam F. Leslie. *California: A Pleasure Trip from*      313
*Gotham to the Golden Gate.* (New York:
G.W. Carleton & Co., Publishers), 1877.
Emma Hildreth Adams. *To and Fro, Up and Down in*      326
*Southern California, Oregon, and Wash-*
*ington Territory, with Sketches in Arizona,*
*New Mexico and British Columbia.* (Cin-
cinnati, Chicago, St. Louis: Cranston &
Stowe), 1888.


REFERENCES      333
FURTHER READING      335

[8]

# Acknowledgements

This book was started as I was doing research in the United States on a Fulbright-Hays Grant in 1975. I would like to thank in particular Mr. Lucien Jambrun, the Director of the Program in France, for his help and support. I am grateful to Professor Guy Bourquin, the Chairman of the English Department of the University of Nancy, France, and to my colleagues there, for making extensive stays in the United States possible.

I wish to acknowledge the courtesy and assistance of the staff of the Beinecke Library of Yale University, and of the Bancroft Library at Berkeley. I am particularly indebted to Archibald Hanna, the Curator of the Western Americana collection in Beinecke, who has offered valuable suggestions regarding the selection of the writings presented here, has made uncatalogued manuscripts available to me, and has always done everything in his power to help me. I would also like to express my thanks to Joan Hofmann, of the staff, who typed the Abby Mansur manuscript and whose tireless devotion has made my work much easier and much more pleasant.

I am deeply grateful to Susan Steinberg, of the Sterling Memorial Library of Yale University, for reading the introduction and helping me improve the style, to James Thorpe III, of the Shoe String Press, who has contributed many pertinent criticisms, and to Professor Marianne Debouzy, of the University of Paris VIII, for her guidance.

My warmest thanks go to Professor Howard Lamar of Yale University, whose work has been a constant source of inspiration and whose advice and encouragement in the past years have meant so much to me, and to Professor Charles Davis, of Yale University, for his sustained interest in my work and for his unfailing kindness.

CHRISTIANE FISCHER

# Introduction

Among recent developments in the study of history, one of the most fascinating is the tendency to look at the daily lives of those ordinary people who laid the foundations upon which great undertakings and achievements were erected. One of the leading scholars of the American West, Howard Lamar, has said: "the story of the frontier is the story of ordinary people dealing with large problems. They overcame the problems and that is a symbol that ordinary man can cope with life. And it further is an example that this country was developed by small, ordinary men, and not by supermen."[1] As scholars increasingly begin to use the massive resources which are in fact available for the study of the American West and its social history, a fair number of myths and theories will have to be reevaluated. One of these is the tendency to imagine that the frontier, and the West, were inhabited largely if not exclusively by men. (There are also, of course, many other versions of the West, some of which began before the advent of Hollywood and television; such commercial *folklorique* ventures are well outside the scope of this book.)

One wants to know about the real lives of the real people who went West. One wants to delve more deeply into their stories, to discover who they were, what their aspirations were. One wants to know what they thought about their new homes, and what they thought about the lives (and friends and family) they had left behind. One wants to know how they coped, how they failed, how some of them succeeded, and what they thought about themselves.

[11]

## Let Them Speak for Themselves

This book will focus entirely on the women who went west. Their story is very largely unknown, and what we know of it tends to come through filters which are for the most part ignorant, patronizing, or blatantly commercial and self-serving. The women here will speak for themselves. Some of them are, by our standards, just semiliterate. Some of them write very well indeed.

As the writings in this collection are generally personal, and sometimes opinionated, one will want to read a fair number of them before drawing conclusions. This book will not try to argue the case for any general ideas concerning the experiences of women in the West, nor will it present any particular ideology; it will, rather, offer the opportunity for a fairly wide variety of women to tell you what life on the frontier and in the American West was like in the second half of the nineteenth century.

The women whose writings have been selected here came from many different American states; three of them came from Europe: one from Switzerland, one from Ireland, and one from England; finally, one was an Indian from the Piute tribe. They represent a wide range of backgrounds and conditions. Most of them came from families of average means and moved West because their fathers or their husbands wanted to earn a better living. Their feelings as they left were extremely varied and ranged from a state of near prostration to the wildest enthusiasm. Many of them did not show any particular interest in the distant place they were heading toward and tended to look backwards: for them, leaving meant being torn from the places in which they had taken root and parting from relatives to whom they felt closely linked. Among the women represented here, very few had participated in the decision to go West. And even fewer could act upon their husbands or their fathers once they had chosen a course of action.

The conditions in the West elicited a variety of responses. The great majority of the women who went there in the early years of the development nearly lost heart upon seeing the way things were. Ray A. Billington has summarized the immigrants' particular brand of "difficulte d'être" in the following manner: "To some degree all pioneers, even those who succeeded most rapidly, felt a sense of social deprivation, based on their failure to establish comforting social relationships with their neighbors, the absence

[12]

of defined social norms, and the failure of the new land to meet their unrealistic expectations."[2] A period of adaptation was necessary as conditions were bound to be different from those previously known, and also from those people imagined they would find. Some recurrent themes in the writings of women who experienced life in the West in the early stages of the development are loneliness, insecurity, anxiety, homesickness, and dismay at the primitive conditions. The way in which they adjusted seemed to depend much on the kind of life they had known before their departure; the more "genteel" their background and education, the more repelled they were by their new environment. The nature of the attachments they had formed in their earlier places of residence also mattered much; some of them could not accept the severance of close family ties which going West entailed.

If I had to point out one single factor which made the adaptation of women in the West so difficult, I would say that it was the prevalent ideology centering on women's place in the home. In so many of the writings by pioneer women that I have read, one sees uprooted people clinging in such a pathetic way to their former homes. As they went away, leaving some of their relatives and their friends behind, they found themselves in totally new surroundings, were deprived of the protective environment in which their lives had been framed, and felt bereft. One has the constant sense that moving West for them did not mean that a new dimension was given to their lives or that new horizons were opened to them: most of them experienced basically a great sense of loss.

Many women's constant concern with "civilization" also grew from their dominant desire to reconstruct around them the meaningful environment that the open spaces of the West could not replace.[3] For they had never been told to look for adventure, excitement, freedom; the essential things in life, for many of them, were sentimental relationships with other people, and cultural, social, and religious activities. In many of the writings selected here, the fundamental contrast between primitive conditions and civilized life is constantly referred to; the most articulate authors explore it in depth.[4]

While some women tended to look backwards and to hang on to objects which reminded them of former homes, others tried to

[13]

see the positive aspects of their new situation and to immerse themselves in the present in order to make use of the opportunities which could help them improve their situation. The great majority of the women presented here had difficulties adjusting in the beginning, but gradually became used to the conditions; a few managed to turn them to their advantage.

The way in which these women coped with their problems depended greatly upon their specific circumstances, and this is why testimonies by women in the same basic situation have been grouped together in this book. The various reactions which can be found within each section show the types of behavior that the new conditions brought out in these women, and the way in which their personal backgrounds influenced their responses. Some were fascinated by the beauty of the landscape, loved the open spaces, and were ever ready for exploration. Some found solace in books, music, or painting and tried to create within their homes a culturally satisfying atmosphere. Some were sustained by the hope of visits or outings. A few tried to set up businesses of their own and devoted all their efforts to making a success of their enterprises. And then there were those who were totally absorbed by the chores in their households and were at a loss to find something to brighten their days; in many instances the dominant problem was isolation, which served to reveal the barrenness of their lives. The basic pattern in many writings by women is one of attraction and repulsion for their new conditions of life, and the various shapes which this constant tension assumed is one of the fascinating aspects of the study of women's responses to the West.

Men generally showed a much greater readiness in adjusting to the new environment. They were much freer to explore the world around them, to participate in the business schemes which were set up daily, and to choose among the various kinds of amusements. The lives of most of the women presented here were circumscribed by their homes. Some made comparisons with their husbands' possibilities and envied the greater variety in the activities they had access to.

Women, generally, did not seem to expect much from their husbands' company, nor from their understanding. A theme which recurs in many of their writings is the importance given to female companionship; it appeared either in the form of a longing

[14]

for visits with other women, or in the expression of the great pleasure they found in those. There seemed to exist a common bond among members of the female sex, which came perhaps from the consciousness of the basic similarity in their fate. Burdens were lighter if they could be shared with other women. In some of the testimonies selected here, women's contributions are stressed specifically as they rarely merge with those of men. Besides, most of the women have a tendency to speak in their own name, even when they describe joint undertakings with their husbands, whom they only occasionally bring into their narratives.

The reverse is true too: many autobiographical accounts left by men never mention women, or if they do, it is only in passing. The themes treated are very different too. While men's testimonies often center on political and municipal events, business schemes and economic conditions, and general evaluations of manners and morals, the narratives left by women usually concentrate on the many problems of daily life and on individual and specific situations, and these have preserved many minute items that men often overlooked. Writings by women are generally close to the basic elements and rituals of life, and only occasionally rise to the general; they present the stuff that daily life is made of. They seem to bring reality within reach and give it such a concrete aspect that one can almost feel it.

Women's records of their experiences in the West exist in many forms: diaries, notes written in scrapbooks, letters sent to friends and relatives, memoirs, oral narratives put down into writing by another person. The testimonies selected here are all from personal narratives by women and are expressed in their own words. No attempt has been made to change the spelling or the punctuation, as the very individualistic way in which these are used in some writings give a distinct flavor. (The great majority were not intended for publication.) Among them, the most vital and compelling are those in which events were recorded at the time they happened; often, the process of putting these down into writing acted as a sort of outlet for pent-up feelings and perhaps gave the writers strength to deal with the many problems in their lives. Generally speaking, the question of truthfulness and sincerity is less acute than with books written for the public; many of the women presented here made no attempt to appear different from what they were. This is not to say, however, that their testimonies should be taken at their face value. They often reflect widely different personalities and offer different perspectives on matters and situations which were often basically the same for many of them.

What changed widely from one woman to the next were the external elements which made up the framework in which their lives unfolded. The physical environment, the climatic conditions and the economic resources were not at all the same in the areas they described and gave rise to different patterns of life. All the narratives selected here except for one are set in California, Nevada, or Arizona, three adjoining territories which presented a great diversity of conditions.[5] In California the economy was based at first on the extraction of precious metals and branched out into many other directions. The population was a "motley crowd,"[6] the immigrants coming from many different places and with particular traits and customs. The basic contrast was between urban and rural modes of living, and as the state developed progress brought great changes in the aspect of society. Life, which had once been close to nature and to the hard core of reality, became more sophisticated and refined, and sometimes artificial: instead of being a serious task, it took on frivolous aspects. A new gloss covered everything and a greater distance was established from the basic necessities of life. A chronological arrangement has been adopted within each of the sections to make the changes more apparent; a list of the times and places described has also been provided to make it easier to assemble quickly the texts concerning each of the three regions.

An important issue in California was the state of morality; differing views are offered in the various accounts, and an effort has been made to include some data on an aspect of life which was not discussed much in writings: prostitution. A sense of the emergence of distinct social classes can also be felt while going through the selections concerning California. Whereas the earlier narratives stress the indiscriminate aspect of society and the fact that exterior appearances revealed nothing about people's status, it is obvious from the later writings that the influx of money had created distinctions and extremely different life-styles, that bar-

[16]

riers among the various classes were being erected, and that the progress of civilization also meant the stratification of society.

In Nevada, specific problems were created by the wasteland aspect of the environment and the isolation of the settlements. Many of the women who lived there commented upon these two aspects and on the melancholy and depressing character life sometimes assumed. Much misery and unhappiness existed: "Men and women, the young and the old, and particularly the foreign-born resorted to self-destruction in such numbers that Nevada's suicide rate rose to more than twice that of the national average."[7] The incredibly fast economic development created a society in which the spectrum of conditions was extremely broad: total deprivation coexisted with fabulous wealth. The pace of life was fast, and in the cities people searched frantically for intense pleasures and excitement. There was a striking absence of stability: many immigrants had no intention of staying permanently, so that the concern was not with building long-lasting structures, but with making the best use of immediate opportunities. Speculation was very much a part of life in the towns, and schemes were constantly being devised to make quick profits. The insecurity owing to the frequent occurrence of fires and the uncertainty resulting from the sudden turns of fortune (one could get rich one day and lose everything the next) created a particular atmosphere. Personal relationships tended to lack stability too: certain towns such as Dayton had a reputation for easy divorce. The economic development in general had a jagged aspect, with a pattern of mining excitements which subsequently died down.

The situation in Arizona stood in total contrast to that in California and Nevada. The development was slow, and conditions remained primitive until the beginning of the twentieth century:

> Both [New Mexico and Arizona] were held back by a highly adverse combination of hostile Indians, poor transportation and a geographic environment made harsh by aridity and topography, and mineral resources in which complex and refractory ores were too prevalent for quick exploitation on an isolated frontier.[8]

Most of the women who left records of their experiences in Arizona dwelt at length on the rough aspect of life, the lack of conveniences, the hard work, the isolation of the settlements. Many women felt totally alienated in such uncongenial surroundings. Life on the frontier offered compensations: rowdy entertainments, a gregarious atmosphere in the camps, freedom from constraints. But these were available to men only. Women were forced to lead very restricted lives; the violence and danger which were part of daily life made them prisoners in their homes. As the communities started growing, conditions improved, and women gradually began to emerge toward the end of the century.

The adaptation of women depended much on the area in which they found themselves. Those who had to live in mining camps in the first years of the development usually had extremely negative feelings. As they gradually found ways of coping with the situation, and as the years went by, they began finding life more tolerable. Many documents have been printed on life in the mines; the best known from a feminine pen is probably Dame Shirley's *Letters*. The texts reproduced here are different, perhaps, because they were written by women who were extremely close to the problems they described and could achieve no distance between themselves and conditions in the mines. They were part of this life, and their reactions are sometimes very intense. The differences in their status provide grounds for comparisons among the ways in which they organized their lives.

Women who lived on farms or ranches also had to deal with elementary problems in the beginning. But their situation was different, for they were part of a self-sufficient unit. When a family rose to prosperity, women were fully conscious of the importance of their contribution and derived great satisfaction from it.[9] Life had its hard aspects there too; tasks were distributed according to sex, and men and women frequently led separate lives in the daytime. Isolation was also a problem, as the settlements were distant from one another. As communities emerged, women had new avenues of participation; in some of the narratives selected here, their contribution in the religious, social, and cultural fields, as well as their devotion to others and their charitable undertakings, are stressed. They were at the basis of development, and their work was as essential as that of the men.

The narratives of women who married into the army and followed their husbands West have many common characteristics.

[18]

*Introduction*

Their authors were often cultivated women, who explored their problems in depth and could establish a distance between themselves and their experiences. The excerpts published here show a variety of responses to similar situations. One trait which they have in common is that husbands play an important part in the narratives. The insights they provide into personal relationships give a fascinating dimension. They also offer a great wealth of literary expressions and styles.

The shape women's lives assumed depended much on the amount of independence they could achieve. Married women who had jobs often had considerable control over their lives. In the early years, it was easy for women to find paid work which they could do beside keeping their own houses. The wages they could command were high; there are allusions to this aspect of the situation in many of the excerpts in this book. As conditions became more settled, however, traditional ideas were reinstated, and married women had to care exclusively for their own homes. Women who were on their own generally had to find some way of supporting themselves, as the custom of harboring dependent relatives gradually disappeared. The problems working women had to face and their difficult emergence in the professions are given detailed treatment in the books excerpted here.

Information on life in the growing cities can be gleaned from narratives in each of the sections. Part 5 has been devoted to this theme so that special aspects could be included, in particular descriptions of the situation of women from the upper classes and information on the "sophisticated" tones of urban life. An attempt has also been made to show the emergence of small towns and the participation of the inhabitants in the rise to prosperity; this aspect can be further documented from material in the other sections.

An interesting contrast is provided by the memoirs of women who discovered the West as children or young girls, or who were born there. They generally looked back to that time of their life with great pleasure and tell with much zest of the freedom, the fascinating discoveries, the joys of life close to nature. Having no experience of a different life, they were not constantly making comparisons and regretting past conditions. Whereas many of the testimonies written by women who moved to the western states in their mature life and had to adjust to primitive conditions would constitute excellent material for a study of the various forms human unhappiness can take, the accounts of childhoods spent in the West are refreshing and full of joy.[10] This results partly from the nostalgia with which many human beings come to their youths. It also shows how the color of one's testimony depends on the time it was written: generally speaking the diaries and letters presented here are much starker than the reminiscences. Another element which must be taken into consideration is the intention the writer had in mind: Sarah Hopkins, who wanted to present a certain view of reality to the readers, has painted an idyllic picture of the Piutes' life in Nevada which calls to mind all the mythical projections which presented the West as the new Garden of Eden. It has been included here primarily because it is a feminine view of the Indian experience. It provides some information on the principles which governed the education of Indian children, and in a way one can see a form of the process of socialization emerge: but here the aim was to enclose the children within the tribe. In the other narratives one can see glimpses of this process at work, as when mothers are shown trying to prepare their daughters for their future roles in society and to mold them into the feminine pattern.

The last section presents views on the West from people who travelled around and never took root there. The aim here has been to provide information on unusual topics or provocative comments on life in the areas visited.

The general intention which has guided the selection has been to offer a wide variety of feminine responses to conditions in California, Nevada and Arizona in the second half of the nineteenth century, to open up as many avenues as possible, and to show that women's lives assumed many different shapes. As there is a huge amount of material to choose from, well-known books have been omitted in favor of narratives which have not had a wide circulation.

It seems to me that none of the women in this selection corresponds to any of the simplistic images which have been devised of women in the West; it would be hard to see any of them as the subdued woman in the sun-bonnet, for instance. Although most of them were devoted to their husbands or fathers and had to abide by their decisions, few could be described as submissive; there is a striking undercurrent of rebellion in several of the narratives. There were a number of things which they found hard to accept, and they were not prepared to pretend that they were content. Quite a few emerge as strong-willed women who knew what they wanted and found some means of obtaining it. In comparison, Sarah Royce appears as a very tame and traditional woman, which does not make her any less interesting, however.

All the women included here had rich and complex personalities. An attempt has been made in the prefaces to each of the excerpts to provide the basic biographical details (when they were available) and to place the passages within the context of the whole narrative. Each of the writings, furthermore, can make a claim to originality, as each of these women had a particular way of expressing herself, which depended on her level of literacy, on her personality, and on her view of life: each of the testimonies has its own flavor, and they are all lively reading. Many times they say more than what is explicitly expressed. Many areas were not openly explored in writing at that time, and this applies in particular to the relationships between a man and a woman. To form an idea of what these were like, it is necessary to read between the lines and to draw inferences from the facts stated. This is probably one of the most difficult, but also one of the most interesting, problems presented by these writings.

Too many interpretations have been built on the records men have left of their experiences in the West. It is time to let women speak for themselves and to examine what they can show us of the society they lived in. The study of their testimonies should greatly alter our perception of what life in the West was really like. It is my belief, furthermore, that their narratives, and particularly those chosen here, are more than rich sources of social history. Many of them bring the reader in close contact with personal experience. Others are lyrical recreations of childhood days. Still others are well-composed books and fine specimens of autobiography. In the prefaces, I have endeavored to suggest some of the authors' ways of expressing themselves which have particularly drawn my attention; however, many other evaluations and interpretations are possible, of course. It has not been my intention to make judgments nor to set down any definite pronouncements, but simply to share the enthusiasm and the delight I have experienced in reading these highly diversified narratives.

[21]

# Let Them Speak for Themselves

1. This quotation is borrowed from a discussion between Gene M. Gressley and Howard Lamar on the theme of "A Shrinking Frontier?" which has been recorded in *The American Issues Forum: A National Bicentennial Discussion.* Voice of America, 1976.

2. Ray Allen Billington, *America's Frontier Heritage* (New York: Holt, Rinehart and Winston), 1966, p. 53.

3. For a detailed study of the meaning of "home" and "civilization" for women who went West, see John Faragher and Christine Stansell's article, "Women and their Families on the Overland Trail to California and Oregon, 1842-1867," *Feminist Studies* vol. II (1975), 150-166.

4. On this subject, see also *Apron Full of Gold:* the Letters of Mary Jane Mecquier from San Francisco, 1849-1856. ed. Robert Glass Cleland (San Marino: The Huntington Library), 1949.

5. The passage from Mrs. Churchill's book is set in Denver, Colorado. It has been included because the conditions she described are relevant to the West in general.

6. *Luzena Stanley Wilson, '49er*, p. 15.

7. Wilbur S. Shepperson, *Restless Strangers: Nevada's Immigrants and their Interpreters* (Reno: University of Nevada Press, 1970), p. 151.

8. Rodman Paul, *Mining Frontiers of the Far West, 1848-1880*, (New York, Chicago, Toronto, London: Holt, Rinehart & Winston, 1963), p. 155.

9. Their situation appears similar to that of colonial women who lived on farms. See for example Nancy Cott's analysis in *Roots of Bitterness: Documents of the Social History of American Women* (New York: E.P. Dutton & Co., Inc., a Dutton paperback), 1972, pp. 6-7.

10. Another example of a lively account written by a young girl is Victoria Jacobs's *Diary of a San Diego Girl* ed. Sylvia Arden. (Santa Monica: Norton B. Stern Publisher), 1974.

# Times and Places
## Described in the Excerpts

*Part 1*

| | | | |
|---|---|---|---|
| Behrins: | 1851 | Quartzburg, Calaveras County | California |
| Ballou: | 1852 | Negro Bar | California |
| Mansur: | 1852-1854 | Horseshoe Bar, Miner's Ravine | California |
| Haskell: | 1867 | Aurora | Nevada |

*Part 2*

| | | | |
|---|---|---|---|
| Ivins: | 1853 | Petaluma | California |
| Compton: | 1853-1900 | Marysville - Chico | California |
| Teeples: | 1879-1880 | Gila County | Arizona |
| Hafen: | 1891-1900 | Bunkerville | Nevada |

*Part 3*

| | | | |
|---|---|---|---|
| Boyd: | 1868 | Camp Halleck | Nevada |
| Biddle: | early 1870s | Camp Halleck | Nevada |
| | | Fort Whipple | Arizona |
| Summerhayes: | 1874 | Camp Apache | Arizona |

*Part 4*

| | | | |
|---|---|---|---|
| Wilson: | 1849 | Sacramento - Nevada City | California |
| Mathews: | 1870s | Virginia City | Nevada |
| Churchill: | | Denver | Colorado |
| Doyle: | 1890 | Sodaville | California |

Part 5
| Larowe: | early 1850s | Nevada City | California |
| | | San Francisco | " |
| Ackley: | 1852-1857 | Sacramento | California |
| Saxon: | 1861-1866 | San Francisco | California |

Part 6
| Bixby-Smith: | 1870s - 1880s | San Juan Bautista | California |
| Hopkins: | 1850s | Humboldt Sink | Nevada |
| White: | 1859-1872 | French Corral, Nevada County | California |
| Kitt: | 1874-1880s | Florence | Arizona |
| | | Santa Catalina Mountains | " |
| | | Tucson | " |

Part 7
| Bates: | 1851-1852 | | California |
| Leslie: | 1877 | San Francisco | California |
| | | Virginia City | Nevada |
| Adams: | 1880s | Pasadena | California |

*Part 1*
LIFE IN MINING CAMPS AND MINING TOWNS

# Reminiscences of California in 1851

Harriet Frances Behrins

(n.p., 1900?)

*From some remarks concerning the progress of civilization in California which appear in the book, it can be conjectured that Mrs. Behrins wrote it around 1900, when she was about 70. Her story starts in 1851 with her departure from home with her young son: she was going to meet her husband who had succumbed to the gold fever in 1849 and was waiting for her in San Francisco. Her frame of mind was far less than cheerful as she took leave of her family and friends; the weather was dreary, and she felt sad and depressed. To her, California was simply a very distant place, and she was obsessed by the fact that she might never see her relatives again.*

*The pages devoted to the journey to San Francisco reveal her interest for other people and her ability to convey her impressions in a vivid manner. Her emotions are expressed with such force at times that we can almost feel their reality: the passage in which she gives way to her joy at seeing her husband again is quite striking. What she could see of San Francisco upon landing dampened her spirits somewhat, and she was torn between two sets of emotions; being with her husband again gave her much happiness, but she was dismayed at the primitive conditions of life she was confronted with. Her first walk in California was in "sand infested with fleas"[1] and her first night took place in a rather dismal lodging-house owned by a Mr. Hunter, to which she refers derisively later in the narrative. She felt so homesick and disconsolate that even her husband could not comfort her. The following*

[27]

pages concern her life in California for the time her husband's involvement in prospecting lasted:

About the first letter I received from home in the uncongenial surroundings of Mr. Hunter's palatial abode was from your dear father. Ah! my children, the preciousness of that welcome missive! Coming all those dreary miles to tell me of the health of our dear mother and other members of the family. A helpful, cheering letter, concluding with these remarks:

"I understand from some of the members of my craft—publishers—that they have established a Vigilance Committee in San Francisco. I can only say, ''Tis true, 'tis pity, and pity 'tis, 'tis true.'"

I did not care to write my brother at that time of the dark side of my life, nor how shocked and grieved I felt the first Sabbath I spent here, when two men were hung from the building occupied by the Vigilance Committee, and I did not dwell upon the scenes witnessed, as I wended my way to the house of God. Bands of music in full blast, marching through the streets. Bulls decorated with gay ribbons, on their way to the Presidio, to fight to the death; a mob at their heels; nor of the open gambling hells, with gold piled conspicuously upon tables in open doorways, to tempt the weak ones, who had earned their money through hard labor.

All these sights I witnessed, and my heart became heavy with the knowledge of so much evil, and a longing for the refined home life which I had left behind me would pull at my heart strings until the church was reached, when "that peace, which passeth all understanding" seemed to fall upon my soul, and the earnest preaching of the Rev. Dr. Mines inspired me with renewed endeavor to rise above my surroundings. I realized then, as never before, the value of true religion.

In the course of a short time some changes for the better took place, for changes were most rapid in those days. Houses seemed to grow in the night, and suitable accommodations were finally secured. We obtained board with a widow lady, where I made the acquaintance of a Mrs. Raymond, the daughter of Mr. Gibbs, the great New York shipbuilder. Mr. Raymond was the agent for a line of steamers; his wife was a cultivated and amiable woman, and we formed a strong friendship.

Having thus seen me established among congenial surroundings, Ferdinand proposed returning temporarily to his adopted profession of prospector, without his family, for, among other attainments, Dr. Behrins was an expert mineralogist, having developed a pronounced taste for this branch of study at the university from which he had been graduated in Gottingen, Germany, but comparatively a few years before.

While chafing at the necessary procrastination in the consummation of his future plans, he had poured into my sympathetic ears tales of thrilling experiences. "He had been on the verge of marvelous results from his prospecting tours time and again," encouraged by spasmodic flashes of success, that held his interest as in a vise; millions danced illusively before his eyes, but invariably eluded his grasp. With the advent of wife and child came the culmination of his plans, which had been held in abeyance in the interim. "Eureka!" was his constant cry.

According to his computation, he had found a top layer of soil which paid twelve per cent. of gold to the pound. Calaveras County held the treasure, which he had located, and the mine eventually became known as the Phoenix.

My husband invested in the enterprise all the wealth of which he was possessed, and assumed the responsibility of the largest stamping mill in California at that time. The firm of Gildermeister, De Frenny & Co., owners of a line of Dutch ships, also invested largely in the prospective Eldorado. Machinery was purchased, delivered with great difficulty, and erected for the purpose of crushing the quartz. Immense weights, from twelve to fourteen hundred pounds each, were worked by machinery to this end. A small army of men were employed, the least competent of which received not less than fifty dollars per month. There was a draughtsman, an engineer, and fifty workmen, including a cook and a baker. No small matter for a novice to handle.

A small cottage was built for my use, at a cost of four thousand dollars, about a mile distant from camp. Thither I was finally conducted, the greater part of the journey made on horseback.

During the two years that followed my establishment in this wild spot, I did not, with one exception, see a white woman. Men on all sides, but none but Indian women. And yet, when I look back to that period of my life, the reflections are most pleasant and sunny; situated as I was amidst beautiful scenes of nature, recipient of the simple gallantry of the men, who catered to my slightest wish.

The enthusiasm and irresistible spontaneity of my partner in life was contagious, and my dear child's good health and budding fancies, whiled away many happy hours. Then, again, my four-legged pets held my interest, chief of which was my little Canadian pony, all my own. Good comrades were we, in our many journeyings to and from camp.

As for our tiny traveler, Walter, the joy of our lives, the pet of the men, he was peacefully slumbering within the tent, the sleep of innocent childhood. On all occasions, a reassuring smile from mother, and the protecting touch of father, made his happiness complete. In every new environment, even in the midst of danger, did these unfailing encouragements obscure from the horizon aught save love, and a sense of security, and so his joyous shouts resounded far and near. Surely, "Heaven lies about us in our infancy." If at times our watchful eyes detected an anxious or tired look upon the dear little face, we hastened to dissipate it. His father would say with intense fervor, always lapsing into German dialect for endearing terms:

"Isn't this great sport, *mein liebling?*" or "Are we not having a fine time, *liebchen?*" with a positiveness that was beyond dispute.

The little fellow would invariably answer in the affirmative, with a smile, a little hand would creep into a big one, a little head would rest upon the broad shoulders in perfect faith; thus the young life intrusted to our care expanded unbeknown to him, under most unusual conditions for a well-born baby.

Now to go on with my story, after this digression of a fond parent. The next day we started again upon our journey, which was not so arduous an undertaking, and toward night arrived at the "diggings." The doctor named it "Fiddler's Green," and I have heard that it still retains the name.

The men went to work vigorously, putting up log cabins, and within a few days all was completed, and another kaleidoscopic view was presented of our little colony, in a somewhat new phase of pursuit, for placer mining, instead of quartz, was not to be the shape of their labor.

My furniture suffered the indignity of being packed high against the sides of the small room, with the exception of the lounge, which was arranged for my comfort, and there I lay, day after day, trying to get thoroughly rested after the long and tedious journey.

The spot was rich in placer gold. Almost the first day, as I sat in the doorway of my cabin, I saw something moving and shining. I ran to investigate, and found that it was a "pocket," as the miners call it, broken loose from the dirt on the bank of the ravine, and soon would have been washed beyond reach by the stream.

I took a horn spoon and extracted from the lump what proved to be an ounce of coarse gold.

The men would dig from these banks, and fill their sacks with the diggings, about fifty pounds to a sack; they would then carry this on their shoulders to a rocker up the creek, and work it. The gold thus rocked out of this quantity of earth, in a wooden cradle, would represent from two to three dollars a sack.

All went pretty well with us until the rainy season set in; then commenced the hard times with the miners, for there were about fifty of them all told, settled around us, whom necessity forced to buy their provisions from week to week. When cut off from the base of their supplies by the swollen tide and lost boat, we supplied food to the most needy, some of whom were on the verge of starvation, until finally our own rations were reduced to Indian meal and brown beans. I could not eat this coarse food, and consequently often went hungry.

My little son became very thin, and my anxiety sharpened accordingly; yet never was there a complaint from the child. He would come to me in his loving, tender way, his big brown eyes going straight to my heart, and say, "You sick, mammie?"

Then I would reply, "Only a little tired, dear boy."

"Well," he would respond, partly relieved, "I will tover you up, and then I will do and make you some dold."

He had fashioned for himself a small canvas bag, with a little help, and would trudge along behind the Frenchmen, back and forth, with his bag of dirt, by the hour, and imitate their every movement, throwing me a kiss as he passed the door—a little streak of sunshine amidst the gloom.

At last our condition became desperate. The doctor came to me one day, saying:

[31]

"Lend me your gold chain, dear; I am going to try an experiment."

I handed it to him, and watched him tie a small cord to the end. He then proceeded to the bank of the river, and shouted with all his might. Some one finally heard him, and then the doctor explained to this man, who came to the rescue, that he would shoot the long gold chain across from his gun, and retain the cord in his grasp. If it proved a success, they could tie a heavier cord, and then a rope, and in that way make a cable that would carry over to us some provisions.

This experiment proved a success, and a mode of transportation was thus established. Still our situation was scarcely less deplorable. The food was so often damaged to uselessness, being soaked in the water on the way; so the two captains before mentioned, Mr. Burr and the doctor, after serious controversy, decided that they would make the attempt to go over the mountains and seek relief from that direction. One was to bring back potatoes, another flour, etc., etc. They must make their own trail, which meant hard labor and patience, but there seemed no alternative.

I was kept in ignorance of the true purport of their mission.

Very early in the morning they started, fully realizing the dangers that would beset them. Still, to relieve the desperate situation, they concluded to take chances of returning late, or may be never. So I was told "they were going off to prospect, and would be away all day."

I did not dwell seriously upon this, as it was rather a common occurrence; but when the sun went down, and the blackness of night enveloped us, I began to wonder. I put my boy to bed, had a big fire made on the hearth, locked and bolted the doors, making all secure as possible; then sat down to wait and listen.

I was alone now, as our attendant occupied his own quarters, and had gone thither, confident of the doctor's momentary return.

Seven, eight, nine, ten, struck the clock, and yet they came not. I piled on the wood, until the flames fairly illuminated the room, and tried to compose my nerves, with which every sound began to play havoc. Ordinary happenings, such as the ticking of the clock, the crackling of the logs from the heat, caused my brain to wildly speculate as to their origin and meaning.

Listening in this frame of mind became acute suffering. I actually awoke my child, to hear his voice, deploring my weakness, but returning somewhat comforted, when, lo! a real sound, a stealthy one, not partaking of the innocent character of those within, startled me.

I crept to the windows and doors, fascinated by the somewhat familiar, clumsy tread of a wild beast! Yes, we had been visited before by venturesome bears, who would come down from the mountains, under cover of the night, and prowl about our abiding place, and I felt sure now that bruin had chosen this inopportune occasion to pay me a visit.

Notwithstanding which, I could almost have laughed to find something tangible to fear. It was the ghostly, supernatural element that had terrorized me—the oppression of a still, dark night, with the additional pain at the heart caused by anxiety for the safety of loved ones.

I peered out into the night, but could discern nothing but blackness. Shambling and snuffling sounds would occasionally remind me of the voracious visitor without, and send a tremor all through me as I stood close on the other side of the rude board partition which alone saved me from his hungry jaws. But even these dread sounds ceased at last, some time before my lonely night vigil stretched out into early morning hours.

"Two!" The clock seemed to toll as for departed spirits, when, in the midst of such torturing fancies, my hearing, unnaturally acute, detected the music of human voices, like a whisper from the mountains, strengthening every second in volume, and sending thrill after thrill of hope and joy to my affrighted senses, growing clearer and more intelligible even unto the threshold of our cabin.

Then the bolt is withdrawn by the silent, expectant creature who stands like a sentinel within, with ear alert at the crack of the door, which is simultaneously flung open from without, and there stands my belated husband, with outstretched arms, while with rather forced gayety, he exclaims:

"*Meine kostbare Gattin*"—my precious wife—"behold your Ferdinand!"

Within his strong embrace, I listened to the details of their perilous journey.

"Many, many times within the past few hours," he said, "I feared that I should never see your dear face again."

It seems they had succeeded in pushing their way over the mountains and reaching the store. Each man was quickly loaded with provisions to his utmost capacity, then they turned their faces homeward without delay. But darkness overtook them on the dangerous trail, which they had cut at random, and they fully realized that one misstep over precipitous edges would hurl them below to their death. So heavily were they burdened that they frequently staggered wearily, and as a last resort they crawled on their hands and knees for miles; but "all's well that ends well," laughed the doctor, as he carried me to the next room and laid me upon my bed, where I soon fell into a deep sleep, but not until I had told of my midnight visitor.

The next morning proved my surmise correct, for the tracks of a huge bear were discovered, and his promenade around the cabin had been a persistent one.

The heroism of the four men brought great temporary relief to the camp, but it was only a question of a few weeks, when we were all in dire straits again.

Two more men made the attempt to ford the turbulent stream, but were drowned, which, of course, had a most disheartening effect upon the colony.

Something heroic must again be tried, however, so Capt. Maston, being a strong man and a powerful swimmer, determined to brave the wicked waters, and, to our great joy, succeeded in crossing. He hastened to the town of Quartzburg, a few miles distant, and sought help; but in this effort he was not altogether successful, for the people there showed a great lack of interest in any affairs save their own. Before leaving the town, however, he obtained some bread, butter and meat, tied them up carefully, to make the parcel as water-proof as possible, with a strong cord, and when he swam back to us he carried the package in his mouth, holding high his head out of reach of the hungry waters.

When he reached camp, he called Dr. Behrins aside and said:

"Here is something the little woman can eat."

When the delicacies were brought to me, and I was told how the captain had managed it, for the first time during all our vicissitudes in the mines, I broke down and cried like a child.

Never shall I forget that brave, good man, who has long since crossed the Great River which leads to our heavenly home.

During these trying times we had in camp a quite distinguished foreigner, *incognito*. He had appeared from no one knew where, with his horse, dog and servant; but as it was not unusual to have unexpected visits from adventurous travelers, this one attracted no especial notice, until one of the Frenchmen in the doctor's employ approached him in a mysterious manner, as if he had a secret to divulge.

"The French gentleman is a great nobleman; I have seen him many times in Paris, in company with Louis Napoleon on state occasions, in regimentals conspicuous with ensigns of royalty."

The doctor's interest having been thus aroused, he engaged the stranger in conversation shortly thereafter, and reported to me that, "whether of high or low estate, he was in truth a gentleman."

"Call me Mr. Philip," he had said, in exchange of courtesies with the doctor. So plain Mr. Philip became his cognomen, and in this wise was he introduced to me some days later, as he accompanied my husband to our humble home.

After a few minutes of polite conversation with me, he looked about the room, and said, commiseratingly:

"Ah, madam, this place too poor for a lady. Before this you nevare been accustom this way to live?"

I shook my head negatively, and replied, smiling: "But it is romantic."

"Romantique!" he repeated, with a shrug of the shoulders; "too much *réalité*."

I laughed outright at the look of disapproval on his expressive countenance.

His acquaintance was a diversion, and became a real pleasure to me. He made me acquainted with his dog, Hugo, and with his horse, which he called Donkeshot, and we all became good friends.

Game was very scarce that winter, but he would frequently present himself at my door, with his gallant bearing, make his graceful French bow, and "request madam to accept a bird or hare," just as he was fortunate enough to shoot them. Sometimes he would send these trophies by his servant, with "Monsieur Philip's compliments."

I would often invite him to come in for a little "conversation," for he seemed to enjoy his *"leçons à l'anglaise,"* as he expressed our attempts at understanding each other. With a limited knowledge of each other's mother tongue, our speech must necessarily be halting, but Mr. Philip conversed fluently enough in the German language with my husband, and once or twice drifted into politics, as a result of which the doctor gathered that our Frenchman, during the revolution in France in 1848, had given offense to President Louis Napoleon by openly sympathizing with a noted statesman, a member of the legislative assembly, who represented the people; consequently opposing the president. The legislator was thrown into prison, and it is likely that our young friend would no doubt have met the same fate had he not fled from the country; or, possibly, he had been banished to the United States.

After a while, when the rain ceased to pour down so incessantly, he took his departure, much to our regret, although I was beginning to have fears of his health breaking down, for he had become so thin, almost emaciated, with the hardships, to which he was evidently unaccustomed, and did not have the physique to endure.

Years afterward, while the doctor and myself were traveling down the Sacramento River, a gentleman on board the steamer approached us, claiming acquaintance. It was our old friend, "Mr. Philip," but, oh! so changed—the picture of health and prosperity, faultlessly attired in the fashion of the day, and altogether metamorphosed.

He told us that he had returned to his home in France, that his titles and lands had been restored to him, but that a spirit of restlessness had seized upon him, and that some inexplicable charm in the atmosphere of our new country had wooed him again thither.

On parting, he handed the doctor his card, with a smile, saying: "My name has grown with my *embonpoint*, but my great pleasure to see you both is the same as of old."

He was quite profuse in extending to us an invitation "to visit his chateau, should we ever visit France," but we never had that pleasure, nor did we ever see "Count Phillippe" again. The string of Christian names to which he was entitled has escaped my memory.

But now we must return to "Fiddler's Green," where I left in my narrative.

We waited impatiently for the angry waters to subside, and as soon as the river was once more navigable, my husband hastened to the town of Quartzburg, and endeavored to find suitable accommodations for a lady in a critical condition, as my strength was well-nigh exhausted.

It was his good fortune to succeed in this respect beyond our most sanguine expectations. Mr. Goddard, the superintendent of the Gaines Mills, was going East with his family on a vacation, and offered to rent his cottage, situated a short distance from the town, on a lofty hill, surrounded by trees and shrubbery. The house was tastefully furnished, and my woman's heart leaped at the prospect of a home with comforts, and even luxuries, which I had long been denied.

Satisfactory arrangements being consummated, we took possession of these attractive quarters. It was here that my little Adrian was born. My convalescence was most peaceful, and my heart filled with thanksgiving that we had entered what seemed to me such a haven of rest, not dreaming of the lawlessness that ran riot through the town.

Several weeks had passed most blissfully to me, with my precious baby, an additional joy in our home, when the quiet of our lives was again disturbed, but in a good cause. The doctor, while passing a cabin on the outskirts of the town, thought he heard a groan. He went to the door and peered in. There lay a young man on his bunk, tossing wildly with fever and delirium.

The doctor hastened to me with this information, saying: "The poor fellow will surely die, left there alone."

We saw no alternative than to bring him to our home. So, acting upon the impulse of the moment, the doctor removed him as carefully as possible, and soon he was comfortably installed beneath our roof. This accomplished, his cabin was securely nailed up, to keep out trespassers. In the course of a few weeks our patient was nursed back to health and reason.

Astonishment was in his eyes as he rationally gazed for the first time into new faces and viewed listlessly his strange surroundings. Weakness checked any expression of his sensations at first, but as he rapidly convalesced, under the doctor's skillful treatment, his gratitude was unbounded.

At last he could brook no further delay, and pleaded with my husband to help him in his still feeble condition to return to his cabin. He desire was so intense and persistent, it was thought best to humor the invalid, so the doctor almost carried him to the wagon, and accompanied him to his former abode, on reaching which, he said:

"Doctor, I have gold buried under the floor, for which I have come near giving my life in exchange. I beg your assistance to unearth it."

By this time he was overcome by exhaustion.

The doctor took the pick and spade and dug up the boy's treasure, for he was not more than nineteen years of age, and by his own unaided exertions had been struggling to obtain a fortune, that he might return to Pennsylvania and enrich his dear ones—a father, mother and sweetheart.

He had accumulated four thousand dollars in gold, and so we urged the lad "to rest on his laurels and return to the East at once."

With many affectionate expressions of gratitude, he yielded to persuasion, and with joyful anticipations he left for his far-away home, and I could hardly help envying him as he turned his head in that direction. But ten long years passed before I started back to the loved ones left on the Eastern shore, and then only for a brief visit.

Quietness and tranquillity again reigned in our little home, but only for a brief period, when one day I was startled by a loud knock at the door.

I answered the summons in person. Outside stood a man with wild eyes and disheveled locks. He talked so rapidly, in Spanish, that I could not understand. I took it for granted that he had called for a physician's advice, as he looked wan and sickly. I raised my voice and almost shouted:

"Doctor not at home," forgetting that he was not necessarily deaf because he could not understand the English language. "One o'clock," I said, raising my forefinger as if talking to a child, he seemed so bewildered. "Back at one."

He stared vaguely, pathetically at me, then turned and left. His face haunted me, with the suffering written there.

The doctor, returning to his noon repast, an hour later, passed through the town. There lay the body of my caller, stiff and stark on the street, riddled with bullets.

I learned that the poor fellow was recovering from a fever, which still clouded his mind at times. Perhaps in some lucid interval he had sought the doctor, whose fame had spread among these people. This, of course, is speculation. We ascertained, however, that after leaving me he had wandered into a store in the town, on this last forenoon of his life, muttered some incoherent words to the woman in attendance, taking her hand, saying, "Come!"

This was construed as an insult, imaginary though it proved to be, and must be wiped out with his blood by the lawless mob that infested the place, without investigation, until too late.

He had been the only support of his poor old mother, whose grief was heartbreaking. I was sick with regret that I had not detained him.

Such incidents were more or less common, but always a terrible shock to me.

Most of the settlers of Quartzburg were from Little Rock, Arkansas, gamblers by profession, and irresponsible as citizens.

After this deplorable affair I became restless, and with a more intimate knowledge of conditions abroad, my desire to escape from an atmosphere so tainted with crime became so urgent that I could no longer school myself to contentment. My husband, unable to counteract my uneasiness, as in times gone by, and realizing the strain under which I had lived so long, abandoned further pursuit of gold, and we returned to comparative civilization.

The year 1852 found us back in that city of magical growth, San Francisco, which proved to be the doctor's legitimate gold mine, after all. He had been chasing a "will-o'-the-wisp," it seemed, and the fascination of the chase had blinded him to the practical side of life, and the possibilities of his profession.

Physicians were few on the coast, and disease stalked abroad in search of victims. As usual, Ferdinand was equal to the exigencies of the times, and put his whole heart and soul into the relief of the sick, winning confidence and friendship daily. In return for his services, he received princely remunerations in many cases, wholly voluntary gifts of gratitude, and gold filled his coffers without the labor of mining, panning and refining. He actually rolled in wealth, and every luxury was heaped upon me and my children, as if to compensate us for past privations. Still, a Bohemian at heart, my husband often sighed for the freedom of the hills and vales, and, I fear, was not altogether appreciative of a fortune that came to him through a channel so fraught with pain and sadness; yet he was always indefatigable in his efforts to alleviate suffering or sorrow, which, of course, was the secret of his professional success, coupled with a strong personal magnetism.

*The theme most often sounded in these pages is her inability to accept the primitive conditions in which she had to live: she deplored the violence which erupted from time to time and missed her past life among the comforts of civilization. This attitude is typical of many women who lived through the early stages of the development of the West. Harriet Behrins had the traditional attachment for the home that was popularized in so many writings of the time. The evocation of the joy she felt in her children calls to mind Sarah Royce's delight in hers; a strong religious bent and the ability to derive solace from faith in God also characterizes both authors.[2] Another theme which recurs in many writings by women at that time is the importance given to female companionship. The most unusual feature in Harriet Behrins's narrative is perhaps the frequency of the allusions to her husband and the openness with which she describes their relationship. She responded to his strong personality, his zest for life, and his cheerfulness. But there was a basic contrast in their attitudes toward life: whereas he valued freedom and the open spaces, she longed for comfort and the good life. The constant ambivalence which marked her way of coping with the situation is quite interesting: she tried to adjust to the circumstances in order to please her husband, but could not disguise her difficulties in doing so. Her compelling personality comes over very vividly, and the lively way in which her life was set.*

*Very quickly after the tribute paid to her husband, she brings her narrative to a close, stressing the wonderful changes which took place in California in the second half of the nineteenth century, and hoping that her account of her experiences would keep her memory alive among her descendants.*

1. Harriet Behrins, P. 14.

2. See Sarah Royce, *A Frontier Lady: Recollections of the Gold Rush and Early California,* ed. R.H. Gabriel (New Haven: Yale University Press), 1932.

# *"I Hear the Hogs in My Kitchen"*: A Woman's View of the Gold Rush

Mary Ballou

Edited by Archibald Hanna (New Haven: Yale University Press, Printed for Frederick W. Beinecke) 1962.

*Mary Ballou's brief but evocative record of her trip to California in 1851 and of her experiences there in 1852 is partly a letter, partly a journal, and consists basically in an outpouring of emotions and reactions to various situations and circumstances. It has preserved all the immediacy of personal experience noted down without any attempt at striking a pose. The letter she wrote to her son Selden gives a sense of daily life in the mining-camps as it really was:*

California Negrobar
October 30 1852

My Dear Selden

we are about as usual in health. well I suppose you would like to know what I am doing in this gold region. well I will try to tell you what my work is here in this muddy Place. All the kitchen that I have is four posts stuck down into the ground and covered over the top with factory cloth no floor but the ground. this is a Boarding House kitchen. there is a floor in the dining room and my sleeping room coverd with nothing but cloth. we are at work in a Boarding House.

Oct 27 this morning I awoke and it rained in torrents. well I got up and I thought of my House. I went and looket into my kitchen. the mud and water was over my Shoes I could not go into the kitchen to do any work to day but kept perfectly dry in the Dining so I got along verry well. your Father put on his Boots and done the work in the kitchen. I felt badly to think that I was detined to be in such a place. I wept for a while and then I commenced singing and made up a song as I went along. my song was this: to California I did come and thought I under the bed I shall have to run to shelter me from the piercing storm.

now I will try to tell you what my work is in this Boarding House. well somtimes I am washing and Ironing sometimes I am making mince pie and Apple pie and squash pies. Somtimes frying mince turnovers and Donuts. I make Buiscuit and now and then Indian jonny cake and then again I am making minute puding filled with rasons and Indian Bake pudings and then again a nice Plum Puding and then again I am Stuffing a Ham of pork that cost forty cents a pound. Somtimes I am somtimes I am making gruel for the sick now and then cooking oisters sometimes making coffee for the French people strong enough for any man to walk on that has Faith as Peter had. three times a day I set my Table which is about thirty feet in length and do all the little fixings about it such as filling pepper boxes and vinegar cruits and mustard pots and Butter cups. somtimes I am feeding my chickens and then again I am scareing the Hogs out of my kitchen and Driving the mules out of my Dining room. you can see by the descrption of that I have given you of my kitchen that anything can walk into the kitchen that choeses to walk in and there being no door to shut from the kitchen into the Dining room you see that anything can walk into the kitchen and then from kitchen into the Dining room so you see the Hogs and mules can walk in any time day or night if they choose to do so. somtimes I am up all times a night scaring the Hogs and mules out of the House. last night there a large rat came down pounce down onto our bed in the night. sometimes I take my fan and try to fan myself but I work so hard that my Arms pain me so severely that I kneed some one to fan me so I do not find much comfort anywhere. I made a Bluberry puding to day for Dinner. Somtimes I am making soups and cramberry tarts and Baking chicken that cost four Dollars a head and cooking Eggs at three Dollars a Dozen. Somtimes boiling cabbage and Turnips

[43]

and frying fritters and Broiling stake and cooking codfish and potatoes. I often cook nice Salmon trout that weigh from ten to twenty pound apiece. somtimes I am taking care of Babies and nursing at the rate of Fifty Dollars a week but I would not advise any Lady to come out here and suffer the toil and fatigue that I have suffered for the sake of a little gold neither do I advise any one to come. Clarks Simmon wife says if she was safe in the States she would not care if she had not one cent. She came in here last night and said, "Oh dear I am so homesick that I must die," and then again my other associate came in with tears in her eyes and said that she had cried all day. she said if she had as good a home as I had got she would not stay twenty five minutes in California. I told her that she could not pick up her duds in that time. she said she would not stop for duds nor anything else but my own heart was two sad to cheer them much.

now I will tell you a little more about my cooking. somtimes I am cooking rabbits and Birds that are called quails here and I cook squrrels. occasionly I run in and have a chat with Jane and Mrs Durphy and I often have a hearty cry. no one but my maker knows my feelings. and then I run into my little cellar which is about four feet square as I have no other place to run that is cool.

October 21 well I have been to church to hear a methodist sermon. his Text was let us lay aside every weight and the sin that doth so easely beset us. I was the only Lady that was present and about forty gentleman. So you see that I go to church when I can.

November 2 well it has been Lexion day here to day. I have heard of strugling and tite pulling but never saw such aday as I have witnessed to day the Ballot Box was so near to me that I could hear every word that was spoken. the wind Blows verry hard here to day. I have three lights Burning and the wind blows so hard that it almost puts my lights out while I am trying to write. if you could but step in and see the inconvience that I have for writing you would not wonder that I cannot write any better you would wonder that I could write at all. notwithstanding all the dificuty in writing I improve every leishure moment. it is is quite cool here my fingers are so cold that I can hardly hold my pen. well it is ten o clock at night while I am writing. the people have been Declareing the votes. I hear them say Hura for the Whigs and sing whigs songs. now I hear them say that Morman Island has gone whig and now

[44]

another time a cheering. now I hear them say Beals Bar has gone whig now another time cheering. well it is getting late and I must retire soon there is so much noise I do not expect to sleep much to night. there has been a little fighting here to day and one chalenge given but the chalenge given but the chalenge was not accepted they got together and setted their trouble.

I will tell tell you a little of my bad feelings. on the 9 of September there was a little fight took place in the store. I saw them strike each other through the window in the store. one went and got a pistol and started towards the other man. I never go into the store but your mothers tender heart could not stand that so I ran into the store and Beged and plead with him not to kill him for eight or ten minutes not to take his Life for the sake of his wife and three little children to spare his life and then I ran through the Dining room into my sleeping room and Buried my Face in my bed so as not to hear the sound of the pistol and wept Biterly. Oh I thought if I had wings how quick I would fly to the States. that night at the supper table he told the Boarders if it had not been for what that Lady said to him Scheles would have been a dead man. after he got his pashion over he said that he was glad that he did not kill him so you see that your mother has saved one Human beings Life. you see that I am trying to relieve all the suffering and trying to do all the good that I can.

there I hear the Hogs in my kichen turning the Pots and kettles upside down so I must drop my pen and run and drive them out. so you this is the way that I have to write—jump up every five minutes for somthing and then again I washed out about a Dollars worth of gold dust the fourth of July in the cradle so you see that I am doing a little mining in this gold region but I think it harder to rock the cradle to wash out gold than it is to rock the cradle for the Babies in the States.

October 11 I washed in the forenoon and made a Democrat Flag in the afternoon sewed twenty yards of splendid worsted fringe around it and I made whig Flag. they are both swinging acrost the road but the Whig Flag is the richest. I had twelve Dollars for making them so you see that I am making Flags with all rest of the various kinds of work that I am doing and then again I am scouring candle sticks and washing the floor and making soft soap. the People tell me that it is the first Soft Soap they knew made in California. Somtimes I am making mattresses and sheets. I have no windows in my room. all the light that I have shines through canvas that covers the House and my eyes are so dim that I can hardly see to make a mark so I think you will excuse me for not writing any better. I have three Lights burning now but I am so tired and Blind that I can scearcely see and here I am among the French and Duch and Scoth and Jews and Italions and Sweeds and Chineese and Indians and all manner of tongus and nations but I am treated with due respect by them all.

on the night of Election the second day of November was Burnt down and some lives lost. Adams express office was Broken open by a band of robbers a large quantity of money was taken. they took one man out of bed with his wife took him into the office and Bound him laid him on the floor and told him to give them the key to the safe or they would kill him. one of the robbers staid in the room his wife his face was muffled and Pistols by his side and told her that if she made any noise for so long a time he would kill her. only immagine what her feelings must be. I lived close by the office. I went in to see her the next morning she told me that she nearly lost her sences she was so frigtned.

I immagine you will say what a long yarn this is from California. if you can read it at all I must close soon for I am so tired and almost sick. Oh my Dear Selden I am so Home sick I will say to you once more to see that Augustus has every thing that he kneeds to make him comfortable and by all means have him Dressed warm this cold winter. I worry a great deal about my Dear children. it seems as though my heart would break when I realise how far I am from my Dear Loved ones this from your affectionate mother

Mary B Ballou

*Many themes are suggested here, which have been given detailed treatment in more elaborate narratives: the hard work which was necessary to improve the primitive conditions; the absence of comforts, which was aggravated by exposure to unpleasant weather; the violence which erupted from time to time; the homesickness which resulted from the severance of close family ties; the feeling of closeness to other women, with whom burdens and sufferings could be shared; the solidarity of the pioneers and the ideal, upheld by women especially, of doing good, of being of service to others and helping them; the respect shown to women. In a way her pages are an epitome of the life of poor women, with an underlying current of fatalism and acceptance of one's lot. There is much courage, and humor too, in her attempt to overcome her discouragement, by inventing a song about California for instance. Religion probably played an important part in her life and was a source of strength for her. Finally, some interesting information concerning conditions in the mines can be gleaned in her pages: she shows that it was possible for women to make money by performing several kinds of manual tasks.*

*What makes her narrative particularly endearing is the way in which her impressions are set down. The homely style is in accordance with the conditions described and restores the flavor of her life. The juxtaposition of widely different notations, and the incongruity which sometimes results, the constant intrusion of animals and the disturbances they create, the absence of logical links between the loose and incomplete sentences, the very individualistic spelling and use of capital letters make the narrative humorous and attaching. A whole variety of moods is suggested; the amusing aspect is offset by a rather pathetic trend and a moving evocation of mother love and tenderness. This fresh and lively account of life in the mines bears a close similarity to an oral narrative; the sentences blend into one another, there is an abundance of concrete details, popular language is used from time to time, and the pace is brisk. The overall effect which is created, and in particular the mixture of humor and pathos, the theme of violence; the recurrent use of the word "mud" which acquires a symbolic dimension very early in the narrative as it follows close upon the word "gold," call to mind the manner used by Mark Twain in some chapters of* Huckleberry Finn. *But here it is not a contrived style: everything is genuine. This is just a simple woman speaking.*

# MS Letters Written to Her Sister, 1852-1854

Abby Mansur

*The following letters were written from Horseshoe Bar, Miner's Ravine, California, by a pioneer woman to her sister in New England. They are part of a series of twelve autograph letters, the first of which was written on the ship "Ohio" on January 10, 1852 and the rest from Horse Shoe Bar; the last is dated March 16, 1854. The collection of letters held at the Beinecke Library also comprises letters written by her son James to his aunt; in one of them, he indicated that he would be 19 in February, 1862.*

September the 12 - 1852

Dear sister
    it waz with much Joy i received your letter last evening    you cannot imagein what pleasure it give me to learn you was all alive and in good health    i cannot say that i am well yet but i am a great deal better than i was when i wrote you last    i had rather a sick spell after i wrote you before    i got so tired out a writeing to you that i did not set up any more for a long time    you did not say any thing about aunt Martha in your letter    i do not know whether she is well or not    i have not had a letter from her yet    i must tell you a little about the country here    i suppose it will interest you as much as any thing    we have not had any rain here since last april nor any thing but fair weather since that time not even a cloudy day and

some of the time hot enough to kill the devil      the thermometer stands 112 hundred in the shade and about 150 in the sun      you find out how it stand there in those hot days and then Judge how hot it must be here i will tell you i get homesick some times for the want of rain      i do not know but i shall do as Mrs french has      i suppose you have not heard how that is      she has left French and gone to the city boarding out for her health      i espect every day when she will come home for she started for there when she left but the captain would not let her go for she had not money she thought when she left French that he would carry her home for nothing      they fell in love with each other comeing out here or he made her beleive that he was in love with her and she loved him all most to death and left French for him as near as i can find out and he would not have anything to say to her when she got to the city and so she had to stop there but keep mum you will here about it i think likely      but i must quit for i want to say something else      i am very glad to here you are so happy      i wish i was home i would give all the gold in California for the flees are thick enough to eat anybody up      you need be thankful you are where you can sit down and not have the fleas eating you up      i am so homesick i do not know what to do but i am afraid i never shall reach my native shore again      if i could have your minature and Eds and mothers and Phebes i should feel a great deal better do make mother have hers taken without fail and Phebe to      i trust you will have regard enough for my feelings to not fail to put them up to it and do not neglect yours and Eds while in health for health is not promised us      you cant think how happy it would make me to receive your minatures all at once      O how happy i should be      when i read your letter to little Jimmy he says tell aunt Hannah i wish i could see her and aunt phebe and grandmarm      he often says he does not see what made me come out here where the fleas was so thick but it cant be helped now but if i ever do get home again i shall know how to appreciate it      i will(   )      Jimmy is well and so is Horace      Jimmy has not been sick a day since we got here      give my love to Ed and tell him i wish him much joy every year a girl or a boy      i want you to write next time how Phebe gets along if she is steady or not      i hope she is      we will send that money as soon as we can      if any thing should happen to mother or Phebe they should be sick or any thing Just write and you can have the money and as much more as you want     i suppose you will have a husband to take care of you so you will not want any help from any body else     Jimmy says I wish you would write for aunt Hannah and grandmarm to come out here for he wants to see you     i wish you would write about Charles Manderville if he is comeing out here again and if his wife is going to have another baby     i expect she is by this time     i must give you a little of a short scetch of the good of this country as well as the bad     i have had watermelons the most splendid watermelons you ever saw     they would weigh from 20 to 30 pounds a peice     i have pine apples all the time in the store put up in tin cans Just as fresh as though they was Just cut up and stawberys and cherrys and peaches     i had some pears 3 or 4 weeks ago and some apples and peaches as fresh as though they were Just picked off     we have some of the most splendid grapes and pears in the store now you ever saw     we have not gone to farming yet and i do not know when we shall for we can not sell out here but we have got 2 cows that gives milk now and 2 heifers calfs and 9 hogs and 5 horses and about 45-0 hundred hens we have Just as much milk and as many eggs as we want all the time     we have from 50 to 60 boarders now all the time     we cook about 40 eggs into custard every saturday     you send your minatures and see that mother sends hers and the first pretty specimen i get worth about $7 or $8 i will send it to you for a bosom pin     i saw one the other day the prettiest thing i ever saw     he said he was a going to send it home to his wife or he would sell it to me     i tried to buy it and he said he would not sell it for 50 dollars     i must he is a going to send it to you to pay you for makeing his soon     from you affectionate sister

Abby T. Mansur

Horse Shoe Bar<br>Dec the 12 1852

Dear Sister and Brother
    I received your letter with the pattern of your little dresses and it give me much pleasure, so much so, that i had to answer it

the first mail and i wish you would do the same     we are all well
at present and hope when this reaches you it will find you the
same     i wrote you a letter the last mail and sent a piece of my
silk dress in it to see if you would get it and then i was a going to run
the risk to send some of Jimmys gold that he paned out     he says
he is a going to send it to you to pay you for makeing his
Briches     Jimmy wants to see you all very much and sends his
love to uncle Ed     he says he knows him     he used to work in
the room with aunt Hannah     i very glad to here that you was all
well     i suppose you let mother know that you hear from
me     if you do not you write and let me know and i will write to
her and you both, I hope you will remember those minatures     i
will willingly wait for the lord knows I do not know but i will go
out of my skin when i receive them     may god spare my life to
enjoy the scene     when you wrote me you was keeping house
and living so comfortable it seems as though my heart leaped
home with you and life was extinct     you cannot think my
feelings Hannah for it tell you i often think can it be possible that i
shall ever put my foot on my native shore once more     o god
forbid i must not think of it     it carrys me away     o Hannah
my feelings is better imugcined than described though i take
comfort here when i do not think of home i have every thing i can
wish but when i think of home it cast a gloomy feeling over all i
enjoy     all i live for is in hopes that i shall meet you once
more     Hannah you never need caution me to write for i shall
certainly write let my buisness be ever so urgent     now i am Just
as busy as i can be but i leave all and write for my Husbands
partner is going to the city to day and i am hurring with all my
might to get this done     i received your last night and the
steamer leaves next wensday and today is sunday

. . .

Horse Shoe Bar Cal
May the 28, 1853

Dear sister
     i received your letter yesterday May the 27th and i will assure
you it gave me much pleasure for i had almost given up the idea of

hearing from you again but i was happyly disappointed      i have not wrote you before for some time but i will write you as often as you do me sick or well if i cannot write i will get some one to, i cannot say that i well for i am not      i have not been well for some time but i am in hopes i shall be better soon      i am hardly able to write      i have a swelling on the side of my face and it is very painful      i do not know what it is but it give me so much pleasure to get that little lock of hair that i could not delay a moment i kissed that more than 20 times and then i could not feel satisfied      i sit down to write a few lines and send a speciment to that darling      though it be rather small i hope it will be acceptable      i cannot imagein what mother is made of to stay away from that beauty      o my god it seems as though i should fly into another world when i think of it Hannah and what is worse than all the rest god only knows when we shall come home for we are as far from it as we was when we first got here      i sometimes think that Horace never will come home but i will tell you i shall come home without him      you tell me i must be contented with my Husband but i cannot agree with you although i would like to,      i am glad to here that you are enjoying yourself so well but i am far from it      I have almost made up my mind to leave California any how      all is wanting is money      when i get that you will see me leave      dont say anything about it      i hope you will hurry up about them minatures for some of our Gentlemen boarders are in a great fix to see my sister for they think considerable of me and i told them they had ought to see my sister      especially my Husbands partner he says if ever he comes home to the states he shall certainly meet you      he takes a great liking to me      i tell you the woman are in great demand in this country no matter whether they are married or not      you need not think strange if you see me coming home with some good looking man some of these times with a pocket full of rocks      you may rest assured that i shall not take up with no common stalk it is all the go here for Ladys to leave there Husbands two out of three do it      there is a first rate Chance for a single woman      she can have her choice of thousands      i wish mother was here she could marry a rich man and not have to lift her hand to do her work, you did not write any thing about Phebe where she was or what she is doing      well about Ed i want you should tell him from me if he comes to this country he will repent it untill the day he dies     it is too late now for a man to come to this country to make a fortune but it is a first rate place for a man to come if he has his wife with him and calculates to spend his days here he can live a great deal easier and better but what is that he has enough to annoy him to make it up you cannot take any comfort for the fleas if you sit down to rest or go to bed there is no comfort for you the flease are biting or the bedbugs or both and you might Just as well be in hell     i never swore so much in my life     i always swore bad enough but if i should die now god only knows that would become of me     i cannot describe it as bad as it is     there is hardly a night i go to bed but what i think of you how nice you can go to bed and sleep and here i am sometimes i have to get up a half dozen times in the night to hunt flease and besides bear the punishment they inflict on me     i am sore the whole time from the effects of there bites     i tell you there are not many that would bare it as i do     they do not bite Horace at all but Jimmy and i have to take it     Some folks they do not bite as bad as they do others     i have a large minature of our house and boarders     i will send it if you would like it     Jimmy says he would give all the money hes got to see that Cousin Hannah     as far as that name is concerned if you do not like it you must choose for yourself     i am a going to write to mother and phebe to day and send them a specimen so if you get yours first tell them there is one on the way for them     dont neglect writeing and let me know if you get this     there is one piece of gold for Ed looks like a boot or a deformed foot     the next largest piece is for you and the two Cucumber seeds and the other little pieces is for that dear little nephew of mine and i will send him something better if these reaches you safe     that smallest piece is a little quartz in with the gold     this is from your unfortunate sister give my love to Ed and kiss the boy Just as many times as you can afford to for me     Jimmy and Horace are first rate     they never was better have not been sick a day since they been here     Direct those Minatures to Sacramento City to Horse Shoe Bar

Abby T. Mansur

[53]

Horse Shoe Bar Cal.
March the 6 1854

Dear mother and sisters

I seat myself once more to write you as i have some little news
to tell you that might be interesting     I have been very busy
lately or I should have wrote you before     Mr Harrab has been
very sick with the rhuematic fever and I have been sick the last
week with one of my sore throats such as I used to have at
home     I have not been sick untill now since my long sickness
when I first came here     I have not enjoyed so good health since
I was 15 years old as I have since I have been here   .  I am getting
so that I like this country as well as Horace does     if my friends
were out here I never would leave the country     the fleas are
getting scarce and bedbugs are getting scarce     it is getting
settled amazeingly     ladys are plenty and I have been getting
acquainted since I have been well and I go to a ball or private party
every week or to and enjoy myself first rate     we have not been
keeping boarders the last 3 or 4 months and we have been takeing
comfort     we are about to leave Horse Shoe and going on to a
farm about a mile and a half from here     we bought it a few days
ago and it is a nice place     it has a nice house built new this last
summer     it has a kitchen parlor and two bedrooms, two large
shade trees one on the front of it the other on the back so it is
shaded all day in the summer and it is very pleasant and the fleas
will not bother me any hardly it is only in boarding houses they are
so thick     that is what makes me in such good spirits     Horace
is a going to sell milk this summer     he can get a dollar a gallon
for Just as much as we have to spare     we have got now 10 cows
that give milk and more calfs all heifers but 2 and shall have 3 more
within 2 months     we have some 75 hens and 7 turkeys     9
young turkeys one more a setting and two more laying     they
lay and hacth two broods a year in this country and they sell for 20
dollars a pair     I do not expect we shall be at home for 3 years
for we want something to bring with us when we do
come     Hannah I want you to remember those minatures and
mother and Phebe I want them to have theirs taken together

. . .

Just imagein yourself way out here away from all your friends and I had never had a baby and should write to you what a handsome little creature it was and all this think for a moment how you would feel and then you can imagein something about how I feel    I know it must be pretty for it has got a handsome father and that is the most principle part    I would like to know how Herd flagg is getting on    has he seen that boy    have you seen or heard of him lately    do write me about him    has he got married or has he died of a broken heart    i expected to have seen him in California before now to drowned his troubles    this is a first rate country for that they say    Mrs French is in san Francisco and has been ever since she left French    she had had a baby and hires a Ducth woman to take care of it or the man she lives with does    she is liveing with a man that is married and has a wife and 4 children at home    that is the way the men do here    she was stopping first with one man and then with another when she first left French but when she got in family way she had to stop it and since she had her baby she has been living with this man    I would like to know how William Hart is getting on    has he found his wife    I had a downright laugh when I read that for it was nothing more than I expected    I am wrighting you a good long letter    you dont know how different I feel when I write you now it seems as though I am writeing to you all not one seperate    I will assure you it give me pleasure to learn that mother had come to her senses once more I can write you a good long letter instead of writeing two or 3    I bleive I have wrote you all the news and must bring my letter to a close by wishing you all good health and prosperity    give my love to Ed and all the rest of my friends which are few and far between I ex-pect    Deborah foss wanted to come to California when we did or said something about    if She had she might have made her fortune before now at dressmakeing    we have to pay 20 and 25 dollars to get a nice satin dress or silk made and 5 dollars for cutting and basting even now we have to pay that and they find the triming which costs only from 3 to 5 dollars    they trim dresses but very little    3 dollars a dozen for washing Just as much as you can do all the time cash down when they take the cloths    the is a lady lives close by me that takes in wash-ing    she has good health    she has no children herself and

[55]

husband and their partner in buisness they are farming    she has
them to wait on and her work to do and she makes from 15 to 20
dollars a week washing when she has all she wants to do so you can
see that women stand as good chance as men    if it was not for
my heart I could make a great deal but I am not stout enough to do
it    I am a going to put you in a piece of my new dress    I
suppose you think me silly but i have no little babys dress to send
so I am going to send you piece of mine as I think it pretty nice

from your Daughter and sister    A.T.M.

*The same themes recur in the first letters of the set. Abby
Mansur tended to revert constantly to her homesickness and her
desire to leave. She insisted very much on keeping her links with
her relatives in the East alive, and tried to project herself back to
her old home; she constantly asked questions about her family and
friends there, and was forever begging her sister to send her
miniatures. She could not adjust to certain aspects of life in
California; one of them was the presence of fleas, which becomes
a symbol of the absence of comfort and the primitive conditions in
the mines. Her feelings were not totally negative, however: she
was aware that there existed many ways for women to make
money. But in the letters dated 1852, the feeling which emerges
most strongly is despair. In one of them, there is an interesting
allusion to the advice her relatives gave her, which was that she
must be content, that is to say, accept her lot. This was the kind of
comfort which was usually given to unhappy women.*

*The letters dated 1854 stand in marked contrast to the earlier
ones: Abby Mansur expressed a greater appreciation of life in
California. Her change in attitude was linked to two elements:
conditions had improved, the place was being settled, more ladies
had arrived and social life was becoming more interesting. She
was still yearning to see her relatives again, but also looked
forward to living in a comfortable new home.*

*But she was not to enjoy her newly-found peace of mind for
long; she died in August, 1855, of heart trouble and exhaustion. In
many of her letters, she alludes to her health problems and regrets
not being able to work as much as she would have liked to. It is so*

*ironical, and so pathetic too, that she died precisely when she was starting to like life in California better.*

*Her letters tell much about conditions in the mining-camps. Her remarks concerning the looseness of ties and the frequent breakups which occured among married people are particularly significant. According to her, it was women who tended to desert their husbands: it is the world reversed! In the years which followed the gold discoveries, society was not stratified. Moral and religious principles were often disregarded, especially in the mining camps, and all kinds of irregular situations could be found. The references to the scarcity of women and the wide choice they had among eligible men are noteworthy too: this was at a time when women did not often get to do the choosing. Women were eagerly sought after, in California in the early days, and their work was necessary too: a wide variety of manual tasks such as washing, cooking, mending, and making clothes had to be performed, and women could command good wages. Furthermore, these were jobs they could do besides keeping their own homes. Abby Mansur's very specific information is especially valuable, as our knowledge of the life of women in the mining camps is still sketchy.*

*Her letters are not only informative; they are extremely vivid: the realities of life in early California, and her own feelings and reactions are expressed with such intensity and immediacy that they become almost tangible. The evolution in her response to the conditions is most interesting as it shows how she gradually managed to find a more comfortable place for herself within the existing pattern. Her frank and straightforward manner of presenting her experiences is thoroughly enjoyable.*

# "A Literate Woman in the Mines: the Diary of Rachel Haskell"

Rachel Haskell

Edited by Richard Lillard, *The Mississippi Valley Historical Review*, vol xxi. no. 1 (June 1944) 81-98.

*The following text covers a rather limited span of time (one month exactly); it constitutes what remains of a diary kept by Mrs. Rachel Haskell, who lived in Aurora, Nevada, where her husband was a toll-keeper, in 1867.[1] Despite its brevity, it is an extremely rich and lively record of daily life in a small mining town in the decade which was marked by the discovery and exploitation of fabulous mineral deposits in Nevada:*

Sunday Mar. 3rd. Got up late as usual these stormy times. Breakfast noon. I washed boys, a good scouring all over, dressed them, then went thru my own toilet. Ella read Gulliver's Travels aloud to boys. While Mr wrote in sitting room Mr. H. read in kitchen. I lay on sofa and enjoyed myself in said quiet position reading a book called "Light" by Alfred Mondet, till supper was nearly ready. Mr. H. keeps it going on stove. Washed dishes alone. Mr. H. talking in kitchen, Ella playing on piano some pleasant airs. Both ministers sick, so no church today. Came to sitting room, sat on a stool near piano while Ella accompanied songs by the family in chorus. Drew table in front of stove, resumed reading of "Light" while children with bright happy faces filled up the gaps. Mr. H. after playing on floor with two younger ones lay on the lounge and read likewise. Finished my book, pleasant writing but not extra deep. Ella read colored pictures.

Monday 4th. Looked a bit calmer and cooler, brighter in the morning. Sun shining cheerfully. Work thru, gave Ella lesson on new page of Linda March. We have been rather musical today, piano open all the time. Bud played a waltz wonderful, we had no idea he had caught even the air of. Is very fond of picking out tunes. Changed my calico dress and lay on sofa, while Ella read aloud some back pages of this. Have taken it easy today. Not sewing, only read "Enterprises." Seemed inclined to snow a little again this evening. Table mountain invisible and even Chalcedony somewhat hazy. Supper waiting on the gents who stay rather late up town. Mr did not come to supper. In evening Mr. H. read at table, while I lay on sofa and heard Dudley and Harry recite the multiplication table and count figures. Did not feel very brisk so took Maney and went to bed. In the night Mr. H. waked up eloquent in repeating a speech he dreamed he was delivering to a Nev. assembly. Sacto was the especial theme.

Tuesday 5th. Baked bread. Papered John's shelves nicely, put back border on outer edge, then he nailed them up. I paste up all the unsightly places broken in paper on the wall. Was just putting on boiled dinner in kitchen when Miss Poor and sister called. Ella entertained them on piano and Miss P practised some. We waited long time for Mr. H. but had to sit down without him. How badly I felt fearing—fearing. Came home about eight o'clock, read Enterprizes aloud. I went to bed early again. Did not sleep very continuously or Mr. H.

Wednesday 6th. Breakfast over I washed dishes and washed floor, intending to write home, but the sun shining clear thought I'd go to town and make some calls. Dressed in silk shirt and red waist, hat and red shawl. Had rather a hard tramp thru the snow. Called on Mrs. Levy, quite a pleasant chat and looked at her numerous sisters nine I think and fine portraits of her father and mother from Strasburg on the Rhine. Went next to Mrs. Poors met Mrs. C. there. Would have me stay and spend afternoon. Sent for Mr. H. to eat supper and we had a lively pleasant time till dark. Spent the evening at Mrs. Coopers, quite a number of friends there, and the jest ran high and the laughter loud. Had some good refreshments and returned home. Found Ella and John with

Maney in his arms asleep, waiting our return. Had a headache. Talked the day over and went to bed.

Thursday 7th. Woke with dreadful headache, breakfast over felt still worse, pale as a sheet. Had to lay on sofa, could not sleep, tried to play some on piano, but no go. Mr. H. did all he could to relieve me, sat reading Esther or Job in the Bible keeping room quiet. I got some camphor and lay on the bed, had a sleep at last which stopped the throbbing in my brain; so long since I had a heavy head ache I had forgotten the misery. Kimball and Carlton called in during afternoon. Felt better and got up. Went to table and ate some supper. Mr. Givin came in. Ella and John went to spend evening up town. Had a social chat in front room with the visitors, Maney very cross running from Mr. H. to me. He still reading Job. We ate some pine nuts. Ella and John returned much pleased with their visit. Ella got Thackerys "Newcomes" which we have in perspective for good reading.

Friday 8th. Pretty bright morning. Kept the house open for a while. Washed after arranging the shelves more to my liking, put specimens, shells, etc. on them. Washing easy today. Mr. H. cleaned up stairs. Kept water and fire up and scrubbed kitchen floor, when I got thru. Wrote up this book from Tuesday while waiting supper. Snow falling lightly and tops of hills slightly invisible.

Saturday 9th. Exceedingly deep snow, the deepest of the season. Breakfast over and work was made easy today. Sat down to complete the dear little velvet breeches commenced so long ago. Gave Ella another lesson on Linda de Chamernix, who had an easy time all day between the Piano and "Newcomes." Had a boiled dinner, of cabbage, potatoes and carrots, which were cooked on the front room stove. Ate our supper alone, Mr. H. not coming Felt very much concerned thereat, worried in mind a good deal. Completed Birdie's suit, put him in them, admiring him as he ran up and down in his first male habiliments. Hemmed some ruffling on machine to put on bottoms. Received a present of handsome carving knife and fork, from John D. Papa came home very late with a dreadful headache. He laid on the sofa saying "He never was so sick in his life." Threw up. And I went to sleep with Ella (that's me you know).

Sunday 10th. Almost snowed in, snow very very deep. 2 feet.

John D. started home; gave me a nice, large platter to go with carving knife and fork, and side-board, both of which he bought of Mrs. Cooper. We were very very sorry to part with him having had a most brotherly visit of several weeks. The snow was so heavy we feared it would crack the kitchen roof, as it groaned once or twice, which made us all scute. Papa ascended the roof and removed the weight. I washed Dudley and Harry and they went to morning service single file through the snow with their Father. Washed up the floor which looked rather soiled, while Ella (that's me and you) washed and dressed Birdie and Manie. We then gave our selves the usual sunday toilette. While getting Manie to sleep looked at "Gulliver's journey to Brobdinag." Pop and boys home in good season. I made plum pies and cunning little tarts, latter which pleased the five children exceedingly. Enjoyed our Sunday dinner. The children did not go to sabbath school. Donned my usual short grey to commence my rest just at dusk. Papa went to town, promising to come back soon with peanuts. I read aloud to Dudley and Harry the "Spectre Bride-groom" and "Legend of Sleepy Hollow" from "Sketch book." Ella (that's me again) in same Sunday blue dress still absorbed in the "Newcomes." Boys enjoyed their stories exceedingly. Mr. H. returned in good season, peanuts all safe which we enjoyed, with the addition of a few pines. Finis to Sunday.

Monday 11th. Sprinkled last week clothes for ironing, made yeast. Ella (me again) ironed while I cut out new fashioned sacque. Paid $1.00 for schooling on bublining [?]. Was interrupted by the arrival of one of the newly arrived Carsonites; Mr. Medley (really) looking fat and rubicund as Kris Kingle. Mr. Chapin came in shortly after bearing a loaf of very nice cake made by himself. He stayed to Supper. How comfortable and cozy the sitting room did look this evening by twilight. The shelves laden with books, specimens, minerals, shells. The Piano, the Sewing Machine, comfortable sofa and easy chair, with healthy, happy, prattling, chippy, little children all from Manie to Ella (again). I with Guitar in hand and Mr. Chapin looking at pictures in "Home Scenes." I played on the Piano for Mr. C. Later Mr. Mac Naten and Tannahill came in. Sat up late for return of Mr. H. I reading "Newcomes" and Ella (again) "Cripple of Antioch." We heard a most piteous wail of wind that seemed like a groan of the Spheres or the wail of a lost soul. Twice or thrice repeated, then died away into a perfect calm. We went to bed without Mr. H. who did not return till after 12 o'clock, ostensibly waiting for the mail.

Tuesday 12th. After breakfast set bread. Made Cup Cake Ginger bread and currant cake of light dough. Scoured kitchen and entry floor. Mr. H. returned from up town early in the day and wrote letters up stairs while I was so engaged. Ella practised in the front room and took care of Manie. Mr. H. went to town before supper, promising to return in season. But we had already sat down when he made his appearance. Mr. Medley knocked before we had risen from the table. Sat in kitchen all evening finishing the remnant of my baking and reading the book I began previous evening. Boys around me at the table. Went to my bed and began to recline Manie and Birdie jumping around me so I could take no pleasure reading. Ella (poor girl) Papa and visitor sat in front room.

Wednesday 13. A sleigh and two horses passed down this morning. Charlie R—driving came back in course of an hour. The first vehicle for a long time. Cut out grey cloth sacque for self to be trimmed with plaid. Mr. Haskell at home reading enterprises in kitchen. He went up town did not return to supper which meal we ate alone. We are sitting in the kitchen this evening. If I turned my head once I turned it fifty times to the window to see if he is coming. Got my daughter (not son) Ella to act as amanuensis writing this up from Sat. 9. Have my sacque nearly completed. It looks quite bright. It is very cold tonight when the door is opened a chill is sent through my frame. Heard Mr. H. E. DeLong had the smallpox. Graciosa! How cold chilly and horrid it was when we went to bed. Ensconced myself with Ella, Maney and Birdie in Ella's bed. Mr. H. came home at 3 o'clock, said he'd been at Winter's Mill. Ate supper he said at Micks, and the rest of the programme I can easily grip. Slept alone in his cold bed for home penalty.

Thursday 14th. Washed. Mr. H. coming down from town was surprised to see me thus engaged and surprised me by saying he had invited couple gents to dine. Hurried thro with washing, scrubbed kitchen paint work. Skimmed thru front rooms, taking a little from one place, adding a little to another and getting all to harmonious whole. Dressed myself and proceeded to make some plum pies. Gents arrived. Ella played for them while I busied with Papa's assistance in getting dinner on table. Had a pleasant enjoyment in the same by all the palates surrounding the board. Mr. H. spread himself in his usual verbose manner, knowing it was his legitimate put in. (Mr. H. brot home the side board). Adjourned to front room, passed a jovial evening adapting ourselves to the humorous propinqities of one of our visiters, by singing odds and ends of humorous songs, negro melody, etc. Mr. Givin also called in evening. Mr. H. went up town with them, staid very late. I fell asleep on sofa waiting for him, but waked to find he had not yet come. Went to bed and fell asleep. Getting so blunted now on that subject it don't keep me awake, suffering in mind as formerly. Waked me up, he in great sweat running home fast as he explained, not realizing in the masculine gabbing he'd been indulging how advanced the night was.

Friday 15th. We all felt worn out and sat in kitchen. Mr. H. reading "Sketch book." I sewing at my sacque. Ella ironing. Fell asleep in my rocking chair holding Maney, was awakened from said nap by entrance of Mr. McNaughton who sat all afternoon, staid to supper. Spent evening telling boys of incidents in the Washoe Indian war of '60. Ella and Harry went to P. Office after dark. Brought Harpers Mag. for March and a volume of Hawthorne "Our old Home." I finished my sacque and entered it to live therein till its last days arrive. It is real Scotchy. We put our extra dishes in side board. Enjoyed so exclusive a retreat much.

Sat. 16th. Scrubbed kitchen again which looked terrific by this morning. Made bread, and set doughnuts—all tardy in rising. Sat in entry and read the Dodge Club in Harper, Ella sewed some on machine while I sat at back window in sitting room enjoying the view and sewing Birdie's velvet pants which proved too short in legs. Jim Poor went to skating pond on horseback. Waited supper on Mr. H. who did not come. While seated at table, Mr. Ricker, his man Josh, and Chapin called. Made to give up frying doughnuts and sit in front room. Passed a pleasant evening. Mr. R. brot us a nice mince pie, had quite a talk with him. Mr. Chapin recd two pieces of music, both of which he presented to us, "What are the wild waves saying" and "Bonnie Eloise." Also a pack of author cards to the children which we played with much zest. After our callers left we sat up quite late children and all, warmed our mince pie and enjoyed eating it much. I read "Newcomes" in bed till three o'clock in morning. Birdie and Maney awake playing around me. Mr. H. did not come home all night. But I thought of other things. Ella's dress I must make for Odd fellows ball and so forth so I experienced no particular harassment.

Sunday 17th. Waked with rather a forlorn, angry feeling at heart. No matches. Dudley started up town to get them and see where papa was. Met him coming home. Had a sharp talk on these growing peccadillos, but went to church together. How wearied and haggard he looked. Small turn out of ladies at Church. Snowy path to church. Had to fry my cakes after return. Mr. H. lay down and slept till dark, supper over, Mr. Medley spent evening and I read my book till my eyes grew heavy and I threw myself on the bed and had good sleep. Mr. H. seems much more affectionate.

Monday 18th. Everything to arrange in cupboard and kitchen. Scrubbed floor and made every thing look neat. Read Hawthorne while resting. Ella making Maney a frock of some old plaid. Put on beans. Had liver and onion, pickles Mr. H. brot down. After supper Mr. H. read near the stove in kitchen while I cut out flannel shirt for Dudley and sewed the seams. Ella writing some in her never ending style. Ball up town tonight, lot of boys came down to skating pond, our Dud got out of bed and joined them. Maney cross; could not sew or read so went to bed. Boys staid out long time. We did not hear them come in, but they were disgusted with the big boys who drank liquor from a bottle.

Tuesday 19. Had some liver for breakfast, which all enjoyed, cleaned the floor again, was reading a "Brace of boys" when Mr. H. came home. He wrote at table in kitchen fire and I sewed at my shirt. Our beans boiling all this while with bacon nicely scored in pot were fit for supper, a dish savory enough for Jupiter. Made fire in sitting room after supper. Mr. H. stretched on sofa reading "Hawthorne." Boys round the stand writing with pencils. Practised the new song, got it started in my head somewhat, think it very grand. Mr. McNaughton came in on way to Mill, had been snowing a little. Told us he was trying to start home in three weeks. Hasn't seen his family for ten years, little girl only 3 months old when he left. Much noise and confusion with lively sleepless children.

Wednesday 20. Snow blowed over, plenty of last fall on the

ground to make everything look wintry. Piutes left this morning. We shall miss them looking in our windows. Mr. H. painted kitchen today. I cat stitched one shirt and finished it. Medley and Ella froze themselves playing and singing in cold front room all the songs they knew. I enjoyed it all by the kitchen fire. Supper over washed dishes. Then went to front room and amid pulling of Manie—noise and constant interruption, wrote this up since last week. Mr. Chapin called and played the author game with children. Mr. H. finished his last evening volume and back to his "Sketch book." Reed Magazine from Hayhugh. "Sabbath at Home," and Ella a flash novel from same source. Am neglecting my "Newcomes" and ought to be practising on piano, too.

Thursday 21st. Swept and dusted house prior to beginning the great domestic dread of the household; washing. Made bread and washed, back ached thought I should not attempt to do this another week but suppose when the day comes shall do so rather than send clothes up town. Mr. Holton came down to tell Mr. H. the Piutes had broken into his bill receptacle and taken bills, etc. Had beans cooking all day. Made rolls to eat hot with them. Bread rather a failure, would not rise well. Scrubbed kitchen nicely and read Harper by stove while waiting Mr. H.'s return to supper. Enjoyed our beans much and spent evening in front room. Children playing their author game. Mr. H. joining them and provoking them considerably, by getting the better of the game. Quite a noisy party. I read "Laura's lovers" and finished "Brace of boys" in Harper. Mr. H. retired to bed early as did the rest of us. Ella broke chimney of lamp.

Friday 22nd. Snowed again last evening. The like was never known, snowing continually. Began the homely employment of making stockings for the boys out of old ones of large size. Sat in the kitchen beside table while Mr. H. wrote. Doctored one loaf of bread by soda, restored it tolerably. Mr. H. working at a ham, but had to give it up too dry to boil into eating state. Had a large tongue on likewise. Mr. Holton brot some drawings of his to Ella and remained all afternoon. Took supper with us, also Willard Markley, Ella's friend. Had roasted potatoes nicely browned, slaw, tomatoes, ham and eggs. Judge Bonny and Mr. Avard called while we were at table. Ella had them all playing the author game when we arose from table. All animated and happy. Mr. H. and

Judge B. left for town shortly. I had a long and pleasant chat with Mr. Avard who gapped considerably tho I did my best to interest him. Mr. Holton good naturedly played with the children. Ella and I washed dishes in cold kitchen after every one left. Not so pleasant a finishing for company, but unavoidable when there is no Chinaman in kitchen. Mr. H. home soon. Practised my song.

Sat. 23d. No end to pot, kettle and pans to wash, plunged boldly into them. Made gingerbread, two pans of custard pie, while Ella ironed, cleaned chimney lamps a hard operation always in this house. Washed and combed and after supper went up town in company with Mr. H., taking a white rooster with him and called on Mrs. Mack. Learned a new way of making a tidy of serpentine braid and cotton thread. Enjoyed talking with a lady, Mr. H. looking over her books. Mrs. Edwards, her mother, Mr. English and Jameson came in; also met a Mr. Wise going home to Philadelphia, will call and see Papa and family. Mrs. Mack showed me some new things she got for late pasty. Snowed while we were there, but we got home pleasantly enough. Stopped in Mitcheners Store looked at "Ladys Almanac" some pretty pictures one "Bobeep" most cunning to a Mother's eye. Coming home found boys, Ella and Mr. Gwin keeping them company. Ate some of our gingerbread, looked over Enterprises.

Sunday 24th. Made some milk toast for breakfast. Ella took charge of boys to wash. I fixed up rooms and Mr. H. superintended kitchen which he cleaned to a high degree of nicety. Ella went to S. School taking Bison in his new pants and green coat of olden time. Snowed, of course. Willard M. carried him home, Manie nicely washed and dressed. Myself in new corsets and dressed, proceeded to make biscuits for supper. Didn't Mr. H. excel himself in making a codfish balls—only he baked them in an entire cake in the oven. This with custard pie to top off with satisfied our inner man and we sat around the table till late in evening all reading. Ella touching some pictures, Little Birdie reading too, as he imagined, with leg crossed like his Father. Their faces looked a pleasing sight as they ranged on opposite side of table from me, to a parent's eye. I read hard enough to hurt my right eye which I had taken a little cold in previous evening.

Monday 25th. Waked this morning with blood running out of my nose. Rather odd for me. After breakfast which Ella cleaned away cut out a long nightgown for self and tried to run it on machine, but the belt would slip. Mr. H. spent an hour fixing it and ran up the sides for me. Sewed it by hand after vainly trying to get good stitch on machine. Mr. Gwin came in during afternoon to get our names for "Good Templars." Mr. H. refused and so the rest of us thought it not best to join. He staid to supper with us. Were setting in kitchen when Mr. Chapin came in, brot us a pie of his own making. Mr. Medley came in later for Ella to go to a dance gotten up impromptu in honor of Mr. Mack & Binson returned Hot Springs. Decided Ella was better off at home than to walk up thro snow and mud such a night. Staid talking some considerable length of time. Both eat ginger bread and having a lantern started back. I finished my gown, a nice heavy one and we separated for the night.

Tuesday 26th. Birdie was dreadfully croupy last night. His breathing intensely labored. Put a wet cloth on his chest which did not relieve him so promptly as it does generally. It was a great drain on my sympathy all the hours of the night. He talked excitedly too a great deal. My eyes were shut, and so very sore when I waked. This eternal covering of snow which continually meets the gaze so glittering must prove hurtful to an organ whose natural color should be green to look upon. Rooms to order and I write this journal up since last Thursday. Hardly think it worth the while, but yet it methodises ones thoughts and actions in a measure, especially when the pen is so seldom employed in letter writing as has been the case with me for past year and more. Snowing again and a mist shrouding the top of hills till theres but a shadowy indistinctness of outside objects, but good fire, and cheerful sitting room, with quiet children today make it cheerful within. Mr. H. uptown and I'll practice my "Waves" a little, and leave development of further incidents of this day to a future summing up. Put supper on in sitting room and did not build a fire in kitchen, waited for Mr. H. and then ate alone at dark in sitting room. Birdie asleep on lounge, put two stands together and though the meal was simple children thot they were having a grand time from the novelty of eating in another room. Cleaned our dishes up there also, all in quick time. Mr. H. came home about 8 o'clock, brot bacon and fried some for his own supper and ate beside stove.

[67]

Wednesday, 27th. Birdie still very croupy and choked at night. Harry is affected in same manner. He and Dudley have sore eyes and colds as well as myself. Mr. H. got new book from Lyceum Library entitled "The Coward" a novel title, story laid in time of late rebellion, language and style very exciting he says. Mr. Gwin called in on way up from mill with a stiff neck. Said the preliminary meeting of "Good Templars" was well attended, thirty names appended for charter. I sewed at a large dress for Ella to wear to Odd Fellows ball which is coming off next month. Only sewed the belt on I believe. Mr. H. down early hurried to get supper which he started at rather fiercely. Instead of sitting down to supper thought I would experiment with my hair. Had it ready to fold round a waterfall when a knock was heard at door and two gents, Jameson and Mitchener made their initiary call. I resumed my plumfer and net, wound braid of plaited hair around my head, and abandoned the waterfall experiment. Had a spirited evening. It was exciting to meet two new gentlemen both good looking and interesting. We had not talked them out as some of the usual callers are—Talked of books, Mr. H. of his Hawthorne, of Washington Irving, of Shakespeare, Goldsmith. They looked at our children thought they healthy. Ella in cunning pocketed white apron put in a word naivly and interested as usual. All joined in the game of authors which was new to them, with enthusiastic zest and all played a long time. Ella and Mr. Jameson coming out ahead mostly. I was generally the Jonas not getting a single trick. Mr. H. had brought some nice apples down so we handed in old fashioned style, a silver basket of apples, plate of gingerbread, which all enjoyed becomingly. Mr. Mitchener asked Ella to play which she did very well. Afterward she and I sang "Would I were a bird" and by request "Twilight Dews" which Mr. J. said a delicious little sweetheart had sung for him nineteen years ago. Mr. J. liked slow stately music marches best.

Thursday 28th. Got up late, later than usual, which is not necessary. Disturbed Mr. H. by preparing for washing said weekly business being repugnant to his nerves. Swept rooms first and got thro well enough with the Herculean task which women all dread, but which is a diversion to me, and proceeded to getting supper. Made oyster soup which children hailed as glorious. Mr. H. ate his sour with vinegar. I washed dishes to let Ella get ready to attend of "Master Mason's daughter," up town. Our guest of previous evening Mr. Mitchener came for her. I never saw her looking prettier than when she came in soon ready to start, expectation in her countenance health in her cheek and nobleness in her manner. Left to ourselves had a quiet evening. I removed traces of the days work from my face and hands, dressed in sober chairs. I sewed at skirt of Ella's dress. Had cabbage boiled for with them as my eyes were too weak to read and hands too tender to sew. Mr. H. in mourning gown read his "Coward" occasionally giving me benefit of a fine simile or peculiarity of description. Ella returned looking pale, had spent latter part of evening at Moling. The ladies from Lodge had adjourned there to play cards! Ella of course refused to sit down to table but her gallant was entrapped and she amused herself playing on the piano. Had to keep her "dagsee" [?] a secret which was rather hard work.

Friday. Ella ironed in sitting room while I sewed anew at the dress, put new sleeves in and ruffle on, bertha on neck; had beans for supper which boiled on stove in sitting room, to finish out from boiling day previous. Mr. Medley asked in evening. I washed dishes. Ella went on with ironing in evening. Cut the puff half off skirt of dress and began rebinding it. Mr. M. told some gossip spoken of Ella by her S. S. teacher in P. office.

Sat. 30th. Mr. H. gathered wood off the hills much to his satisfaction, boys accompanying him. Squaws engaged in same business packing off loads their backs. Scrubbed kitchen and chairs. I sewed at skirt of Ella's dress. Had cabbage boiled for supper and bacon. Mr. H. washed entry and stairs down rather surly till supper was over when he beamed forth a little. Maney so cross and fretful and my eyes so painful I took her to bed quite early. Mr. Lytle and Chapin called shortly after but I fell sound asleep.

Sunday 31st. So muddy determined not to let children go to S. School. Washed Maney and boys in kitchen and Willard Markley came in. Recd. four "Sunday Mercurys" from Carson with numerous stories therein. Ella got "Leslies pleasant Hours" a magazine of light literature. Ella and self had just gone to dress when Medley came in kitchen to see Mr. H. Made raised yeast biscuit which would have been nice, but got a little too light. We read papers all day. Mr. H. went to town a while in evening. Did not dare to read too steadily my eyes warning me. Mr. H. went up stairs and slept with bub as he coughed good deal.

Monday Apr. 1st. Before quite completing morning work Mr. Holton called. Ella made fire in front room. I put on clean calico dress and entered. Went to sewing on the everlasting dress, took out some of the skirt which was soiled. Ella talked some then retired into her capacious portfolio and wrote all afternoon at some mysterious piece of composition. I sewed and talked to our visitor who is not very loquacious. Had a piece of beef on the boil. When Mr. H. came from town hurried to kitchen, made two large pans of biscuit, slaw, potatoes and the beef was very tender. Mr. Holton at supper with us. Mr. H. brot down "Enoch Arden" and Widow Bidott papers" which latter he read aloud to our great amusement. Mr. Chapin came in looked at magazines etc and Mr. H. read aloud some more. Talked of hydraulic power in raising buildings. When Holton left Mr. C and Mr. H. talked of cleaning up the amalgam of a removed mill below us, when the weather cleared up. We sang the "Waves" over by note. During evening I gathered the skirt of dress ready to sew on the waist. Have to do my sewing by snatches. Mr. H. quite infatuated by Widow Bedott, read it aloud till I fell asleep.

Tuesday Apr. 2nd. Storming again. Snowing but melting soon as it touches Terra Firma. Mr. H. getting wood. I swept and made bed after getting breakfast then thought I should write this up from last Tuesday before I forgot events which are so slight it is hard to keep the sum. Mr. H. in and eating a lunch which his exercise on the hills has no doubt given him appetite for. I am still troubled with soreness and weakness of eyes. Do nothing for it. I must write some letters. Was writing balance of afternoon to my father. Mr. McNaughton came in which interrupted me some-what. Mr. H. writing, too, so we talked by turns to visitor. Got up and hurried supper on table, mashed potatoes, bacon, eggs and slaw. Mr. Mc N. sat down with us. Maney very cross after supper. Made poor head way in writing tho tried to stay at it. Mr. H. put his face in window on return from town to view his family frightened me and amused children very much. Read the Enterprises and continuation of Clark-Rees breach of promise case, verdict with five thousand dollars for her. Read also of Mr. Peabodys continued munificence and was struck with an insane idea which I revolved all night, scarcely sleeping. Heard a step in the night which filled me with intense fear for few moments.

Wednesday Apr. 3rd. Not an agreeable morning, or breakfast. Felt wearied and excited and no appetite. Maney crying as usual for the breast refusing other food. Mr. H. washed dishes. I mixed bread, have made biscuit for couple of weeks. Tacked and patched torn place on Ella's room carpet. Gave some clothes to washman, mended a little while nursing Maney whom Ella kept on porch seesawing long while Mr. H. read Enoch Arden aloud to me. I cried, he laughed at me but I saw his eyes were filled with tears also. We both blubbered over the story and laughed at each other for so doing. Have my bread baked; looks nice. Before getting supper wrote the letter I revolved in my mind last night. Have not yet dispatched it but most assuredly will. Have some hope!—Fried doughnuts after supper, children poking in dough of their own cutting. We sit around the table, they looking at maps and I writing this, with Maney squealing so. I must stop and take her—

*Many of the entrances start with a description of weather conditions, which are often linked to the writer's mood and feelings. The atmosphere created by the wild environment is sometimes powerfully suggested, as at the end of the description of an idyllic evening at home which acquires an almost poetic quality (see March 11). The evocations of nature and the landscape constitute but the framework, and the diary's main interest lies in the recreation of the warm and cheerful atmosphere which animated the home itself. Daily life for most women who lived in mining towns was an endless routine of back-breaking and time-consuming chores. Quite remarkable is Mrs. Haskell's ability to include cultural and artistic pursuits in the life of the family. Her notations show a wide range of interests and a capacity to relate to other people, and to her children in particular. There are constant shifts in the tone, and a great variety of emotions are expressed. Sometimes Mrs. Haskell projected negative feelings on such chores as washing, and at other times she performed them without displeasure. A most attaching element in her narrative is the pride which can be felt from time to time in her achievements in cooking and sewing, and of the manner in which they were enjoyed by the family.*

The only disrupting note occurs when she mentions her husband's evenings on the town, which she disapproved of but was nevertheless able to describe with a touch of humor sometimes. It was the custom for married couples to go their separate ways in the evenings, according to Louis Palmer, who depicts her own situation in the following manner:

> John seldom finds time to go to balls and parties, and it used to trouble me at first, especially as I had an unnatural craving for such things, caused by the many evenings John's business calls compelled me to remain alone. But presently I found that the unmarried men were not so closely employed as their encumbered brethren, and that it was their allotted duty to become the escorts of the ladies, while their lawful knights remained in billiard halls and club rooms to battle on their behalf with the fickle goddess fortune.[2]

*Louise Palmer's remarks were inspired by life in Virginia City, which was certainly more sophisticated than in Aurora, where women probably had no place to go at night.*

*Despite this problem, Mrs. Haskell seems to have had a pleasant relationship of mutual affection with her husband, who helped her from time to time in the house. One of the words which recur in the diary is "enjoy." Mrs. Haskell's wonderful gusto and cheerful disposition constantly come through in the narrative, which gives a sense of the rhythm of daily life with its ups and downs, its joys and disappointments, in those past times.*

1. This information has been gathered from the introduction (p. 83) written by Richard Lillard in his edition of the diary. He also indicates that Mr. Haskell was a member of the first and the second sessions of the Nevada legislature and that he advertised in 1867 and 1868 in the *Esmeralda Daily Union* (Aurora) as an attorney-at-law.

2. Louise Palmer, "How we live in Nevada, *Overland Monthly* II (May, 1869), p. 461.

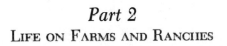

*Part 2*
LIFE ON FARMS AND RANCHES

# Pen Pictures of Early Western Days, 1905

Virginia Wilcox Ivins

*Virginia Wilcox was born around 1827. She lost her parents when she was still a child. In 1840, she came to Keokuk, Illinois, and made her home with her uncle, Dr. Isaac Galland. She attended Edgeworth Seminary in St. Louis from 1845 to 1848. She was married to William Ivins, who was in charge of his father's boarding house, in 1849, and they left Keokuk to go to California with their small son in the spring of 1853. Both shared the same enthusiasm and were eager to embark on this new venture; this was a rather uncharacteristic situation, as women were often loath to part from their families and former homes. They were hopeful indeed:*

> *Blessed with the fearlessness of youth we started bravely forth to seek fortune and a new home with but slight conception of the dangers, difficulties and hardships we were to encounter and knowing little of the sterner realities of life upon the more remote frontier.[1]*

*Her narrative includes a detailed account of the tiresome trip which brought them to Marysville in September, 1853, and during which she gave birth to a girl. Her husband rented a ranch five miles from Sacramento, but was persuaded to give up this arrangement by an acquaintance of his whom he met by chance in the city. This Mr. Hunt invited him to join his party and go with them to a place on the coast which he described in idyllic terms.*

[75]

*Mrs. Ivins did not like the idea at all, but was powerless to change her husband's mind. She became severely ill during the trip in the crowded wagon and, fortunately, her uncle, Dr. Galland, over-took them and brought her back to health. They finally arrived at Petaluma:*

I was put to bed and my uncle watched over me for two weeks, when, thanks to his skill, I began to improve. By this time my children were both sick and my husband down with mountain fever. And altogether we were in a most deplorable state. We were paying twenty-five dollars a week at the hotel with very poor accommodations. Our cattle were turned loose in the hills with no one to look after them but Carl, and he just a half-grown boy. As soon as he could leave us my uncle hurried back to Marysville, sold his outfit and brought my aunt back to Petaluma, where they at once rented a house, and took us all home to nurse us back to health; and most gently and tenderly did they care for us and help us regain our exhausted strength. Had it not been for them, my more than father and mother, this family would have ended then and there. As it was, with all their care, the month of February found me just able to begin housekeeping in a small cottage of two rooms which my husband had built, lined with cloth and papered; poor and cheap as it was, it was a veritable palace to me, for was it not my home, after six months spent in an ox wagon. The cosy nest was our home for eight months.

The town which contained only four hundred inhabitants when we arrived there grew quite rapidly. But change was the order of events, and we kept pace with them. Our cattle were still in the hills, but the owner could now see to them, and they were fat and fine.

We had made many friends, mostly men, but gentlemen who were enterprising, enthusiastic and who never said fail. My husband now decided to go into the stock and dairy business. He took a ranch about two miles from town, suited to the purpose, built a house and we were soon at home to our friends there. The hills closed in on every side, although the road to town was perfectly level, going through the valleys. It was beautiful to look at, but lonely in the extreme. We were nearly a mile from the nearest neighbor, and they only men. I was alone with my children most of the time for the first four months, my husband being away attending to business interests. There was an Indian village about two miles further on called The Rancharee, and so many Indians passed the house drunk and disorderly that I was in a constant state of fear. There were also California lions in the hills about, and coyotes so bold that they stole our provisions, which I tried to keep in a sort of cage hung outside; to say nothing of grizzly bears, for a mother and two cubs were killed only half a mile from the house soon after we moved out there, and just across the road was a ledge of rocks which I was sure sheltered rattle snakes. Mr. Ivins ridiculed the idea, but going there one day to gather wild roses I heard a sound that I could not mistake, so I charged little Charley not to cross the road. Time proved that I was right, for two years afterwards a person going there heard the same sound and set fire to the bushes covering the ledge, when hundreds of the reptiles crawled out and were killed.

It was some time before we got into running order for cheese and butter making, but when we did found it a most lucrative business, a great deal of work but fine profit. A dollar a pound for butter and fifty cents for cheese will do very well when you have eighty cows giving milk, to say nothing of the growing calves and pigs, and money flowed in plentifully.

Mr. Ivins was so well pleased that he wanted to build a better house and make it a permanent home. but I could not think of spending my life and raising my children there, and was dissatisfied and homesick for companions and more refined surroundings.

We were constantly having some grand scare or hairbreath escape. An incident worth relating occurred soon after we moved out to the ranch. Mr. Ivins had bought three hundred chickens, paying a dollar apiece for them, and had built a chicken house of red wood slabs on the hillside back of the house, near a clear spring which gave us our water supply. In a short time they began to disappear. It was a mystery where they went as the door was locked at night, and there was just an opening less than two feet square for them to go in and out. One night I was awakened by the excited breathing of my husband who was dressing himself as fast as possible. He said there was a commotion among the fowls, and rushed off to see what it could be. While he was gone I dressed myself and called the hired man. In a short time Mr. Ivins came back and told me that there was something in the chicken house, and that he had fastened up the small door, and for us to go with him and see what was the matter. So John took the ax, Mr. Ivins his gun and I a piece of candle, and proceeded to the scene of action. The only noise was the fluttering of the chickens. Mr. Ivins opening the large door, set the candle on the ground inside, and as he did so saw the blazing eyes of some animal. Stepping back quickly and fastening the door he took aim straight at the eyes and fired. The chickens flew in all directions putting out the candle. At the same moment there was a terrific crash and something came across the house almost knocking off the slabs. We all ran in different directions. After waiting a while as there was no more noise we proceeded to investigate. We had no more ammunition, so it was rather a dangerous undertaking. Procuring another candle Mr. Ivins opened the door by degrees, and seeing the creature still immovable went in and found it to be an immense lynx, as large as a six months old calf. His solitary load of shot had taken effect directly between the eyes. We dragged his catship down to the house setting him up on the back porch where he was an object of much curiosity. My little boy called it the big pussy.

One lovely day in the latter part of the summer Mr. Ivins went to Tomales for a load of vegetables. It being fifteen miles out he started very early, taking the ox team which served for all occasions, sometimes as a carriage. After he left the hours dragged slowly, and it seemed as if the day were a week long, that night never would come. Drunken Indians rode past making the air hideous with their whoops and howls, but no other human being came in sight. After what seemed a day almost interminable the night closed down. I put my little ones to bed and waited. Outside the cloth and paper house the coyotes barked, and there were all sorts of alarming sounds. I felt as if I should almost die of fright. I could not leave or carry my children, and the nearest neighbor was almost a mile away. It was midnight when I heard a shout on the hill back of the house, and shortly after my husband came, driving the big ox wagon straight down a steep hill a half mile high, without any signs of a road. He had turned off the main road to find a shorter route and had driven over hills and ravines, which he could do as there were few trees. But I think it was the only time that a loaded wagon was ever driven straight up and down those Petaluma hills. All the vegetables in the state would not have tempted me to live over again that dreadful day. I knew of the grizzly bears that had been killed so near the place, and although my husband assured me that dead grizzlies would not hurt me, I was afraid there might be live ones left.

While we were waiting for affairs to get into running order for business, we had leisure to take many short trips to places of interest in the vicinity, one of which was particularly enjoyable. Quite a party was arranged to go on a clam bake to Tomales Bay on the ocean, fifteen miles distant, camping over night. There were about thirty in the party. We started at ten o'clock one lovely June morning, a merry party, in all sorts of conveyances, even to a lumber wagon bedded with hay—mostly men, as women were scarce.

The ride was through the foothills of the coast range of mountains which were covered with wild oats, California poppies and other wild flowers, with now and then live oak trees looking very like orchard trees, with wide spreading shade. We stopped at noon in a convenient spot with a small spring for our picnic lunch. Driving on just before sunset we arrived at the top of the last hill. On reaching the summit a magnificent sight met our eyes. No words can express the grandeur of the scene. Beyond the small promontory which makes the bay, the Pacific stretched one grand expanse of water, smooth as glass, the sun hanging red above it, and in the foreground the little bay with its green borders coming close to the shore. We drew up and waited to see the sun sink like a ball of fire into the water, then driving on down the hill, made our camp, and while the men were putting up the tents got supper and made the beds before dark. There was little sleep for we sat by the camp-fire and told stories and sang songs till far into the beautiful moonlight night; then after the women and girls had retired the men serenaded us until almost morning. After breakfast most of the party went across the bay to the main shore, leaving a Mrs. Thompson and me at the camp, as we both had children with us. They crossed the bay in small boats, taking baskets to bring back the spoils, returning about four o'clock in the afternoon, loaded down with clams, muscles, sea weed and beautiful shells. Mr. Ivins had found a number of beautiful shells commonly called sea eggs, fine specimens, not large but perfect. On reaching the camp as he took his basket down from his shoulder where he had carried it he crushed all but two. I still treasure one of them as a memento of a most enjoyable trip. After having a fine dinner of clams and other fish, we started home about six o'clock. The moonlight ride was beautiful, as we did not reach Petaluma till after midnight.

A friend of ours, Mr. Hulet, had married the daughter of an old Spaniard, Signor Bohockus, who owned many leagues of land, one of the early Spanish grants. Those old land owners kept many retainers dependent upon them, and when money was needed he would have his flocks, herds and manather of horses which roamed over his broad acres of hill and meadow driven up, and as many as were needed sold, at which time money would be plenty. The round-up generally lasted two weeks, after which there was a good time, ending with a fandango and barbecue. Everybody for miles around was invited. Mr. Hulet had asked us to come to the next one, which would be in the spring. One night about nine o'clock a spring wagon drove up with a message from Mr. Hulet to come to the fandango, that he would send us home whenever we wanted to come.

We at once dressed and taking the baby, left Charley with John. After a drive of five miles we arrived at the place of festivities. The whole house, a large adobe, was thrown open and brilliantly lighted, and dancing was going on to the music of Spanish guitars. We entered and were most cordially greeted by the host, and introduced as Signor and Signora Ivins. The baby was taken to the nursery, a long room having beds and cradles, with nurses in attendance, where there were at least thirty babies being cared for. The little Sierra was a most accommodating child, and opened her big blue eyes very wide to see the small Spanish boys of six months old or less dressed in short pants, bolero jackets, and the finest of linen cambric shirts, trimmed with dainty thread and Valenciennes lace, and cunning silk socks and slippers. They were too comical and pretty.

We returned to the salon and joined the throng. Mr. Hulet brought up a tall Spaniard, mentioned my name and his. He bowed and offered his arm which I took, and we stepped into the circle of waltzers. One could not help dancing with such a partner, so round and around we went. I could not ask him to stop, but we did when the music ceased. Later Mrs. Hulet took me to the supper room to see the tables before they were demolished, and to the kitchen where the waiters were carving a whole ox, which had been roasted and was steaming hot. It was all so interesting to me, but strange; so like a foreign country. At one o'clock I took my sleeping baby and the conveyance took us home after a most delightful evening. One of my friends sent me a fine pony and I was getting quite independent, riding into town often, also going with my husband to hunt cattle, and it was delightful riding over these beautiful hills. One day I was going into town; the wind was blowing a gale, there was a long ravine to pass through where the sweep was greatest; when about the middle of this I saw a carriage coming out, and what was my surprise and delight to meet our friends, Mr. and Mrs. Cram, on their way out to visit us. They had a big laugh at my expense. I suppose that I looked the perfect country woman, my hat blown onto the back of my neck, my riding skirt filled with wind and the pony, Flossy, going at a keen gallop. I turned back with them, glad to welcome them, and we had a week to be remembered, filled with reminiscences of our never-to-be-forgotten journey, and anticipations for the future.

And now work began in earnest. Making butter and cheese is no child's play, although I had plenty of help and every convenience for making it as easy as possible, and it brought in lots of yellow gold. The knowledge of our prosperous business became known and visitors were numerous at the ranch to see the process which I had learned from an eastern cheese-maker, and to eat the curd and drink the milk and cream. One August day, when we felt more tired than usual a purchaser came, and in an hour's time everything was sold, including four tons of cheese on the shelves. In another hour I was getting clothes ready for my children and preparing to leave that land of grizzlies, coyotes and rattle-snakes—the latter a local institution, however.

In a few days we bade good-bye to the lonely ranch, which I even then began to regret, spending the last two weeks at the home of my uncle, Dr. Galland, in Petaluma. Our passage was engaged on the steamer Sierra Nevada, which sailed September fifth. Our friends, when they found that we had decided to leave, did everything in their power to keep us, and I began to fear that we had made a mistake in leaving the state, but my uncle and aunt intended to return east in the spring, and there were other dear friends at the end of the anticipated journey. If my husband engaged in business again it would be permanent, for as he said he never put his hand to the plow and looked back. The days passed all too quickly. The dear friends just showered us with kindness, but they could not hold back Father Time.

*In the last part of her book, Mrs. Ivins relates the return trip to Keokuk; they brought back with them a small fortune in gold. She describes conditions there, mentioning in particular the boom of 1856 and the subsequent crash in 1857. Her narrative ends with an account of life in Keokuk during the Civil War.*

*One rather striking element in the last chapters is the nostalgia with which she kept thinking of California; she tried to convince her husband to go back for a visit, but he would not consent. After their departure, she realized how fond she had become of the ranch which had been her home there. From the preceding pages, however, it is evident that while she stayed there she entertained mixed feelings. She was dissatisfied and often unhappy because she had to spend so much time alone in the first months. She felt remote from civilization, longed to talk with other women, and was beset with anxieties and fears, especially at night. On the other hand, she enjoyed the lovely landscape and derived much pleasure from rides and outings. She contributed to the development of the family business and rejoiced in its prosperity.*

*The ambivalence in her feelings should perhaps be ascribed in part at least to the necessary adjustment to conditions which were very different from those she had known in her former life. She did not tell all in her narrative, however, and one is left to wonder what her relationship with her husband was really like. These puzzling aspects and omissions show that it is necessary to read behind the lines, and leave much room for interpretation.*

1. Virginia Ivins, pp. 52-53.

# Mary Murdock Compton

Henria Packer Compton

(Privately Published)

The record of Mary Murdock Compton's life is based primarily on an oral narrative she made to her daughter-in-law through many evenings they spent together in their ranch near Chico. Her reminiscences were supplemented by those of her son concerning his early years and those of one of her daughters, as well as by notes made by Dr. Coolidge after an interview with her.

She was born in November, 1827, in Ireland, to a family of peasants who owned about fifty acres of land. As more and more children came, the older sons started emigrating to America. Mary went to school until she was 10; but as her mother was not well she had to say at home to help. Her father did not think it necessary for girls to get an education. After his death, she remained with her mother and her brother John on the family place until 1851, when they left to go to America; it was a hard decision to make as it meant they would never see their Irish relatives again. They were met in New Orleans by one of the older brothers, Hance, and then went on to Arkansas where he bought 500 head of cattle. In March, 1853, they undertook the long overland trip to California. Mary was entrusted with the cooking. As the journey had been carefully planned by the older brother, they did not meet with any particular problem, apart from the usual hardships and anxieties generated by the crossing of uncivilized territories. In November, 1853, they settled in Marysville:

How good it must have seemed to them to be once more

[83]

under a roof. I have often wondered what became of the sturdy wagons that had been their homes for so long, and had brought them over the rough roads and across the streams. I also wonder what happened to the dear old oxen that they surely had learned to love for their strength and performance if for no other reason. Hance probably sold them for a little money at least. And what about all the men they had brought with them? I never heard Mary mention any disagreement or trouble such as many other wagon trains had between the leaders and the men. They most likely struck out for the gold diggings as soon as they landed.

On their arrival they turned Hannah Strain over to her brother, Gawn. They arrived on the thirteenth of November, 1853, I think.

Mary and her mother lived in Marysville for some time. Her brothers, Hance and William, were running cattle close by and Marysville was their headquarters.

Mary did housework for a family for a while to help out with the finances, but not for very long. Her brother, William, took over the responsibility of providing for her and their mother. She did not say, but I imagine she kept house for him.

Mary met Henry C. Compton about 1858, and they were married on November 30, 1859, in Marysville. He had come to California from Dearborn, Michigan, in 1850, by way of the Isthmus to San Francisco. He tried mining with some success around Hangtown (Placerville), but did not like it. He then turned to ranching and livestock raising.

The Comptons established themselves in Butte County soon after their marriage. They took up land near the Sacramento River, nine miles below Chico, expecting to get it patented. It was not very far from a bend on the river called Grizzly Bend because of the great number of Grizzly bears found along the river in the thick jungle-like growths; willows, oaks, and cottonwoods all hung heavily with wild grapevines. Other animals were found in abundance also. Deer, wildcats, and raccoons were plentiful, and of course, skunks.

The Comptons farmed and raised cattle. Then their first son, Adam Murdock Compton, was born on October 3, 1860. He was named for his mother's brother who had settled in Texas. Four more children were born at this ranch: Elizabeth in 1862, Henry C.

[84]

on January 18, 1864, Ira Lorenzo 1866, and Mary Ellen, known as Mollie, 1869.

When the Comptons had lived here for six or eight years it was established that this land was part of a Mexican Grant given to Sebastian Kayser in 1845, and was later confirmed to Chas. J. Brenha in 1852. The patent was issued in 1861.

Since the Comptons had settled here in 1859 or 1860 one wonders why they did not know of the very doubtful possibility of acquiring the land. Many other families had also taken up land here.

The grant was acquired by John Parrot who was a merchant and trader of some importance in Matzatland, Mexico. He was exceedingly fair to those who had settled on the land and gave the various families the privilege of living there long enough to adjust themselves; a period of three years or more. This gave them time to find new locations. This ranch of 18,000 acres is still owned by the Parrot family, and is called the Llano Seco Rancho.

Mary often said that during the eleven years she lived there she was in Chico about twice. It was not really necessary to go into town often since much of what they needed they made or produced at home.

Mary did all of her own housework including cooking, baking, washing, ironing, mending and making practically all the clothes they wore. So there was not much time for her to go or even to think of going to town.

There were itinerant merchants who came by at fairly regular intervals, and a shoemaker who came twice a year. He stayed until he had made and repaired the shoes that kept the family in footwear for another six months.

At least one trip the family made to Chico was forever imprinted in the mind of the small boy Henry C. Jr. On July fourth 1870 there was a big parade and a big crowd for the small town of Chico. It was a history making event. The Central Pacific Railroad, as it was then called, had built as far north as Chico, and on that day passenger service was being inaugurated.

Henry Compton Sr. loaded his family into the wagon to take them to town to see the train, and to take part in the festivities. It was a long way and they had started a little late. As they were nearing the town the father hurried the horses along the Dayton

Road. Just as they neared the railroad crossing they heard the locomotive whistle. They whipped up the horses and approached the crossing just in time to see the train steam into Chico. It was the first train the children had ever seen, and the first passenger train to come to Chico. It carried many railroad officials and other notables from San Francisco and Sacramento who were coming to celebrate the importance of the occasion.

Sometime prior to the Comptons leaving the Parrot Grant, William Murdock had begun the purchase of parcels of land in Glenn County. He combined these into what he called the Stone Valley Ranch, and it is still known by that name. This ranch is still in the family and the great grandchildren of Mary Murdock Compton are now living there. In October 1871 the Comptons moved from the Parrot Grant to this ranch. At that time the northern part of the county had not withdrawn to form Glenn County so the ranch was then situated in Colusa County. The Comptons lived here until the early spring of 1872.

During the winter Mary's last child was born. Because of high water and bad roads they knew a doctor could not get out to the ranch. So Mary's good neighbor, Mrs. O'Brien, took her over to the O'Brien Ranch before the baby arrived. When the baby girl was born they lost her due to the lack of skill in delivery. Mary named this baby Jane after her sister who had died in Ireland. The O'Brien Ranch is now a part of the Milton French Company.

The winter of 1871-2 was very dry and the drought in the valley was very bad. There was no feed for the livestock, and the ranchers had to move their stock out to other sections of the country. A lot of them went to Idaho and some to Nevada. At this time Henry Compton Sr. was running about 2,500 head of sheep and about 200 head of cattle. In the early spring of 1872, like the other stockmen, he had to hunt for pasture elsewhere. So he moved his family and livestock to Modoc County in the extreme northeast corner of California.

It took them twenty-eight days to make the trip. They went from Stone Valley Ranch to Red Bluff, north and east to Jelly's Ferry, then through the section of the country known as Manzanita Chutes, and by way of Hat Creek to the Pitt River area. They settled on a little creek about five miles east of Fall River Mills. All the livestock made the trip successfully, and came through in very fine condition.

The elevation there was rather high and the weather quite cold. They had a very cold winter that year and Mary said that on snowy nights the snow would sift between the unbattened boards of the cabin and leave a light cover of snow on their bed covers. They had built this cabin in an isolated but rather open place. The ground about was strewn with huge, low rocks. They were quite fortunate to find a cleared spot close to water for their small house.

They had fine grazing higher up on land that was rather like a mesa. The sheep would be taken up through the day to feed, but were brought down every night and bedded in a corral near the cabin because of danger from coyotes and other predators.

Usually Adam, who was thirteen years old, would go with his father to look after the stock up on the mesa, and Mary would be left all day with the three younger children. Lizzie, the older daughter, had remained in Marysville at the convent so she could attend school. There were no other resident schools at that time. They had an old Indian, Toshey, who worked for them and stayed around the buildings to help with the chores or any other work that Mary and the children had to do.

Often it would be late when Mary's husband and Adam would get down off the mountain with the sheep. Once they were lost with the sheep in a dense fog. Mary put a lighted lantern in a wagon out in the flat. She hoped they could see the feeble light and so find their way down. Then she would go out into the cold, foggy night at frequent intervals and call to them. At last they heard her voice and, directed by the sound of her calling, managed to get down off the mountain through the brush. They had been far off the trail.

There were rattlesnakes everywhere in that rocky country. Strangely Henry Compton, Sr., was deathly afraid of them and would become almost paralyzed with fear at the sight of them. So if Mary was near by it was she who killed them with rocks or a gun.

The Comptons had a small cellar under the cabin kitchen that was reached by a trap door in the kitchen floor. One day she sent Adam to get some potatoes which were buried a little deeper in the cellar and covered with a burlap sack to keep them from freezing. Adam rushed back to tell here there was a big rattlesnake coiled on top of the sack. She got her pistol, lay flat on her stomach on the floor above and shot it through the trap door.

[87]

This was the winter that the famed Modoc Chief, Captain Jack, led his Indians in the uprising known as the Modoc War. There were a great many Indians in this part of California and Nevada. Mary always treated them kindly, which probably saved the lives of her and her family. The Indians all through this winter of 1872-3 had been foraging and stealing as far south as Surprise Valley, demanding food and stealing clothes off the clotheslines. But Mary and her husband were unaware of all this.

One day the Indian, Toshey, came to the door with a big band of Indians in war bonnets and war paint. Toshey assured her they were friendly and would not harm her, but they wanted some food and tobacco. She gave liberally of food, but told them she could not give them tobacco. She had none. Her husband did not use it. She expected them to move on, but they found a dead sheep, took it down to the stream close by and spent the day butchering and cooking it. Later Mary learned that these Indians were a part of Captain Jack's band being hunted out by the United States soldiers who were hiding in the lava beds some distance to the north of the Comptons' grazing territory.

Soon after this, Toshey came one day and told her there was a big fight and made signs that "white man be scalped." This must have been shortly after the real fight started on January 16-17, 1873. News did not travel very fast. Fall River Mills, five miles away, was the first post office and the Comptons went there only when they needed supplies. This was their only source of news.

Everywhere else was open country for miles around them, inhabited mostly by Indians. After Mary's husband and Adam came down with the sheep that evening she told Henry what Toshey had said. Henry then made the trip to Fall River Mills on horseback after supper to get the news. He learned that the Indian trouble was very serious and the white settlers were joining with the soldiers to drive out the disturbing Indians. Henry thought the younger children and Mary must get out of this country at once. So they packed up that night and the next morning he took them out to Redding by wagon. Mary and the children took the train for Chico. This is evidence that the railroad had forged ahead on up the valley toward Oregon.

Henry and Adam went back to take care of the livestock. Mary had no way of hearing from them all the rest of that winter.

She had no idea of what their fate might be with the Indians. Then one spring day in 1873 Henry came down to Chico with Adam. They had over $10,000. They were both sound and well and Henry had sold his cattle and sheep in Modoc County.

In the fall of 1873 the Comptons bought a ranch of 192 acres three miles south of Chico with the money from the sale of his livestock. It was known as the York Place. Mary did not tell me whether $10,000 was the complete price or a down payment. However, they did very well here with their usual thrift and hard work.

For the first time all the children were able to attend school regularly. While Henry and Adam were in Modoc, Mary and the children lived in Chico with Emma Weed, and the younger children had been going to Mrs. White's private school. But after they moved to the York Place they went to the little country school, the York School, only about a half mile from their ranch. Part of the time Henry's brother, Ben, was their teacher.

Again Henry Sr. raised grain and some sheep. Sometimes in the early summer he would take his sheep to the mountains. They would go up the Humboldt to Big Meadows, which is now under Lake Almanor. Henry Compton Jr. often recalled these trips as he traveled over the road by automobile many years later. He would tell me how, as a boy of about ten years, he had slept beside a big rock in Jonesville, now on Hugh Baber's lot. He had been impressed, and no doubt a little scared, by the short turns in the descent on the east side of the summit. There was a big, rocky formation known as Robbers' Roost where, a few years before, a band of robbers had hidden and held up a stage coming from the west. Their haul was considerably large.

Henry Jr. liked to stop at the Bruce Place just east of the summit where he had spent the night as a lad; and also at Fanianis' of the olden days in Big Meadows where he remembered they had camped. Sometimes they had been able to buy the sweet mountain butter put up in firkins. He would recall what a beautiful mountain meadow the Big Meadows was at that time.

While they were living at the York Place Mary's brother, John, and his wife, Sarah, came to live with them. John had become paralyzed and unable to work, so they lived with the Comptons until he passed away.

Mollie was just a little girl then and she remembered that her
Aunt Sarah pierced her ears, and an old man who worked for them
bought her a pair of earrings with bright, blue stones in them. This
same man built a flour bin for Mary. It was on wheels and could be
moved about the kitchen. She was very proud of it. The Chinese
cook noticed this and said, "I think you take that box with you
when you die." Small wonder it is that she prized that little luxury
for there were very few conveniences in this pioneer country.

About this time Mary had a letter from her brother, Robert,
from whom she had not heard for years. He was married and lived
in Yreka. He was mining near there. He wanted a picture of Mary,
so she had one taken with herself and Mollie, and sent it to him.
Later he sent a silver nugget to Mollie and some mineral samples to
Lizzie, but he never came to see them as Mary hoped he would.

In November 1878 Henry Sr. and Mary bought a ranch of
1,900 acres on the Sacramento River about nine miles north of
Colusa, and moved there with their family. It was part of the
Thomas O. Larkin children's grant. They farmed here, raising
wheat and sometimes barley. They did very well indeed. Mary
often spoke of her raising chickens and making butter. She was
able to sell enough of these to supply the ranch with provisions,
thereby making it possible to pay their net profit on the purchase
of the ranch. I do not know just how much this ranch cost them,
but it must have been a very good amount for those times.

The Compton ranch on the river was known as the Compton
Landing. The river at that time was navigable all the way up to
Red Bluff. Their place was known by all the rivermen and also on
the plains back of them for miles north and south. They had put in
scales for weighing grain and the ranchers for miles around hauled
their grain there on wagons with eight-mule teams. The drivers
used what was called a jerk line. That meant driving the mules
with a single rein and guiding the lead mule which was trained to
respond to a jerk of the line. The grain was weighed and loaded on
barges. The loading was done usually by Indians who lived on a
ranchero close by. The barges were towed down the river by tow
boats. The Comptons charged for this service and made considerable money in this way.

An interesting feature of the life along the river was the
trading boat that made the trip up the river about every two

weeks. It stopped at each ranch landing along the river bank. The people from what they called "the plains" back of the river would be waiting for it. The boat signaled its approach by a long, loud blast of the whistle, and on its arrival men, women, and children would be on hand to come on board. The boat was, in fact, a floating country general merchandise store. It had everything in hardware as well as clothing bolts and shoes, groceries, millinery, ribbons, notions and everything else one could imagine; even candy and toys. The storekeeper would take orders for fence posts and wire, which he would bring up on a return trip. The ranchers could trade in their products—sometimes bacon and lard too old for their own use—or anything else they wanted to get rid of. The boats were still going up and down the river in the early 1900's. Practically all the grain, hides, wool, and so forth went by barge down the river to Sacramento or San Francisco.

The Comptons still kept the ranch south of Chico and let it out to others to farm for cash rent.

Each of the children attended Pierces Christian College at College City, Colusa County, at some time.

Henry Compton Sr. died at this river home in 1888. Mary and her sons carried on until 1891. During this year Ira, with family funds, built what must have seemed to them a luxurious home on the ranch south of Chico. When it was completed Mary and her daughter, Mollie, and Ira went up to this ranch to live. Adam took over the Colusa County ranch to farm for his mother.

By this time Adam and Henry had been farming as partners on their Uncle William's ranches. There was the Stone Valley Ranch and also a ranch known as the Adobe which was seven miles west of Willows. When William died in 1894 Adam and Henry disolved partnership as Adam had been made one of the executors of his Uncle William's estate. Adam continued farming the Colusa County ranch for his mother on shares, and Henry Jr. took over the management of his Uncle William's two ranches.

Mary lived the remainder of her life on the York Place. Her daughter, Mollie, married John Deter of Colusa County. They lived with her, and farmed that place as Ira had found other interests. All of her children were married and established in their homes. Henry and I lived on the ranch south of Chico known as the Briscoe Ranch, and it was here that Mary related so many of the adventures of her life. Later when we moved into Chico she was often with us.

Mary died in our home after a very short and seemingly slight illness in her 88th year on May 24, 1915. Thus ended a life full of adventure, toil, and achievement. She was certainly a remarkable little woman. She was not more than five feet tall, and never weighed more than 120 pounds.

While she did not have much schooling, she was self-educated. She often said even in her busiest days and no matter how tired, she just had to spend some time reading, and after supper when her day's work was over and the small children put to bed, she spent an hour or so thus. She did not care for fiction, but loved her Scotch and Irish poets. She was well informed in history, and kept up on current events.

Mary was firm in her principles and loyal to her friends. She was sweet and womanly, and never lost her natural refinement. She was one whom everyone loved and admired.

After Mary was 70 years old she enjoyed doing French embroidery which she had not done for years, for she had not had the time for it in her earlier years. She had met the hardships of pioneer days with her chin up, and was in no sense hardened by her experiences. She looked upon it all as a great adventure.

She once said to Mary Roberts Coolidge who had a Doctor's degree and was the daughter of a college professor, "I never wanted to go back and live my life any different. I would not give up all I have seen and done for your education."

Though Mary's early life was spent in hard work and close living financially, she accepted the comforts that were available to her in later life very graciously.

She had a keen sense of humor and her brown eyes would twinkle with fun as she gave a quick answer. She was proud of her age and had grown old gracefully. At one time a friend said, "Mrs. Compton, you are looking younger every day." She answered, "It is time. It is time. I have been old long enough."

I look back over the years that I spent with her and consider it a great privilege to have known her. I have a most wonderful and cherished memory of her.

*The most original feature in this narrative, in my opinion, is that it portrays a happy pioneer: Mary Murdock Compton had a deep enjoyment of life and was able to concentrate on its positive aspects only. She was used to hard work and had learned to accept it without complaints. As she had never known another kind of life, she did not look backwards and did not long for better conditions. Her delight in manufactured objects such as the flour bin is evidence that she knew how to appreciate what she had. Despite her numerous occupations, she managed to broaden her horizon and to pursue cultural interests. She preserved throughout her life a remarkable openness and receptivity to experiences. She probably derived great pride from her contribution to the rise of the family and her ability to surmount the difficulties which marked her early years.*

*This brief narrative also provides insights into the way a ranch was run. Theirs functioned as a self-sufficient unit, and the tasks were divided between the different members of the family: the father and elder son took care of the stock, while Mary remained on the farm with the younger children and was responsible for the management of the dairy. This was a traditional organization, which caused the male members of the family to be away in the day time. External conditions brought about a longer separation: when the Modoc War started, Mary and the children were sent to the nearest town and were without news from the rest of the family.*

*So much energy and courage, so much patience and endurance had to be shown! Each time the family moved, it was necessary to adjust to different circumstances. Fortunately, success rewarded them. And when Mary could finally enjoy some leisure, she still had that great ability to derive pleasure out of experiences.*

# "The First Pioneers of the Gila Valley"

Mrs. C.A. Teeples

*Arizona Historical Review*, vol. 1 no. 4 (January 1929), 74-78

*Mrs. Teeple's extremely brief relation has the particularity of centering upon a group, and not just one family. It is set in the Gila Valley in the years 1879-1880, and tells something of the way in which the Mormons organized their settlements:*

Many have attempted to tell who the first Gila Valley pioneers were in Graham County. They have told it in public and have printed it in the valley paper. Most of the earliest pioneers have passed away, but they still live in the minds of all of the true early pioneers, and those who speak of the first pioneers, in most cases, have either forgotten or do not know the facts.

I am taking the liberty to tell who the first pioneers who came to the Gila Valley were; how they were sent and what they experienced after arriving. In 1879 William Teeples came twice to the Gila with two different companies from Northern Arizona, in search of a new home. Some liked the valley, while others did not. Those who were favorably impressed went to Jesse N. Smith, who was then president of the Snowflake Stake of Latter Day Saints, and reported conditions and their desires, and asked for his advice in regard to colonizing the valley of the Gila. President Smith told the men that he would go to Show Low, where their camp was located and organize their colony. President Smith then took with him a company and went to Show Low and held a meeting at the home of Moses Cluff. At this meeting, J. K. Rogers was chosen and set apart as presiding elder in the church, with William Teeples as first, and Henry Dallas as second counselors, and Hyrum Weech, secretary. These leaders were instructed by President Smith to obey counsel and they would get along all right. The little colony then made rapid preparations to start on their journey. With the men, women and children they numbered about twenty-five souls. The men and women drove the teams while the boys drove the loose cattle, and everything proceeded well.

When we reached Camp Apache our men went to get supplies, so that we could continue on to the Gila Valley. When the officers of the camp heard of our travels they desired to secure the names and ages of every member of our company, and also wanted to know of trouble from the Indians, but we did not know of the danger at that time. We continued on and encountered some very bad roads. When we reached Black River we crossed over safely and camped for the night, but the next morning the men and boys had to remove the large rocks from the mountain road before we could go on. It was more of a trail than a road, but after lots of hard work to get the way clear we passed on by hitching nearly every team to a wagon and pulling one at a time to the top of the hill. It took nearly the entire day to get over the hill. In descending the grade, it was necessary to lock each wheel of the wagon and tie a log behind to keep it from running over the horses. We made the journey with only the slight break of one bolt on a wagon and not a single accident, and reached the Gila in safety.

When we got to the Gila River we met a band of Indians. Our company had crossed the river and camped for noon. The men and boys went in swimming, and afterwards caught some fish. I was getting the dinner ready. I had a plateful of nice fried fish and a plate of warm bread ready for the table. There was a young Indian standing near; he watched his chance and when I wasn't looking he grabbed both bread and fish and ran. I then had to cook more bread and fish and this time kept it from the sight of the Indians. After dinner we gathered our belongings together and journeyed on. That night we camped near Mr. Moore's ranch, at Fort Thomas, and the next day, April 8, we arrived at Pima. It was afternoon. The first thing we did was to burn the tall grass for a camp site, where Pima now stands. There were lots of insects, mice and snakes, and burning the grass made it safer for a camp.

Tents were pitched and a townsite laid out into lots, and the men drew tickets for their lots, which were numbered. Each man went on his lot and went to work to improve it. They went to the river and cut cottonwood logs with which to build their houses, and exchanged work in building them. The first house finished was for J. K. Rogers. It had a combination roof of willows, tall rush grass, then finer grass mixed with clay mud, and, lastly, dry earth was put on to keep out the rain. Mr. Teeples' house was the first one built with windows, doors and floors. This one was built with two rooms, with a shed between. By the Fourth of July three more families had arrived. They were Heber Reed, John Busby and Sam Curtis.

We all joined together in celebrating this first "July 4th" on the Gila. There were also three other young men who had come from Show Low and were working for the ranchers. These young men did a good part in helping to make a success of the celebration. They brought some of the provisions to help out with the dinner. While some of the women were preparing the meal others were taking part on a program. After dinner the men and boys played games until chore time. Then came the dance in the evening. Planks were arranged around the rooms for seats. Wm. Thompson played an accordian, while we all joined in the dance. Everybody was enjoying themselves in the promenade when Mrs. Patterson and her friends arrived, or, in other words, "a band of ruffians." We were unaware of their coming until they had unhitched their team and come to the house. There were four women and five men in the company. As our people were leaving the floor for their seats, after a dance, this group came rushing in and pushed to the center of the room. They were invited to be seated until it was their turn to dance. Each of the women had two revolvers and the men had one each. When they went on to dance they removed their weapons and laid them down. While the four couples were dancing the extra man slipped a revolver outside and hid it in the wagon. When it was discovered that the gun was missing the women made a great disturbance and began to accuse us "Mormons," and demanded to know who had taken it. Mr. Teeples asked them to be quiet and told them that it would be found and proven that our people did not take it. They searched the house and then went to the wagon and found it there hidden under some things. They were peaceable the balance of the time, but when they got started home they made a terrible racket and drove like Satan was after them. This was their introduction. They came again afterward.

Mr. Teeples had a good blacksmith shop and the ranchers often came to have their tools repaired; travelers would also stop for meals. Some were clothed like human beings, but had the manners of beasts—as wicked as sin could make them, and those who were with them who would be decent, were afraid to object to their actions for fear of death. One time a gang got into a fight, beat one man until they thought him dead, then rode off and left him. Later, some of them came back and found him still alive and asked our people to care for him until he was well which we did. Another time a man was taken away from the officers and carried some distance up Ash Creek and hanged to a walnut tree. Our people were asked to cut him down and bury him, which they did. Other things were very trying. Our cattle at one time all went blind and our men had a hard time to cure them from this infection. At times the Indians were so bad that some of the men would have to stand guard at night.

Many families came the first fall and winter. Some only remained a short time and then went to St. David, where they could get freighting as employment. Our men bought a threshing machine and threshed their own grain and hauled it, thus keeping them in employment. They made their own flour at a great saving, as at that time flour was eight dollars a hundred. We would get four pounds of sugar for one dollar and other groceries were priced on the same basis. While the men were threshing they contracted malarial fever and were very sick. Mr. Wilton Hawes, whose wife had died before he left Utah, was living on Mrs. Patterson's ranch. He had a large family and they all took the fever and chills, and his daughter narrowly escaped death. Mrs. S. G. Rogers and I were called to go and care for this girl. We stayed all day, and worked with her until she was out of danger. That was on Friday. The next morning (Saturday) my son took sick with the same malady, and on Sunday he died. At this same time we were threatened with having our stock driven off and ourselves driven out on foot. But we weathered it in spite of all the discouragements and trials.

In 1879 our colony erected a log house in which to hold school and church services. In 1880 a number of new families arrived and we felt more secure. Still at times we were threatened. Never were men more faithful to their calling than were Mr. Rogers and Mr. Teeples. They went through all kinds of trials, which cannot be mentioned here. Mr. Teeples' greatest trial brought him to his bed, and he was heartsick when he died. He divided his last foot of land as an inducement to people to stay and help build the colony. He also bought grain for seed, which he gave to them; and he did other things as great. Finally he died trying to do all he could to hold the colony together. And he died penniless. Mr. Rogers was never the same afterwards, for he had to carry a double load. Rueben Fuller and Henry Dall had to taste the bitter pill also, but Mr. Dall later moved to Utah.

In the year 1880 Mr. Collins, of Ft. Thomas, sent a troop of soldiers up to drive the colony away, but Jack O'Neil, who was deputy sheriff of Ft. Thomas at the time, told the soldiers he would come with them and see what was wrong. He had the soldiers stop down in the wash, while he came to talk with the leading men. He found them peacable and that there was no cause to molest us, and he sent the soldiers back.

In the summer of 1880 there was a small colony came from the Little Colorado and settled on the north side of the river. They rented land and planted it to corn and beans. Then they were stricken with chills and there was none well enough to take care of another. While they were in this troubled condition, the Indians made a raid on them. There was but one man able to move and he ran down to the river and started to cross. The river was very high and soon his horse went down and left him to swim for his life. He had a hard time reaching the shore, and when he did it was near Mr. Moore's farm at Ft. Thomas. He called to a Mexican to bring him some clothing, as he had lost his in the river. He then borrowed a horse and rode up to Pima and gave the alarm about the Indians. Our men built a raft and brought the sick people across the river to Pima and cared for them until they were well. Mr. Teeples took three families to his home—twenty-five souls in all—stricken with chills and fever. Mr. Rogers and all others who could take a family did so.

There was a baby in one family and the mother and baby

were very sick and sorely in need of help. When I found this out I helped them. Later that fall and winter there was another company came over the mountains, in great danger from the Indians, but the hand of the Lord guided them and they got through all right. About that time Al Kempton came with a company. The night before they arrived at San Carlos the soldiers and Indians had a battle, and when the company came off the mountain toward the river there were dead horses and dogs lying all around, and the teams had to turn out of the road to get past them. These are some of the things the first pioneers had to pass through the first two years on the Gila. These staunch old pioneers were ready to help all that needed help as long as they had a cent to do it with. With all these trials and hardships they were faithful and strong in the cause of truth, and rich in the spirit of the Lord, our Redeemer. Our men paid for the right-of-way, and made the first ditch, and made it possible for others to make homes here. Through all this, the Teeples and Rogers had suffered many hardships; nevertheless, but few know who the first pioneers were. The first pioneers are dead and forgotten, and others get the praise for something that does not belong to them. But there is still a spark of fire left that will not die, and when the wind blows in that direction it will come to life again. The children know what their parents have gone through. These men should not be forgotten, and when the different organizations of the young gather, these organizations should bear the names of the first pioneers and have the history of the community taught to them. The pioneers should have all the honor due them, for they went through more for the upbuilding of this valley than anyone, for they came here with plenty and died poor men. For the sake of these faithful pioneers, I will close with pleading, as the poet says, "Please don't let me die."

(Signed) MRS. C. A. TEEPLES,

Pima, Arizona.


*Various stages are delineated in the growth of the commu-*
*nity: first, campsites were chosen, tents set up and insects*

*eliminated; then, the land was distributed and houses were built; finally, with the arrival of new families, agriculture developed and public buildings were gradually erected. Throughout the narrative, one constantly has the sense of the solidarity which existed between the pioneers and of their readiness to sacrifice their individual comforts to the common good. The list of the various hardships and misfortunes they had to go through is impressive, and their endurance and strong religious beliefs emerge forcefully; many of them remained poor, but had acquired spiritual riches on which they could always depend.*

*Conditions in Arizona at that time are mentioned: the problem of safety loomed large as Indian bands were still roving; the kind of company that could be found in the Territory was rather bad, and violence was still very much a part of daily life. Despite the many obstacles which had to be overcome, the Mormon pioneers were successful in their attempt to colonize the area because they were united by a common religious faith and a sense of hierarchy and discipline. As Mrs. Teeples says, they paved the way for others and have a right to recognition.*

# Memories of a Handcart Pioneer, with some account of frontier life in Utah and Nevada

Mary Ann Hafen

(Denver, Colorado: privately printed
for her descendants) 1938.

Mary Ann Hafen's narrative is organized around her own experiences and tells much about daily life in a Mormon community. In a foreword dated August, 1938, she indicates that she wrote it for her descendants.

She was born in Switzerland in 1854, to a moderately prosperous family. They embraced the Mormon faith and left their native country to go to Utah in 1860. The following year, they were told to go with the Swiss company to settle southern Utah. The pioneers were hampered in their efforts to develop the area by unfavorable climatic conditions, and suffered much from hunger and cold in the winter of 1862. In Mary Ann's family, every member had to help in procuring means of subsistence: the mother and the children worked in the fields for many years; the children often had to feed and watch the cows, which meant exhausting walks in the scorching sun. The family remained poor for a long time. No task was considered too hard to be performed by a woman or a child - such was the pressure of necessity. The two babies that were born to her mother at that time died. Amusements consisted mainly in social gatherings, games and outings. Polygamy was current among Mormons and men were encouraged to support several families. At 19, Mary Ann was married at Santa Clara; she was happy, despite the fact that she was this man's second wife; unfortunately, he died shortly *afterwards. As her parents did not have much money and were getting old, she was urged to marry again rapidly. She was reluctant at first to accept John Hafen, as his first wife objected to the plan; on her wedding trip, she cried most of the time. An arrangement was worked out after a serious crisis, by which the husband shared his days equally between his two wives. Later, he married again twice.*

*Mary Ann Hafen gave birth to several children and lived according to the Mormon principles. Hard work was her daily lot, and she tried to help support the family by drying peaches and making clothes. After the birth of the sixth child, she moved to Nevada. Her life there is told in the following excerpt:*

Because Santa Clara had so little land for so many settlers, we decided it would be best for me to take my young family and move to Bunkerville, where a settlement had been started and where there was more and cheaper land. My son Albert was already down there helping John's other wife, Anna.

My birthday occurred the day before we were to leave. Our relatives and friends gathered to give a combined birthday and farewell party.

On May 6, 1891, with me and our five children tucked into a covered wagon, John clucked at the horses and drove away from our old home town. Another wagon, driven by young Johnnie, conveyed our household effects. As neighbors, relatives, and friends crowded about to see us off, I with others shed a few tears. I knew I was going to something of the same hardships I had known in childhood days; that my children were to grow up in a strange land with scarcely a relative near; and that they too would have to share in the hardships of subduing a new country.

Our drive was not unpleasant, however. The country was all new to me as I had never been beyond Santa Clara westward. Past Conger Farm, up Conger Hill, and on to Camp Springs Flat we traveled and there camped for the night. The next day we drove past the Cliffs, and down the long Slope where great Joshua trees looked like soldiers with their helmets and spears. The second night we spent at the Beaver Dams on a clear little creek where gnawed young cottonwoods gave evidence of beaver being present. The next day we passed the beginnings of Littlefield. Then we followed the Virgin River bed, crossed Mesquite flat, where a few farms and shanties showed settlement, again crossed the river, and arrived at Bunkerville.

The little town was rather inviting. In the early dusk the numerous young cottonwoods along the field canals and along the town ditches looked like an oasis in a desert. There was only one fence in the whole town and that was around Samuel Wittwer's lot.

Albert was overjoyed to see us. John's other wife, Anna, had supper waiting for us when we arrived. Among other things she served alfalfa greens dressed with white sauce. It was quite a tasty dish.

The next morning we went up to the little place that John had purchased from a Danishman, Brother Jorgensen. It was a two-roomed adobe house with dirt floors and dirt roof. That did not look so inviting, but John promised that he would see that it was soon finished off with a good roof and floors, and probably would put a second story on the house to make more bedrooms.

The big lot already had five or six almond trees growing, and a nice vineyard of grapes. But there was a little wash running through the side of the lot which had to be filled in; and there was only a makeshift fence of mesquite brush piled about three feet high. Besides, the lot was covered with rocks, because it was close to the gravel hill. Our twenty-five-acre farm, about a mile and a half above town, was only partly cleared of arrow weeds and mesquite. It was sandy land with some large sand knolls to be leveled.

The cow we had brought down was dry so John turned her in as part payment on the land. Later another was brought down from Santa Clara. Because of his duties as Bishop in Santa Clara my husband had to hurry back and left Albert, our sixteen-year-old son, in charge of the planting.

As soon as we could we planted corn, cane, cotton, squashes and melons in the field; and vegetables in the town lot. The brush fences were but poor protection from the stray animals that went foraging about. However we got a pretty good crop from everything planted that year. Albert dug up three young mulberry trees from Mesquite and planted them around our shadeless house. Now, after forty-seven years of growth, those mulberry trees completely shade the old place.

I remember how in those earliest years we were disturbed by the hot winds that swept over the dry bench lands from the south.

That first fall John came back bringing a load of lumber to finish off the house. During the winter he and Albert put in the floors and ceiling; built up the adobe walls to make a second story; and put on a shingle roof. There was no stairway up so the children used a ladder out of doors.

From the first we found that the river dam was far more unstable here than at Santa Clara. Each flood that came down the river broke our Bunkerville dam. Nothing but a loose brush and rock dam seemed feasible here because of the soft sandy river bottom, which was quite in contrast to the rocky bottom of the Santa Clara Creek. Because of this softness, teams were often stuck in the quicksand and had to be dug out. Range animals occasionally mired fast and starved to death in the sandy bars of the river.

Before we had been in our new location eight months I became homesick to see the folks in Santa Clara. So when John took a load of grain up to the grist mill in Washington, I went along. It was pretty hard pulling for his little span of mules so I walked most of the way up the fifteen-mile Slope above Littlefield, to lighten the load. When at last we neared the town, at sight of the old familiar creek, I broke down and cried. And yet from choice I would not have given up my new home, poor though it was.

After that, about every year I managed to make the trip up to see my relatives. And for a while John came down every month or so to help Albert and to make small improvements around the place. But being Bishop at Santa Clara, and with his other three families, he could not be with us much. So I had to care for my seven children mostly by myself. He had provided us a house, lot, and land and he furnished some supplies. But it was a new country and we had a hard time to make a go of it.

Though we almost always had grain on hand, we sometimes found ourselves without flour. At such times we had to grind the wheat in a coffee mill until we could take a grist to the mill at Washington, sixty-five miles away. We also ground corn in the coffee mill and made mush of it. With molasses and milk on the mush it made our breakfast for years.

We hauled our loads of cotton to the cotton factory at Washington and received cloth in exchange. I think we got about twelve and one-half cents per pound for cotton in the seed, and paid fifty to sixty cents a yard for jeans—a cotton and woolen mixed cloth.

Sugar, or sorghum, cane we took to the town sorghum mill and got our year's supply of molasses. Sugar and honey were almost unknown in those times, so sorghum served as sweetening. Candy pulls around the shining molasses mill were favorite evening pastimes for the young people. Most every year we made a practice of putting up twenty-gallon barrels of preserves—peaches or green tomatoes. The peaches were washed, dumped whole and unpeeled into the big vats of sorghum. After cooking to a preserves they were put into barrels. Green tomatoes were generally gathered just before frost, soaked overnight in salt water, and then cooked over the furnace fire with sorghum as sweetener.

After we had been in Bunkerville about two years, my last child was born—December 8, 1893. He was a fine husky boy, weighing 12½ pounds. Aunt Mary Bunker, wife of the Bishop, was the acting mid-wife of the town. She came the customary ten days to bathe the baby while I was in bed. We called him Reuben LeRoy. As soon as his father learned of the birth, he came down to Bunkerville. I have never had a doctor at the birth of any of my children, nor at any other time for that matter, and I have never paid more than five dollars for the services of a mid-wife.

When my baby was just a year old, my brother Christian came down on horseback to tell me that mother had died of la grippe. To make a light conveyance, we took the running-gears of a wagon, laid boards across, and padded them with hay and quilts to soften the jolts. Then with my youngest children and with Albert for a driver, we left home at four o'clock in the morning. We arrived at Beaver Dams at sun-up, took fresh horses that my son-in-law-to-be, Henry Leavitt, had taken ahead, and hurried on to Santa Clara by eight that night. The next morning the funeral was held.

Afterwards we divided Mother's belongings into four piles, then drew cuts to see which should belong to each of us four children. In the draw I got Mother's bedstead that she had slept on all these years; and some of her nice dishes. We each got seventy-five dollars from money left her by a relative in Switzerland.

It pained me to see that father was fast losing his eyesight. Ever since he had been caught in a blizzard years before, his eyes had troubled him. Often they were sore and inflamed, and now within a year he was to go totally blind, and to be so the fifteen remaining years of his life. He had always been such a hard worker that the handicap of blindness was very hard on him. He would sometimes cry like a child because he was unable to do much work. But he did a good deal, even though blind. He would feel his way with a stick across the wide ditch and into his lot, where he would cut lucern and carry it to his cows. Once he came down to Bunkerville and stayed with me for a while.

With the $75 received at mother's death, I bought some store goods, brought them to Bunkerville, and sold them off and on for the next two years, thinking I could make a little money in that way. Finally I gave up that venture because it tied me too close. Besides, I did not make much profit, and goods let out on credit were not always paid for, especially those sold to Indians.

I did not want to be a burden on my husband, but tried with my family to be self-supporting. I picked cotton on shares to add to our income; would take my baby to the fields while the other children were at school, for I never took the children out of school if it could possibly be avoided. That cotton picking was very tiresome, back-breaking work but it helped to clothe my children.

I always kept a garden so we could have green things to eat. Keeping that free from weeds and watering it twice a week took lots of time. With a couple of pigs, a cow, and some chickens, we got along pretty well.

In the spring of the year, when the grass sprang up on the hills, almost everybody turned their cows out to graze for the day. Sometimes they failed to return at night, unless there was a young calf to call them back. Often I have walked almost to the mountains, to hunt for and bring back the straying cows. We had alfalfa, or lucern as we called it, in the lot and the children or I always cut it with a sickle or scythe throughout the summer to feed the cows. In the early spring, before the lucern was high enough to cut, we would go to the field and fill sacks with young sweet clover and bring it home to the cows. This clover or young lucern we would mix with straw so the cows would not bloat on it.

[106]

We made good use of the grapes on the lot. The thinskins we dried into raisins on the roof of the kitchen. I always made some batches of jam, usually out of the Californias. The Lady Downings and tough-skins we usually sent fresh with peddlers to the mining camps. Albert frequently took them to Delamar or Pioche.

The year after mother died, my oldest girl married— September 3, 1895. She was only seventeen and I hated to see her go, but she got a good husband and has raised a fine family since.

In the spring of 1896 I took my three youngest children and went up to the March conference. Now that Mother was dead, I always stayed with my sister Rosie whenever I visited Santa Clara. When I walked in with my babies there lay Ella, Rosie's little girl, all blotched with measles.

A week after I got back home with my family they all broke out with measles. One night when I was weary from caring for the sick children, I fell asleep on top of the bed. My boy Wilford, eight years old, crawled out of bed and took a big drink of cold water. The measles went in on him and do what we would we were unable to help him. Smothering spells came on and he jumped up fighting for breath. Shortly before he died he kept looking up to the corner of the ceiling and saying, "I'm coming." And then he left us. I felt somewhat reconciled to his going because of the dream I had had when he was a baby. I believed that his time had come; that God wanted him on the other side.

For years I had longed for a cool cellar and for a kitchen built onto the house. Albert went out to Mount Trumbell and worked for lumber. He chopped trees for a while and then returned with a load of lumber to build the kitchen for us. His father helped dig the cellar and lay up the walls with rock. Then they made a trip to the nearby mountain and got some heavy cedar and pine logs to put over the cellar. These served as joists below the kitchen floor. Adobe walls for a nice big room were laid up and a roof topped them. But the rooms could not be finished until we had more lumber. Again Albert drove a hundred miles to the Trumbell saw mill and worked for another load. The room was finally finished and we surely welcomed the new comfort of more space.

By this time I had become a grandmother. Mary had a fine little baby girl. But it lived only to be a year and a half old and then died. Mary took sick over the strain and was bedfast for six weeks, but she pulled through all right.

[107]

The book constitutes a plain, straightforward and often moving account of the author's experiences. This is life reduced to the essentials, where nothing comes to shield people from the hard realities. The author's and her family's struggle is a truly remarkable show of courage in the face of adversity; the amount of suffering which is hidden behind these simple words is almost too enormous to be imagined. There never seemed to be any respite: misfortunes, illnesses, deaths followed in quick succession. The necessity to unite to bear such blows created a great similarity between men's and women's lots; besides, women were encouraged to be self-sufficient and participated in all the tasks. Toward the end of her narrative, Mary Ann Hafen reveals that polygamy represented a strain for the men as well as for the women. But she adds: "We went into it in obedience to the Lord's command and strived to subdue our jealous feelings and live in accordance with the spirit of the Gospel of Jesus Christ."[1] She alludes time and again to the part played by religion in her life. Staunch convictions, an acceptance of life and of its trials, a belief in discipline and solidarity, and an ideal of doing good were certainly the fountainhead for the Mormon pioneers' wonderful resilience. Such a choice eliminates doubts, hesitations and also the temptation of despair: the pioneers marched on, their eyes fixed toward the future, confident that they would eventually rise.

1. Mary Ann Hafen, p. 91.

*Part 3*
ARMY WIVES

# Cavalry Life in Tent and Field.

Mrs. Orsemus Boyd

(New York: J. Selwin Tait & Sons) 1894.

*Mrs. Boyd's narrative was written after her husband's death while on active duty and was obviously intended partly as a tribute to his courage and selfless devotion to his country. She gives all the particulars concerning his family and career, and says practically nothing about her own origins and early life. They were married in October, 1867, after his graduation from West Point. He was ordered to San Francisco two days after the wedding took place, and was then assigned to Camp Halleck, Nevada, where Mrs. Boyd joined him in the beginning of the following year. Their life there is described in the following pages:*

When courage to look around had at last been mustered, I found that my new home was formed of two wall tents pitched together so the inner one could be used as a sleeping and the outer one as a sitting room. A calico curtain divided them, and a carpet made of barley sacks covered the floor. In my weary state of mind and body the effect produced was far from pleasant. The wall tents were only eight feet square, and when windowless and doorless except for one entrance, as were those, they seemed from the inside much like a prison.

As I lay in bed that night, feeling decidedly homesick, familiar airs, played upon a very good piano, suddenly sounded in my ears. It seemed impossible that there could be a fine musical instrument such a distance from civilization, particularly when I remembered the roads over which we had come, and the cluster of tents that alone represented human habitation. The piano, which I soon learned belonged to our captain's wife, added greatly to her happiness, and also to the pleasure of us all, though its first strains only intensified my homesick longings.

This lady and myself were the only women at the post, which also included, besides our respective husbands, the doctor and an unmarried first lieutenant. The latter, as quartermaster and commissary, controlled all supplies, and could make us either comfortable or the reverse, as he chose.

Shortly afterward another company of soldiers, embracing one married officer and two unmarried ones, joined us; but at first our troop of cavalry was all. The men, instead of living in tents, were quartered in dugouts, which, as their name implies, were holes dug in the ground, warm enough, but to my unaccustomed eyes places in which only animals should have been sheltered, so forbidding and dingy did they seem. The soldiers were not, however, destined to spend the summer in such accommodations, for by that time very comfortable barracks had been erected.

As everything in the life I then led was new and strange, and surroundings have always powerfully influenced me, I took note of many things which it seemed should have been remedied. One which greatly troubled me was the power extremely young officers exercised over enlisted men. If the latter were in the least unruly, most fearful punishment awaited them, which in my opinion was not commensurate with the offense, but depended entirely upon the mercy and justice of the offender's superior officer, who usually but a boy himself had most rigid ideas of discipline.

I have always noticed how years temper judgment with any one in authority, and thus have come to believe that no very young man is capable of wielding it. Situated as we were in tents, so the slightest sound could be heard, we were made aware of all that transpired outside. When an enlisted man transgressed some rule and was severely punished, I always became frantic, for his outcries reached my ears, and I recognized the injustice and impropriety of some mere boy exercising cruel authority over any man old enough to be his father.

Methods have completely changed in the army since that

time, and I am glad to state that for many years past such scenes as then wrung my heart have been unknown; but in those days our military organization was so crude many things were permitted which are now scarcely remembered by any one. Our soldiers, recruited from the Pacific coast, then famous for the demoralized state of its poorer classes, were indeed in need of firm discipline; but it required men with more experience than those young officers possessed to wield it.

I always have had, and always shall have, a tender, sympathetic feeling for American soldiers. In fact, most of the kindly help which made life on the frontier endurable to me came from those men. We were never able to procure domestic help; it was simply out of the question, and for years it would have been necessary for me either to have cooked or starved but for their ever-ready service.

To cook in a modern kitchen, or even in an ancient one, is not so dreadful; but to cook amid the discomforts and inconveniences which surrounded me for many years would have been impossible to any delicately nurtured woman. I recall the delight with which an offer of help from a soldier in that, my first effort at housekeeping, was welcomed. Although I soon became the slave of my cook's whims, because of my utter inexperience and ignorance, yet his forethought when the floor was soaked with rain in always having a large adobe brick heated ready to be placed under my feet when dining, will never be forgotten.

The greatest proof of devotion I ever received was when that man, learning that the laundress declined longer employing her services in our behalf, saw me preparing to essay the task myself. To prevent that he rose sufficiently early to do the work, and continued the practice so long as we remained there, despite the fact that it subjected him to ridicule from other soldiers; and so sensitive was he in regard to the subject that I never unexpectedly entered the kitchen while he was ironing without noticing his endeavors to hastily remove all trace of such occupation.

As the season was severe—the thermometer during that and the succeeding winter frequently fell to thirty-three degrees below zero—a large stove had been placed in the outer tent, and a huge fireplace built in the inner one. A large pine bunk, forming a double bed, occupied nearly all the spare space, and left only just room enough in front of the fire to seat one's self, and also to accommodate the tiniest shelf for toilet purposes. It therefore required constant watchfulness to avoid setting one's clothing on fire; and among other ludicrous occurrences was the following:

In our inability to find suitable places for necessary articles, we were apt to use most inappropriate ones. On the occasion referred to, a lighted candle had been placed on the bed, where my husband seated himself without noticing the candle. Soon arose the accustomed smell of burning, and I executed my usual maneuver of turning about in front of the fire to see if my draperies had caught. The odor of burning continued to increase, yet I could find no occasion for it.

The cause, however, was discovered when I leaned over the bed, and saw that a large hole had been burned in the center of Mr. Boyd's only uniform coat. He had been too intent on shielding me to be conscious of his own peril. It was an accident much to be regretted, for our isolation was so complete that any loss, however trifling, seemed irreparable by reason of our remoteness from supplies. A lengthened account of our difficulties in procuring needed articles during this and many subsequent years would seem incredible.

I had been delighted to purchase, at the stage station where we stopped previous to our one hundred miles' ambulance trip, and for exactly the amount of one month's pay, a modest supply of dishes and cooking utensils. Prior to their arrival we were happy to obtain our meals at the house of the quartermaster's clerk; yet I looked eagerly forward to my first attempt at housekeeping, and daily sought to induce our quartermaster to send for the goods. At last he informed us that they were on the way, and then began tiresome efforts to have some sort of kitchen and dining-room prepared.

All my entreaties resulted only in a number of willows being stuck in the ground and covered with barley sacking. Even the door was composed of two upright and two cross pieces of willow covered with sacking; a simple piece of leather, which when caught on a nail served as fastening and handle, was deemed sufficient guard. The floor was primitive ground, and in time, as it became hardened by our feet, was smooth except where the water from above wore it into hollows. No efforts of mine could ever induce the powers that were to cover the roof so as to exclude rain. At first some old canvas was simply stretched over it; but as the roof was nearly flat this soon had to be replaced. By degrees, as cattle were killed for the soldiers, we used the skins which were otherwise valueless, lapping them as much as possible. However, they formed no effectual barrier to melting snow or falling rain, as later experience proved, when it became only an ordinary occurrence for me to change my seat half a dozen times during one meal.

Young people are not easily discouraged, and I was very happy when informed that our housekeeping goods had arrived and been placed in the quarters prepared for them. An ominous sound which greeted our ears as we opened the boxes rather dismayed us; but we were not prepared for the utter ruin that met our eyes. What had not been so brittle as to break, had been rendered useless and unsightly by having been chipped or cracked; and as we took out the last piece of broken ware I concluded that what was left might be sold in New York for a dollar. On comparing the residue with the inventory, we discovered that half the goods were missing.

The articles had been bought from an army officer who was changing stations, and were not strictly what I should have chosen. Everything, however, was useful there, and I was rather pleased that we had duplicates of nearly every article, although results showed that this had tempted the freighters' cupidity, and they had fitted themselves out with the primary supply; so when by breakages the secondary disappeared, we had really nothing of any consequence left. Bitterness was added to sorrow, when of a dozen tumblers only the *debris* of six were found. The common kitchen ware was too solid to be shattered, but everything at all fragile was in fragments.

The triumph with which we evolved from the chaos a large wash-bowl and pitcher, which though in close proximity to a pair of flat-irons had escaped injury, was equaled only by our chagrin when we found our little toilet shelf too small to hold them, and were therefore obliged to return to a primitive tin basin, though hoping in time for enough lumber to build accommodations which would allow us the luxury of white ware.

I regret to state that the climate proved too much for our large pitcher. One morning we found it cracked from the cold to which it had been exposed in the out-door kitchen, in which we were obliged to keep it. Our basin was cherished; but on the anniversary of our wedding-day I nearly sank from mortification when Mr. Boyd came into our tent, which was filled with friends who had gathered to celebrate the occasion, carrying the wash-bowl full of very strong punch which he had concocted. No thought of apologizing for our lack of delicacies occurred to me, but I felt compelled to explain, in the most vehement fashion, that the wash-bowl had never been utilized for its obvious purpose; in fact, this was the first period of its usefulness.

My housekeeping was simplified by absolute lack of materials. I had, as a basis of supplies, during that and the succeeding two years, nothing but soldiers' rations, which consisted entirely of bacon, flour, beans, coffee, tea, rice, sugar, soap, and condiments. Our only luxury was dried apples, and with these I experimented in every imaginable way until toward the last my efforts to disguise them utterly failed, and we returned to our simple rations. I was unable to ring any changes on rice, for after Mr. Boyd's experience with General Burnside's expedition off Cape Hatteras, the very sight of it had become disagreeable to him.

We had at that time no trader's store within two miles, which was a matter of congratulation, for when we indulged our desire for any change of fare, however slight, we felt as if eating gold. Nothing on the Pacific coast could be paid for in greenbacks; only gold and silver were used; and when an officer's pay, received in greenbacks, was converted into gold, a premium of fifty per cent always had to be paid. That, added to frontier prices, kept us poor and hungry for years. If we indulged in a dozen eggs the price was two dollars in gold. If we wanted the simplest kind of canned goods to relieve the monotony of our diet, the equivalent was a dollar in gold.

I had always disliked to offend any one; but remarking one day that the flavor of wild onions which permeated the only butter we could procure, and for which we paid two dollars and a half a pound, was not exactly to our taste, seriously offended the person who made it. I quite rejoiced thereat when she refused to supply us with any more, feeling that a lasting economy had been achieved without any great self-denial. The taint of numerous kinds of wild herbs of all sorts, during the many years of my frontier life, always made both beef and milk as well as butter unpalatable, especially in the early spring season, and in Texas, where the flavor was abominable.

There were so many motives for economy that we rejoiced continually at our inability to procure supplies. First should be named the fact that a lieutenant's pay, exceedingly small at best, was, when converted into gold, just eighty dollars per month. That reality was augmented by an utter inequality in the cost of actual necessaries. We found, for instance, that we must have at least two stoves—one for cooking and the other for heating purposes. Their combined cost was one hundred and seventy-five dollars, although both could have been bought in New York for about twenty dollars. If we ever rebelled against such seeming impositions the cost of freight would be alluded to; and remembering what the expenses of my poor solitary trip had been we were effectually silenced.

Among the many amusing stories told on that subject, none was more frequently quoted in every frontier station than the retort of a Hebrew trader, who, when expostulated with on account of the exorbitant charge of a dollar for a paper of needles, vehemently replied:

"Oh, it is not de cost of de needles! It is de freight, de freight!"

So when obliged to purchase any article we counted its cost as compared with the freight as one to one hundred.

Shortly after we reached Camp Halleck, a team was sent to Austin for supplies; and being sadly in need of chairs it was decided that if we ordered the very strongest and ugliest kitchen ones they would escape injury, and be cheap. The bill was received before the team returned, and to our dismay we found that the six chairs cost just six dollars each in gold, or fifty dollars in greenbacks. We tried to hope they would be so nice that the price would prove of slight consequence. But lo! the teamster brought but one chair, and that a common, black, old-fashioned kitchen one.

When asked about the other five, the man replied that the roads were so bad, our chairs, having been placed on top of the load, were continually falling under the wheels, and finally, broken in pieces, had been left to their fate. We, however, suspected that they had served as firewood. We frequently joked, after the first pangs had worn away, over our fifty-dollar chair, claiming a great favor was bestowed upon any one allowed to occupy it.

Reading matter was our only luxury, and the weekly mail, always an uncertainty, was just as apt to have been lightened of its contents in transit, if the roads were at all heavy, as any other package. We were never sure, therefore, that we should be able to understand the next chapters in serial stories, which were our delight.

I remember being very much engrossed in one of Charles Reade's novels, the heroine of which was cast on a desert island, where I thought only her lover's presence could reconcile her to the absence of supplies. The story was published in *Every Saturday*, and at first came weekly; but after we had become most deeply interested five weeks passed during which not a single number was received, and we were left to imagine the sequel.

Several periodicals of a more solid nature always came regularly, which fact constrained us to believe that we were furnishing light literature to the poor inhabitants of some lonely stage station on the road; and in that belief we tried to find consolation for our own losses. Rumors of the outside world grow dim in such an isolated life: we were unwilling to become rusty, and hence read with avidity all printed matter that reached us.

There were, however, other diversions. I learned to play cribbage admirably; and as my husband was able to give me a good deal of his time we found it a pleasant pastime. The winter seemed well-nigh interminable, and we longed for snow to disappear, intending then to explore the whole country. I was such a novice in the saddle that the steadiest old horse, called "Honest John," was chosen for me; and by the time pleasant weather had come I was ready to ride in any direction, having learned that my steed was all his name implied.

We found the streams, so small and insignificant during the dry season, enlarged by melting snows from the mountains; and they were not only beautiful, as clear running water ever is, but were filled with the most delicious spotted trout, which on our fishing-trips we caught and cooked on the spot, and whose excellence as food simply beggars description.

Though the country remained almost as dreary as in mid-winter, grass made some improvement. The lovely wild-flowers, in endless beauty and variety, were a ceaseless delight; while our camp, situated on a lovely little stream in a grove of cottonwood-trees, was far more beautiful than I had ever imagined it could be.

Unfortunately there were no trees to cast their shade over our tents; and as in mid-winter we had suffered from intense cold, so in summer we suffered from intense heat. The sun penetrated the thin canvas overhead to such an extent that my face was burned as if I had been continually out-of-doors, or even more so, as its reflected glare was most excessive. Then we were almost devoured by gnats so small that netting was no protection against them. I had never before, nor have I ever since, seen any insect in such quantities, nor any so troublesome and annoying.

In after-years I became accustomed to the most venomous creatures of all sorts, and in time learned not to mind any of them; but while in Nevada I endured tortures from a colony of wasps that took possession of the canvas over the ridge-poles which connected the uprights of our tents. At first we scarcely noticed them; but they must either have multiplied incredibly, or else gathered recruits from all directions, for soon they swarmed in countless numbers above our heads, going in and out through the knotholes in our rough pine door, buzzing about angrily whenever we entered hastily—in fact, disputing possession with us to such a degree that I dared not open the door quickly. Whenever I did, one of the angry insects was sure to meet and sting me. They remained with us during the summer, and when we finally left were masters of the field by reason of their superior numbers.

I have often since wondered why we did not dispossess them by some means, as they were the terror of my life. One day while in the inner tent, where I felt safe, dressing for breakfast, I experienced the most intense sting on my ankle. The pain was so great I screamed, doubly frightened because confident a rattlesnake had bitten me, and too terrified to exercise any self-control. My cries soon brought a dozen or more persons to the scene, who found a wretched wasp, and calmed my fears; but my nerves had been terribly shaken. Since then I have met army ladies who live in constant terror of snakes, tarantulas, and scorpions; though no longer sharing their fears, I always sympathize with them.

I soon became an expert fisher; and the dainty food thus procured was a great addition to our supplies. With all its drawbacks, life in the open air then began to have many charms for me.

We made friends with the neighboring ranchmen, particularly those who were married, as their wives interested us greatly, they were such perfect specimens of frontier women. At first the rancheros were a little shy, but soon made us welcome to their homes and festivities, where we were always urged to remain as long as possible. Gradually new arrivals—always called "sister" or "cousin"—appeard at several of the ranches, and soon a rumor gained ground that though not exactly in Utah, the Mormon religion prevailed to some extent in our locality.

Another source of great interest was the Piute and Shoshone Indians, who were so numerous that I soon regarded red men as fearlessly as if I had been accustomed to them all my life. They were deeply interested in us, at times inconveniently so; for they never timed their visits, but always came to stay, and would frequently spend the entire day watching our movements.

In one of their camps, several miles away, I found a beautiful dark-eyed baby boy, to whom I paid frequent visits, which were at first well received. But one day I carried the child a neat little dress—my own handiwork—and before arraying baby in it gave him a bath, which evidently caused his mother to decide that I had sinister designs upon her prize, for on my subsequent visits no trace of the baby could ever be found. Had his sex been different I probably could have obtained complete possession; but boys are highly prized among the Indians.

We considered ourselves well repaid for a ride of twenty miles by an Indian dance. It was, of course, only picturesque at night, when seen by the light of huge fires; then, indeed, the sight was weird and strange! On such an occasion, when depicting so perfectly their warfare, the Indians seemed to return to their original savage natures. Had it not been for our fully armed escort we might have feared for safety.

It was startling to see the Indians slowly circle around their camp-fire, at first keeping time to a very slow, monotonous chant, which by degrees increased in volume and rapidity, until finally their movements became fast and furious, when savagery would be written in every line of their implacable countenances. I could then realize in some degree how little mercy would be shown us should they once become inimical; but seeing them at all times so thoroughly friendly made it difficult to think of them as otherwise; and therefore, when we afterwards lived among the most savage tribes, I never experienced that dread which has made life so hard for many army ladies.

With the advent of early spring active preparations were made to build houses for the officers before the ensuing winter. We watched their slow progress, hoping against hope that we might occupy one of the cozy little dwellings. All sorts of difficulties, however, seemed to delay their construction, for good workmen were as scarce as good food, and we found that while anticipation and expectation were pleasing fancies, realization was but a dream. All our hopes were doomed to disappointment, for we finally left the post on the following January, just one year after my arrival, with the house we had longed to occupy still unfinished; thus I passed half of the second winter in our two small tents.

*Mrs. Boyd insists much on the primitive and uncomfortable conditions, and on her lack of preparation for such a life. She could see positive aspects in her situation too, and was always intent on bringing about some improvement and on making suggestions as to changes which would render army life easier. She had a rather keen sense of humor and was quick to find some way of making up for the many problems and losses she had to suffer, and of using her imagination to supply what was lacking in Nevada. She even managed to turn the account of her losing battles against insects into an entertaining story, by endowing the insects with human attributes. She had a good command of words and her language shows that she was a cultivated woman. Her ability to enjoy life in circumstances which made artistic and intellectual pursuits difficult is all the more remarkable.*

*Her husband's career was rather checkered and involved constant moves to various posts in the western part of the States. Despite the fragmentation due to the absense of stability in her life, her book acquires a unity from the presence of two threads in*

*the narrative which often appear together: one is her insistence on
the suffering, deprivations and anxieties attendant upon army life
in unsettled territories, and the other her ability to make the best of
trying circumstances and to bring out the attractive character of
that life too. There is a constant shuttle movement between the
pleasant and the annoying aspects of life in the West, and between
the admirable and the undesirable sides of army life. The
following passage is a good example of the twofold perspective
she had on her experiences:*

> *Though a sufferer all my life from discipline, which has
> continually controlled my movements, yet, when chafing
> most against its restraints, I have admired the grand soldierly
> spirit which made nearly every officer uncomplainingly
> forego all personal comfort for the sake of duty.[1]*

*It is evident that she wanted to gain recognition for all military
people and that she thought no adequate compensations were
provided for the hardships they had to endure and the sacrifices
they made. She felt that the services rendered by women should
be acknowledged in particular:*

> *It is notorious that no provision is made for women in the
> army. Many indignation meetings were held at which we
> discussed the matter, and rebelled at being considered mere
> camp followers. It is a recognized fact that woman's presence
> as wife alone prevents demoralization, . . .[2]*

*She traced her enjoyment of life to her ability to draw
pleasure out of insignificant sources and trivial matters.[3] She
delighted in the amusements of social life and had a great
appreciation of the magnificence of some western landscapes:*

> *To mount a horse, . . . and gallop over prairies, completely
> losing one's self in vast and illimitable space, as silent as
> lonely, is leave every petty care, and feel the contented frame
> of mind which can only be produced by such surroundings. In
> those grand wastes one is truly alone with God. Oh, I love the
> West, . . .[4]*

She was a woman of high ideals, who never stooped to self-pity, even when she mentioned the death of one of her babies. Her strong personality and her zest for life endow her account of her experiences with feeling and intensity.

1. Mrs. Boyd, p. 151.
2. *Ibid*, p. 142.
3. *Ibid*, pp. 144-146.
4. *Ibid*, p. 182.

# Reminiscences of a Soldier's Wife

Ellen McGowan Biddle

(Philadelphia: J.B. Lippincott Company) 1907.


*The title of Mrs. Biddle's book is in accordance with her tendency to self-effacement and her great modesty. For she was married to Captain Biddle (who had been a brevet Colonel in the Civil War and to whom she alludes under this title in her narrative, as was then the custom). She had a charming personality, which made her interesting in her own right, and she deserves better than a mere definition as a "wife." It is not easy to reconstruct her early life as she does not mention dates in the first chapters of the narrative, and provides few details concerning her own and her husband's background. At one point, she indicates: "I had been raised very carefully in a quiet little church-going town";[1] it was presumably located in New England. Her book starts with a description of life in the various places in the South to which her husband was assigned, recapturing the fragrance and beauty those days were pervaded with. Her first experience of life in the West represented a total change. Conditions in Brenham, Texas, were most trying; women had to perform hard and exhausting tasks as no servants could be found. Mrs. Biddle became ill from the nervous strain and went back East to see her parents and to recover her health. She then followed her husband to Nevada, and lived in Camp Halleck for a while:*


We reached Halleck station in the evening at about seven o'clock. The Colonel met us. Our luggage was soon put on an army

[124]

wagon and we were comfortably settled in the ambulance drawn by four mules, when the Colonel said: "All set, Price." The mules started on a gallop, which considerably startled me, until the Colonel reassured me by telling me that the Pacific Coast mules always ran and did not trot, as the Eastern mules did. I suppose they, too, imbibed the spirit of the country at that date.

The garrison was thirteen miles from the station, up in the foothills of the Humboldt Mountains. We were glad to reach the little home. The commanding officer's house being occupied, the Colonel took a smaller set of quarters; but they were quite comfortable and better than I had had at either Macon or on my first arrival at Natchez; they were built of adobe, with a hall in the center and two rooms on each side, each twelve feet square. Outside, the back porch had been enclosed, which we used for a dining room; the kitchen was separate from the house, and we had an excellent Chinaman cook, named Joe. We also had a nice wide porch in the front of the house. The morning after our arrival I went on the porch to look at our surroundings. I found the mountains—great rugged peaks—around three sides of us; the country in front of us was a gradual descent to the station, and beyond high mountains rose in the distance. Many times afterwards I stood on the porch and saw the trains passing thirteen miles distant, the atmosphere was so clear.

The officers' quarters were well back, in a straight line against the foothills; facing the parade-ground, on the right, were the adjutant's office, the commissary and quartermaster's buildings; on the left were the long low quarters for the men; at the end, also facing the offices' quarters, were the stables, leaving a square for parade-ground of about five hundred feet. Running just by the side of our house was a most beautiful clear mountain stream. I could hear the sound of the water as it dashed over the stones from my window. Often the Colonel would take his rod and flies and catch a basket of delicious trout for our breakfast. Game of all kinds was to be found in the vicinity and after the Colonel's morning duties were over he would jump into his shooting clothes and go off, often walking twenty-five miles, and bring back from ten to fifty birds, ducks, grouse, quail, prairie-chickens and sage-hens; he would always draw the latter as soon as killed so there was no taste of sage left in the bird. He kept the garrison supplied with game, for he was the best shot in the Department and it always remained his pride to be so in every Department in which he was stationed. I often went shooting with him. We would take the boys and drive out to a stream and spend the day in the open. The Colonel would go off down the stream and the boys would take the seats from the ambulance and make us comfortable in the shade of the willows. By the time their lessons were said it would be noon. I would then make the coffee, the driver, Price, and the lads making the fire and bringing the water. Soon we would hear a shot and know the master was coming. He would broil some quail or a teal duck and we would have a luncheon fit for a king. I was never afraid of Indians in this locality, they always seemed so peaceful and quiet, though troops were stationed at Camp Halleck for the protection of the settlers and the railroad. After our luncheon was over the Colonel would go off shooting down the other side of the stream; we would follow slowly in the ambulance until he was ready to return. The birds would be taken from his pockets (much to the delight of the boys, who were fast becoming young sportsmen), put on the floor of the ambulance, and home we would drive. It was at Camp Halleck I first learned to sew. I had to make all the clothes my children and I wore, besides the household linen. It was a very difficult task for me to make the little trousers that my lads now wore, especially putting in the pockets, and I tried very hard to buy them off, but they were never willing to give them up; they would stand, one each side of me, helping to get them in right.

We often had visits from the officers stationed in San Francisco; they would come on duty of one kind or another. It was always a delight to us to see them, as they brought us news from the outside world.

Had it not been for these occasional visits, life would have been very dreary. Camp Halleck was but a two-company post; there was nothing, but an occasional ride over the sage-brush plains, to relieve the monotony of our life; had it not been for my children, my two boys in particular, who were hearty and thoroughly alive mentally and physically, I think I would have despaired. No one who has not lived an isolated life can appreciate what it is for a woman. The men had more interest in their lives, for when not scouting they had their "companies" to look after, and when the morning duties were over they could swing a gun over their shoulders and go hunting, which is the greatest pleasure a man knows.

Colonel Baker was ordered away and later we moved into the house they had occupied. Here we were much more comfortable, having three large rooms down stairs and two bedrooms above; we had not much furniture, the family being a good size, (and the allowance of luggage small); the Colonel allowed me and the other ladies, each, to have a new iron bedstead from the hospital, in case of a guest coming; otherwise they would have had to sleep there. These bedsteads were kept stored in case they should be needed. After we were settled in our new quarters the Colonel heard that the Inspector General of the Department was coming, so I had the guest room fixed up a little bit. Whatever could be spared from the other rooms was taken in there, fresh muslin curtains were put at the windows, and the canopy I had fixed over the bed covered up the ugly black iron. We had no springs for the bed, but had sacks filled with fresh, sweet hay put under the mattress; it made a comfortable bed, and the room looked very pretty. The Inspector General arrived, and we were glad to see him. He was a charming man socially, was a fine soldier, with a splendid war record, which was considered everything in those days; there was not a better officer in his corps; he was very strict, and almost every post commander dreaded his arrival. The troops and quartermaster's department were inspected, fortunately, the first day; the second day they went to the hospital, which was found in excellent condition, but three new iron bedsteads were missing. The Colonel fully explained their absence; the General listened attentively and then said, "They must be returned immediately; that the Government did not supply beds from the hospital for the use of officers," etc. The bedsteads were at once sent for. Bridget came to me in great distress to know where the Inspector General would sleep? "Make his bed on the floor with the sacks of hay," I replied; "there is no other place." Of course the Colonel thought (if he had time to think of it that day), that I would find some way out of the difficulty, as I usually did when troubles arose. The next morning after the Inspector General's departure the Colonel, in passing the room, saw the bed on the floor and asked what it meant. He was greatly mortified when he learned the Inspector General had slept on the floor, but I thought it just as well for him to realize some of the privations the officers and their families endured who lived on the frontier. Unfortunately the matter got out, as such things do, but it never made any change in our friendship with General Jones, showing he was really a big man. Many years later an officer was presented to me; I bowed, but he put out his hand and said, "I must shake hands with the woman who had the courage to put the dignified Colonel Jones on the floor to sleep."

Not long after this, when we had been at Camp Halleck about eighteen months, I became very ill; our post surgeon did every-thing he could for me; but, as usual in those days, there were no surgical instruments at the place, and no nurses to be had. When Dr. Brierly found himself helpless he telegraphed to General Schofield telling him the conditions and asking that another surgeon be sent as soon as possible. I continued to grow weaker and weaker. The third day after the telegram had been sent the Colonel received a dispatch, saying the new doctor would arrive that evening and to send a horse to the station for him. But it seemed to be too late; there was no hope left; I had taken the last communion, bade my loved ones good-bye and awaited the end. While hovering between life and death I had a wonderful vision; slowly a beautiful form descended; the face divine, like the face of the beloved disciple Saint John. The arms were extended, the flowing robe was of the beautiful blue seen in old pictures; it came lower and lower and seemed to say to me, "All is well!" I had no power to utter a sound nor to raise my hand.

While waiting for the end, the doctor from San Francisco arrived. He had ridden at a hard gallop the thirteen miles when he learned how desperately ill I was, and to this day he carries the scar of a wound made by a buckle in the saddle, which he would not stop one moment to properly adjust. Such was his idea of duty; he had never seen, probably never heard of, either the Colonel or myself. The sound of his voice as he entered the room seemed to arouse me, and some little time after giving me a stimulant there was a slight pulse, and later I was brought back to life—but had lost my child. It was some time before I was able to recognise anyone, but I well remember the morning when my soul seemed to have come back to me and I opened my eyes and found standing beside my bed a stalwart man, with tawny hair and beard, the picture of health and strength. No wonder I came back from the valley and shadow of Death. He had given me of his strength and compelled me to live. The masterful expression was in his face and I knew I would get well, and quietly whispered it to my husband, who sat beside me.

*When she was back in health, she lived in a variety of places in the Middle West; in 1876, she travelled to Arizona, where conditions were still primitive. A taste of her experience there is given in the following pages:*

Fort Whipple was the headquarters of the Department of Arizona. It was situated about one mile from the town of Prescott, which had been established as close to the fort as possible on account of the Indians. There was a good stream of water running through the garrison and some small willows and cottonwood trees, making quite an oasis in the desert. The quarters for the officers and their families were poor and unattractive. General Kautz, the colonel of the Eighth Infantry, then stationed there, was in command of the Department. He was a fine soldier and a man of great integrity; loved not only by the officers and soldiers, but by every one in the Territory. The staff officers all lived on a sloping hill overlooking the garrison, and huge granite mountains were in the distance. Directly facing the house we occupied, but miles away, was a huge mountain of rock towering above all others, called "Thumb Butte," as it was in the shape of a hand doubled with the thumb up.

The staff officers' quarters were better (because newer) than those of the garrison, but there were but two sets that could really be called good. They were all built alike,—low, broad houses with hall in the center, and two rooms about sixteen feet square on each side; pantry and kitchen back, also an attic above. I often looked through the cracks in my house to the light outside. They were built of wood and ceiled (as there was no plaster to be had), and in that dry climate the wood shrunk, leaving great slits for the light and air to come in, and as there was often in winter a difference of fifty degrees in temperature between the day and night-time, we had to keep great fires going continually. We had no stoves or furnaces; only the large open hearth fire, and it is needless to say it was hard at times to keep warm. We bought thin muslin, something like cheese-cloth, and had it tacked over the walls of the living-room, and bed-room and papered them, the muslin holding the paper, a soft gray ground with the passion vine and red flower in full bloom. We had sent to San Francisco for it, and it took just four months to reach us after the order was sent. The Government at that time allowed no extra money to make the quarters comfortable, and I doubt if many of the discomforts we had were realised at Washington.

We were so far from the railway that when officers came from a distance we were so glad to see and to talk with them about what was going on in the world, that our discomforts were for a time forgotten.

We were not long in getting settled. An officer and his family were in the quarters we were entitled to, but as they were expecting to go East soon we made ourselves comfortable for the time in a small house. The Colonel was now on duty as Inspector General of the Department, and was on General Kautz's staff. There were some delightful people at Fort Whipple, among them Colonel and Mrs. Wilkins, whom I had not seen since we left Macon, Georgia, and their beautiful daughter Miss Carrie, whom every officer fell in love with in less than twenty-four hours after his arrival, and it was the same when she went to visit a garrison. All the youngsters fell down before her. Colonel Jim Martin was the Adjutant General of the Department, and I suppose a more competent adjutant general, or more congenial man, was never in the army. His wife was very beautiful. Colonel Rodney Smith was there, with his bride. Colonel Chandler, a bachelor at that time, most agreeable and with a fine war record; Dr. Magruder and his wife and daughters; Captain Simpson and his wife, and dear little

Amy with her beautiful hair like spun gold; Lieutenant Earl D. Thomas and his interesting wife and three little girls; besides a great many others.

It was a very gay post, with an entertainment of some kind almost every day and evening. In fact years after we used to allude to the time when General Kautz was in command, as "the days of the Empire." The officers were going scouting continually, so there was no time for the routine there now is in the army. Soldiers learned from actual experience in the hardest kind of warfare, and strange to say there were fewer desertions. When the officers had their turn to remain in the garrison it was pretty lively with dinners, dances, and the rehearsals of plays, for we had a most excellent Dramatic Society, and presented some very good plays every winter. I have been at a "hop," and once at a play, when we heard the "Assembly Call." Every officer dropped his partner and ran to his troop, and in an hour's time they were in the saddle and off to catch the Apaches, who were on the war-path, killing and destroying everything they passed. Although the Colonel was on detached duty from his regiment as Inspector General, he never let his men go out on these expeditions without going with them if possible. We generally had a little something for them to eat at our house before they left, and a sandwich to go in their pockets; for often they had an all-night ride, and sometimes longer, before they could stop for anything.

The days for the women were all alike. Usually in the morning we rode or drove, and we sewed a part of every day and ofttimes in the evenings, for as I have said we had all our own and our children's clothes to make, besides the adornment of our houses. I remember very well upholstering a lounge and two chairs in pretty light blue cretonne with apple blossoms on it. A soldier in Lieutenant Kingsbury's troop made the frames out of some boxes we had, and he tied in some springs that I was able to get in town, and I did the rest of the work. I also made window-curtains of the same material with fluted swiss ruffles, and lined with a soft unbleached cotton. They were very pretty and when they were drawn at night to keep out the cold, our room was charmingly pretty and cosy. Years after an officer told me there was not (to his mind) as pretty a room in Washington as my dainty little living-room on the frontier. This showed how little of the beautiful we had around us. In fact we would have been starved had it not been for the blue skies, the wonderful rugged mountains, and the mystery of the desert.

I remember one occasion shortly after our arrival at Fort Whipple. There was a great outbreak of the Indians in the Territory. All the troops of the command were ordered out except enough to protect the garrison. The Colonel was away on an inspecting tour, and General Kautz, who was always thoughtful of others, came and insisted upon Nellie and myself going to his house in the garrison to remain during the excitement. We had been there but a few days when the outbreak became so general and the excitement in the Territory so great that General Kautz and all of his staff went to the southern part of the Territory to be on hand in case they were needed, as the General would there be nearer the scene of action. I remained with Mrs. Kautz until the return of the troops and greatly enjoyed her hospitality, as she was a charming hostess.

In the month of June eighteen hundred and seventy-seven we had a son born to us, christened James Harwood, for my great-grandfather. I had been unable to secure a nurse; such a luxury was not then to be had in that part of the country. I was very ill and my child frail and delicate. Dear Mrs. Wilkins, whom I had known in Macon, Georgia, whose husband was the lieutenant-colonel of the Eighth Infantry now stationed at "Whipple," came every morning, gave my little son his bath, dressed him, and did everything for us both, that her generous heart dictated, but my child staid with us only three short weeks. I wept so much seeing his struggles for breath, knowing he was suffering, that trouble came upon my eyes and I was kept in a darkened room. Dr. McKey and Dr. Worthington both feared cataract, but after six weeks the disease yielded to treatment. All of the officers and ladies came during the time doing all they could to cheer me. General and Mrs. Kautz lost their little daughter under almost the same conditions that had cost my child's life.

The following autumn three Sisters of Charity, including Mother Monica, of whom we became so fond, came to Prescott to establish a much-needed hospital, and I went down to see them and ask in what way I could help them, for they had really nothing to begin on. Every one in the place was interested, for it was a fine charity and much needed. When the poor miners in the vicinity met with an accident or were ill there had been no place for them to go for treatment. The officers and ladies at the fort gave a play, "The Two Orphans," charging a dollar admission. The little room was so crowded we were almost scared, and I would give much if I had a photograph of the audience. There were all classes and conditions of men, but all well-behaved and appreciative. We raised considerable money, and added to the amount the good sisters raised in the town and county they were able almost immediately to build the hospital, as the merchants promised generous contributions monthly for its support. Brave, hearty, generous frontiersmen, who does not admire them? I think I must tell that a few gentlemen in town had a game of poker once or twice a week, and when the Colonel was not off on his inspecting tours he used to go down and play with them, though it was a rule of his life while in the service never to play cards when in command of a garrison. One day he stopped at the hospital to see how they were getting along. Some conversation took place about "the game" in town, when the Colonel promised that whenever he made a winning he would stop by and divide with them for the benefit of the hospital, which he did; but some time later when I was there Mother Monica asked: "What has become of the Colonel? We have not seen him for a long time." "Ah! well, then, Mother," I said, "he can't have been winning." While talking of the hospital I think I must tell of an incident that further strengthened my belief in the doctrine of compensation. A few years after we had left Fort Whipple an uncle of mine went to Prescott to look after some mining property. When within a mile of the city, going down the steep hill I have referred to before, some part of the harness broke; the horses ran, throwing the coach over an embankment; my uncle was picked up and carried to the hospital and found to be seriously injured. On his return to consciousness some time later, he inquired for Colonel Biddle, thinking he might be at the garrison. When the sisters learned he was a relative of ours they could not do enough for him, and they nursed him so carefully his life was saved to his family.

At this time there was a very estimable lady living in the garrison, a veritable Mrs. Malaprop. She told us of some jewelry she had lost, and among the things was a topaz chain with a beautiful "pendulum." One Friday evening we went to the hop-room for the usual dance. It had been newly painted, and Miss Wilkins remarked that the odour was not pleasant, when the lady, who was present, said: "Oh! dear, new paint always did make me nauseous." She also told us she had several "relicts" of the Revolution, and she was heard telling a stranger that we had to "irritate" the soil in Arizona to raise crops. Her husband died suddenly and the doctor asked: "Did your husband speak before he died?" "Oh, no!" she said, "he just gave three grasps and died."

Whenever an officer left the Territory it was the practice to have an auction, selling off everything he did not care to keep—even to his clothes sometimes, as they had generally been in the Territory some years and the civilian clothes brought in would not do very well after getting back to the States. The lady I refer to held an auction before leaving, and when some silver-plated knives were put up for sale, she rose, and in a sobbing voice said: "Oh, dear, no! I cannot sell them; they have been in dear John's mouth too often."

These auctions were a great institution. They enabled the settlers to buy furniture and other things at a fair price. Freighting was enormously high—twelve and one half cents per pound when we went into the Territory, and it had been higher. The ladies and officers always attended because it meant a frolic, and besides we always bought something. When we first went into the Territory I should have been delighted to have attended an auction, as I did later, for I had to pay $7 for a washtub, $2 apiece for flat-irons, $2 per pound for butter, $2 a dozen for eggs, and so on. A cook could not be gotten under $50 per month, and a housemaid $25, and everything was proportionately high. I often wondered how the young lieutenants lived on their pay. Perhaps I might give a couple of recipes that we used, showing how one can get along without either milk or eggs.

Custard without eggs or milk: Six tablespoonfuls of corn-starch; enough water to make it creamy thick when cooked; add essence of lemon and sugar to taste; serve in custard-cups.

Apple-pie, without apples: Soda crackers soaked in water, and warmed until soft, but do no break too fine; add essence of lemon and sugar and a great deal of nutmeg; bake in pastry, with a top crust to the pie.

You will feel sure it is apple-pie (if you do not make it yourself). These recipes were handed down from Mrs. Coolidge, who was on the frontier in 1850, and knew more privations than we did; but she is still living and is a most charming old lady, full of anecdote and interest. I had not been long at Fort Whipple before I bought from a lady, the wife of Judge Lieb who had a ranch near, a setting of good eggs, for which I paid $3, and she lent me a hen that wanted to set and I began to raise chickens and turkeys. I sold over two hundred of the former and fourteen of the latter, besides having all we wanted and plenty of both eggs and chickens to give away. We also bought a cow from a man who was driving a herd up from Texas. Poor fellow, he had lost many, and was glad to sell out what remained at Prescott. We sold three cows at our auction, and I had had the pleasure of sending milk every day to both hospitals, the one at the fort for the soldiers, and the one in town erected while we lived at "Whipple."

*She had become used to the discomforts of army life on the frontier, and was able to find compensations in an active social life. Her description gives an idea of the kind of activities which filled her days, the concerns which occupied her mind, and the problems which had to be dealt with. She shows the practical aspect of life and also, in brief glimpses, the quality which it held for her and the deeper emotions which she experienced.*

*More children were born to her in the following years, and her life led her through various posts in the West, and also included several visits with her parents in Philadelphia. In the last chapter, she retraced her husband's career from 1861 to his retirement in 1895, stressing his fine record and his numerous years of Indian service on the frontier. She felt that he had not been adequately rewarded, but added in a post-face that President Roosevelt later corrected this situation.*

*Ellen McGowan Biddle was a warm, compassionate and courageous woman, who never put herself forward and tried to record her impressions of life as she felt them at the time they occurred. She shows the traditional devotion to her husband and to her children. Her narrative suggests more things than it openly states; there is a great delicacy in feelings and subdued expression of the emotions.*

1. Ellen Biddle, p. 55.

# Vanished Arizona

Martha Summerhayes

(Philadelphia: J.B. Lippincott Company) 1908

In her Preface, Mrs. Summerhayes explains that her account
of her experiences in the West was written to comply with her
children's request, and she indicates that she used letters dating
back to those times to supplement her memories. She expresses a
concern for method and structure; in fact, her book is remarkably
well organized and the narrative proceeds very smoothly without
being bogged down by unnecessary details. She has achieved
exactly what she set out to do, which was to record "the
impressions made upon the mind of a young New England
woman who left her comfortable home in the early seventies, to
follow a second lieutenant into the wildest encampments of the
American army."[1] This sentence contains some of the main themes
in the book: the contrast between primitive life and civilization,
the wide gap which separated her early life from her frontier life,
and her unswerving devotion to her husband.

Mrs. Summerhayes was a complex and intelligent woman
who held on to her principles and ideals, but was not bound by a
static and unchanging view of life. Her attitude, moods and
reactions vary much according to the circumstances, and she was
often caught up in contradictions. These stemmed partly from the
double aspect offered by army life which is so aptly summarized
in the expression her German friend used, "glaenzendes Elend:"[2]
On the surface it appeared glamorous, but it held in store many
hardships and sufferings. A similar ambivalence can be found in
her appreciation of life in the West. She admired the magnificence

[137]

*of some of the scenery, but found the barren desert repulsive in the extreme. Her relationship with her husband also contained opposite elements: basically, she cared deeply for him and was always loyal and attentive to his needs, but at times she was irked by his conservative attitudes.*

*Her narrative starts with an account of a visit to Germany in 1871. Upon coming back, she married one of her old friends and in 1874 they departed for Wyoming Territory. Her description of her first experiences with army housekeeping is very entertaining: her mind was full of her memories of Germany and of romantic dreams, and suddenly she was confronted by down-to-earth problems of a very practical nature. Very soon, her husband was ordered to Arizona, where she had difficulties adjusting to the unfamiliar environment:*

CAMP APACHE

By the fourth of October we had crossed the range, and began to see something which looked like roads. Our animals were fagged to a state of exhaustion, but the travelling was now much easier and there was good grazing, and after three more long days' marches, we arrived at Camp Apache. We were now at our journey's end, after two months' continuous travelling, and I felt reasonably sure of shelter and a fireside for the winter at least. I knew that my husband's promotion was expected, but the immediate present was filled with an interest so absorbing, that a consideration of the future was out of the question.

At that time (it was the year of 1874) the officers' quarters at Camp Apache were log cabins, built near the edge of the deep cañon through which the White Mountain River flows, before its junction with Black River.

We were welcomed by the officers of the Fifth Cavalry, who were stationed there. It was altogether a picturesque and pretty post. In addition to the row of log cabins, there were enormous stables and Government buildings, and a sutler's store. We were entertained for a day or two, and then quarters were assigned to us. The second lieutenants had rather a poor choice, as the quarters were scarce. We were assigned a half of a log cabin, which gave us one room, a small square hall, and a bare shed, the latter detached from the house, to be used for a kitchen. The room on the other side of the hall was occupied by the Post Surgeon, who was temporarily absent.

Our things were unloaded and brought to this cabin. I missed the barrel of china, and learned that it had been on the unfortunate wagon which rolled down the mountain-side. I had not attained that state of mind which came to me later in my army life. I cared then a good deal about my belongings, and the annoyance caused by the loss of our china was quite considerable. I knew there was none to be obtained at Camp Apache, as most of the merchandise came in by pack-train to that isolated place.

Mrs. Dodge, of the Twenty-third Infantry, who was about to leave the post, heard of my predicament, and offered me some china plates and cups, which she thought not worth the trouble of packing (so she said), and I was glad to accept them, and thanked her, almost with tears in my eyes.

Bowen nailed down our one carpet over the poor board floor (after having first sprinkled down a thick layer of clean straw, which he brought from the quartermaster stables). Two iron cots from the hospital were brought over, and two bed-sacks filled with fresh, sweet straw, were laid upon them; over these were laid our mattresses. Woven-wire springs were then unheard of in that country.

We untied our folding chairs, built a fire on the hearth, captured an old broken-legged wash stand and a round table from somewhere, and that was our living-room. A pine table was found for the small hall, which was to be our dining-room, and some chairs with raw-hide seats were brought from the barracks, some shelves knocked up against one wall, to serve as sideboard. Now for the kitchen!

A cooking-stove and various things were sent over from the Q. M. store-house, and Bowen (the wonder of it!) drove in nails, and hung up my Fort Russell tin-ware, and put up shelves and stood my pans in rows, and polished the stove, and went out and stole a table somewhere (Bowen was invaluable in that way), polished the zinc under the stove, and lo! and behold, my army kitchen! Bowen was indeed a treasure; he said he would like to cook for us, for ten dollars a month. We readily accepted his offer. There were no persons to be obtained, in these distant places, who could do the cooking in the families of officers, so it was customary to employ a soldier; and the soldier often displayed a remarkable ability in the way of cooking, in some cases, in fact, more than in the way of soldiering. They liked the little addition to their pay, if they were of a frugal mind; they had also their own quiet room to sleep in, and I often thought the family life, offering as it did a contrast to the bareness and desolation of the noisy barracks, appealed to the domestic instinct, so strong in some men's natures. At all events, it was always easy in those days to get a man from the company, and they sometimes remained for years with an officer's family; in some cases attending drills and roll-calls besides.

Now came the unpacking of the chests and trunks. In our one diminutive room, and small hall, was no closet, there were no hooks on the bare walls, no place to hang things or lay things, and what to do I did not know. I was in despair; Jack came in, to find me sitting on the edge of a chest, which was half unpacked, the contents on the floor. I was very mournful, and he did not see why.

"Oh! Jack! I've nowhere to put things!"

"What things?" said this impossible man.

"Why, *all* our things," said I, losing my temper; "can't you see them?"

"Put them back in the chests,—and get them out as you need them," said this son of Mars, and buckled on his sword. "Do the best you can, Martha, I have to go to the barracks; be back again soon." I looked around me, and tried to solve the problem. There was no bureau, nothing; not a nook or corner where a thing might be stowed. I gazed at the motley collection of bed-linen, dust-pans, silver bottles, bootjacks, saddles, old uniforms, full dress military hats, sword-belts, riding-boots, cut glass, window-shades, lamps, work-baskets, and books, and I gave it up in despair. You see, I was not an army girl, and I did not know how to manage.

There was nothing to be done, however, but to follow Jack's advice, so I threw the boots, saddles and equipments under the bed, and laid the other things back into the chests, closed the lids, and went out to take a look at the post. Towards evening, a soldier came for orders for beef, and I learned how to manage that. I was told that we bought our meats direct from the contractor; I had to state how much and what cuts I wished. Another soldier came to bring us milk, and I asked Jack who was the milkman, and he said, blessed if he knew; I learned, afterwards, that the soldiers roped some of the wild Texas cows that were kept in one of the Government corrals, and tied them securely to keep them from kicking; then milked them, and the milk was divided up among the officers' families, according to rank. We received about a pint every night. I declared it was not enough; but I soon discovered that however much education, position and money might count in civil life, *rank* seemed to be the one and only thing in the army, and Jack had not much of that just then.

The question of getting settled comfortably still worried me, and after a day or two, I went over to see what Mrs. Bailey had done. To my surprise, I found her out playing tennis, her little boy asleep in the baby-carriage, which they had brought all the way from San Francisco, near the court. I joined the group, and afterwards asked her advice about the matter. She laughed kindly, and said: "Oh! you'll get used to it, and things will settle themselves. Of course it is troublesome, but you can have shelves and such things—you'll soon learn," and still smiling, she gave her ball a neat left-hander.

I concluded that my New England bringing up had been too serious, and I wondered if I had made a dreadful mistake in marrying into the army, or at least in following my husband to Arizona. I debated the question with myself from all sides, and decided then and there that young army women should stay at home with their mothers and fathers, and not go into such wild and uncouth places. I thought my decision irrevocable.

Before the two small deep windows in our room we hung some Turkey red cotton, Jack built in his spare moments a couch for me, and gradually our small quarters assumed an appearance of comfort. I turned my attention a little to social matters. We dined at Captain Montgomery's (the commanding officer's) house; his wife was a famous Washington beauty. He had more rank, consequently more rooms, than we had, and their quarters were very comfortable and attractive.

There was much that was new and interesting at the post. The Indians who lived on this reservation were the White Mountain

Apaches, a fierce and cruel tribe, whose depredations and atrocities had been carried on for years, in and around, and, indeed, far away from their mountain homes. But this tribe was now under surveillance of the Government, and guarded by a strong garrison of cavalry and infantry at Camp Apache. They were divided into bands, under Chiefs Pedro, Diablo, Patone and Cibiano; they came into the post twice a week to be counted, and to receive their rations of beef, sugar, beans, and other staples, which Uncle Sam's commissary officer issued to them.

In the absence of other amusement, the officers' wives walked over to witness this rather solemn ceremony. At least, the serious expression on the faces of the Indians, as they received their rations, gave an air of solemnity to the proceeding.

Large stakes were driven into the ground; at each stake, sat or stood the leader of a band; a sort of father to his people; then the rest of them stretched out in several long lines, young bucks and old ones, squaws and pappooses, the families together, about seventeen hundred souls in all. I used to walk up and down between the lines, with the other women, and the squaws looked at our clothes and chuckled, and made some of their inarticulate remarks to each other. The bucks looked admiringly at the white women, especially at the cavalry beauty, Mrs. Montgomery, although I thought that Chief Diablo cast a special eye at our young Mrs. Bailey, of the infantry.

Diablo was a handsome fellow. I was especially impressed by his extraordinary good looks.

This tribe was quiet at that time, only a few renegades escaping into the hills on their wild adventures: but I never felt any confidence in them and was, on the whole, rather afraid of them. The squaws were shy, and seldom came near the officers' quarters. Some of the younger girls were extremely pretty; they had delicate hands, and small feet encased in well-shaped moccasins. The young lieutenants sometimes tried to make up to the prettiest ones, and offered them trinkets, pretty boxes of soap, beads, and small mirrors (so dear to the heart of the Indian girl), but the young maids were coy enough; it seemed to me they cared more for the men of their own race.

Once or twice, I saw older squaws with horribly disfigured faces. I supposed it was the result of some ravaging disease, but I

[142]

learned that it was the custom of this tribe, to cut off the noses of those women who were unfaithful to their lords. Poor creatures, they had my pity, for they were only children of Nature, after all, living close to the earth, close to the pulse of their mother. But this sort of punishment seemed to be the expression of the cruel and revengeful nature of the Apache.

### LIFE AMONGST THE APACHES

Bowen proved to be a fairly good cook, and I ventured to ask people to dinner in our little hall dining-room, a veritable box of a place. One day, feeling particularly ambitious to have my dinner a success, I made a bold attempt at oyster patties. With the confidence of youth and inexperience, I made the pastry, and it was a success; I took a can of Baltimore oysters, and did them up in a fashion that astonished myself, and when, after the soup, each guest was served with a hot oyster patty, one of the cavalry officers fairly gasped. "Oyster patty, if I'm alive! Where on earth—Bless my stars! And this at Camp Apache!"

"And by Holy Jerusalem! they are *good*, too," exclaimed Captain Reilly, and turning to Bowen, he said: "Bowen, did you make these?"

Bowen straightened himself up to his six foot two, clapped his heels together, came to "attention," looked straight to the front, and replied: "Yes, sir."

I thought I heard Captain Reilly say in an undertone to his neighbor, "The hell he did," but I was not sure.

At that season, we got excellent wild turkeys there, and good Southdown mutton, and one could not complain of such living.

But I could never get accustomed to the wretched small space of one room and a hall; for the kitchen, being detached, could scarcely be counted in. I had been born and brought up in a spacious house, with plenty of bedrooms, closets, and an immense old-time garret. The forlorn makeshifts for closets, and the absence of all conveniences, annoyed me and added much to the difficulties of my situation. Added to this, I soon discovered that my husband had a penchant for buying and collecting things

[143]

which seemed utterly worthless to me, and only added to the number of articles to be handled and packed away. I begged him to refrain, and to remember that he was married, and that we had not the money to spend in such ways. He really did try to improve, and denied himself the taking of many an alluring share in raffles for old saddles, pistols, guns, and cow-boy's stuff, which were always being held at the sutler's store.

But an auction of condemned hospital stores was too much for him, and he came in triumphantly one day, bringing a box of antiquated dentist's instruments in his hand.

"Good gracious!" I cried, "what can you ever do with those forceps?"

"Oh! they are splendid," he said, "and they will come in mighty handy some time."

I saw that he loved tools and instruments, and I reflected, why not? There are lots of things I have a passion for, and love, just as he loves those things, and I shall never say any more about it. "Only," I added, aloud, "do not expect me to pack up such trash when we come to move; you will have to look out for it yourself."

So with that spiteful remark from me, the episode of the forceps was ended, for the time at least.

As the winter came on, the isolation of the place had a rather depressing effect upon us all. The officers were engaged in their various duties: drill, courts-martial, instruction, and other military occupations. They found some diversion at "the store," where the ranchmen assembled and told frontier stories and played exciting games of poker. Jack's duties as commissary officer kept him much away from me, and I was very lonely.

The mail was brought in twice a week by a soldier on horseback. When he failed to come in at the usual time, much anxiety was manifested, and I learned that only a short time before, one of the mail-carriers had been killed by Indians and the mail destroyed. I did not wonder that on mail-day everybody came out in front of the quarters and asked: "Is the mail-carrier in?" And nothing much was done or thought of on that day, until we saw him come jogging in, the mail-bag tied behind his saddle. Our letters were from two to three weeks old. The eastern mail came *via* Santa Fe to the terminus of the railroad, and then by stage; for in 1874, the railroads did not extend very far into the

Southwest. At a certain point on the old New Mexico road, our man met the San Carlos carrier, and received the mail for Apache.

"I do not understand," I said, "how any soldier can be found to take such a dangerous detail."

"Why so?" said Jack. "They like it."

"I should think that when they got into those cañons and narrow defiles, they would think of the horrible fate of their predecessor," said I.

"Perhaps they do," he answered; "but a soldier is always glad to get a detail that gives him a change from the routine of post life."

I was getting to learn about the indomitable pluck of our soldiers. They did not seem to be afraid of anything. At Camp Apache my opinion of the American soldier was formed, and it has never changed. In the long march across the Territory, they had cared for my wants and performed uncomplainingly for me services usually rendered by women. Those were before the days of lineal promotion. Officers remained with their regiments for many years. A feeling of regimental prestige held officers and men together. I began to share that feeling. I knew the names of the men in the company, and not one but was ready to do a service for the "Lieutenant's wife." "K" had long been a bachelor company; and now a young woman had joined it. I was a person to be pampered and cared for, and they knew besides that I was not long in the army.

During that winter I received many a wild turkey and other nice things for the table, from the men of the company. I learned to know and to thoroughly respect the enlisted man of the American Army.

And now into the varied kaleidoscope of my army life stepped the Indian Agent. And of all unkempt, unshorn, disagreeable-looking personages who had ever stepped foot into our quarters, this was the worst.

"Heaven save us from a Government which appoints such men as *that* to watch over and deal with Indians," cried I, as he left the house. "Is it possible that his position here demands social recognition?" I added.

"Hush!" said the second lieutenant of K company. "It's the Interior Department that appoints the Indian Agents, and besides," he added, "it's not good taste on your part, Martha, to abuse the Government which gives us our bread and butter."

"Well, you can say what you like, and preach policy all you wish, no Government on earth can compel me to associate with such men as those!" With that assertion, I left the room, to prevent farther argument.

And I will here add that in my experience on the frontier, which extended over a long period, it was never my good fortune to meet with an Indian Agent who impressed me as being the right sort of a man to deal with those children of nature, for Indians *are* like children, and their intuitions are keen. They know and appreciate honesty and fair dealing, and they know a gentleman when they meet one.

The winter came on apace, but the weather was mild and pleasant. One day some officers came in and said we must go over to the "Ravine" that evening, where the Indians were going to have a rare sort of a dance.

There was no one to say to me: "Do not go," and, as we welcomed any little excitement which would relieve the monotony of our lives, we cast aside all doubts of the advisability of my going. So, after dinner, we joined the others, and sallied forth into the darkness of an Arizona night. We crossed the large parade-ground, and picked our way over a rough and pathless country, lighted only by the stars above.

Arriving at the edge of the ravine, what a scene was before us! We looked down into a natural amphitheatre, in which blazed great fires; hordes of wild Apaches darted about, while others sat on logs beating their tomtoms.

I was afraid, and held back, but the rest of the party descended into the ravine, and, leaning on a good strong arm, I followed. We all sat down on the great trunk of a fallen tree, and soon the dancers came into the arena.

They were entirely naked, except for the loin-cloth; their bodies were painted, and from their elbows and knees stood out bunches of feathers, giving them the appearance of huge flying creatures; jingling things were attached to their necks and arms. Upon their heads were large frames, made to resemble the branching horns of an elk, and as they danced, and bowed their heads, the horns lent them the appearance of some unknown animal, and added greatly to their height. Their feathers waved, their jingles shook, and their painted bodies twisted and turned in the light of the great fire, which roared and leaped on high. At one moment they were birds, at another animals, at the next they were demons.

The noise of the tomtoms and the harsh shouts of the Indians grew wilder and wilder. It was weird and terrifying. Then came a pause; the arena was cleared, and with much solemnity two wicked-looking creatures came out and performed a sort of shadow dance, brandishing knives as they glided through the intricate figures.

It was a fascinating but unearthly scene, and the setting completed the illusion. Fright deprived me of the power of thought, but in a sort of subconscious way I felt that Orpheus must have witnessed just such mad revels when he went down into Pluto's regions. Suddenly the shouts became warwhoops, the demons brandished their knives madly, and nodded their branching horns; the tomtoms were beaten with a dreadful din, and terror seized my heart. What if they be treacherous, and had lured our small party down into this ravine for an ambush! The thing could well be, I thought. I saw uneasiness in the faces of the other women, and by mutual consent we got up and slowly took our departure. I barely had strength to climb up the steep side of the hollow. I was thankful to escape from its horrors.

Scarce three months after that some of the same band of Indians fired into the garrison and fled to the mountains. I remarked to Jack, that I thought we were very imprudent to go to see that dance, and he said he supposed we were. But I had never regarded life in such a light way as he seemed to.

Women usually like to talk over their trials and their wonderful adventures, and that is why I am writing this, I suppose. Men simply *will not* talk about such things.

The cavalry beauty seemed to look at this frontier life philosophically—what she really thought about it, I never knew. Mrs. Bailey was so much occupied by the care of her young child and various out-door amusements, that she did not, apparently, think much about things that happened around us. At all events, she never seemed inclined to talk about them. There was no one else to talk to; the soil was strange, and the atmosphere a foreign one to me; life did not seem to be taken seriously out there, as it was back in New England, where they always loved to sit down and talk things over. I was downright lonesome for my mother and sisters.

I could not go out very much at that time, so I occupied myself a good deal with needle-work.

*In April, 1875, Mrs. Summerhayes left with her husband and their small son to undertake a most strenuous trip which was fraught with rigors and anxieties and finally led them to Ehrenberg, a forsaken and desolate place. She felt so uncomfortable there that she begged her husband to let her adopt the Mexican way of life; but he insisted on keeping up the appearance of civilization. Mrs. Summerhayes experienced frontier conditions in a great number of places in Arizona, Nevada, New Mexico and Texas, with from time to time the relief of a visit with her parents in New England. She could never really make up her mind concerning army life: at times she decided that young wives should definitely not follow their husbands to uncivilized places, at others she felt that her life was linked to that of her husband and that she wanted to be always near him. Her book ends with her husband's retirement and their subsequent establishment in the East; it closes on a positive note, as she was able to see the enriching aspect of her experiences and admired the ideals which sustained military life at that time.*

*Reading her book is a wonderful experience. It is probably one of the most sensitive, searching, lively and entertaining books about frontier life and one of the very few which can make claims to literary merit.*

1. Martha Summerhayes, p. 2.
2. *Ibid*, p. 18.

*Part 4*
WORKING WOMEN

# Luzena Stanley Wilson, '49er. Memories recalled years later for her daughter Correnah Wilson Wright

Luzena Stanley Wilson

(Mills College, California: The Eucalyptus Press) 1937.

In 1881, Luzena Stanley Wilson recounted her experiences to her daughter, who wrote them down in longhand; they were later typewritten and bound.[1] The particular manner in which the book was made accounts perhaps for the brisk pace of the story and its compelling character. The narrator's personality emerges strongly, and the reader soon becomes involved and shares in the excitement of the times and events described.

Luzena Stanley Wilson was 28 when she and her husband went to California, taking along with them their two small children. They had been living in a log cabin on the prairie, and as they had nothing to lose and everything to gain, they were particularly receptive to the news of the gold discoveries:

My husband grew enthusiastic and wanted to start immediately, but I would not be left behind. I thought where he could go I could, and where I went I could take my two little toddling babies. Mother-like, my first thought was of my children. I little realized then the task I had undertaken. If I had, I think I should still be in my log cabin in Missouri.[2]

They were so eager to leave that it took them but a few days to make the necessary arrangements. In a lively, sometimes humor-

[151]

*ous, always graphic manner, Luzena Stanley Wilson described the strenuous and monotonous trip and the incidents on the way. She stressed the courteous and friendly way in which she was treated by the travellers they encountered, who were almost all men. As the sentences unfold, the reader gets a feel of the particular quality of life in those days and the scenes appear with the vividness of animated pictures. The variations in the moods and feelings of the characters are suggested and the reader has the sense that he participates in it all. As soon as they reached Sacramento, all hardships were forgotten and the future looked bright and promising. They were in rags, they had no money, but their strength was in their intention to work hard:*

The daylight woke us next morning to the realization that if we were to accomplish anything we must be up and stirring. The world around us was all alive. Camp fires crackled, breakfast steamed, and long lines of mules and horses, packed with provisions, filed past on their way out from what was already called a city. The three or four wooden buildings and the zinc banking house, owned by Sam Brannan, looked like solid masonry beside the airy canvas structures which gleamed in the October sunshine like cloud pictures. There was no credit in '49 for men, but I was a woman with two children, and I might have bought out the town with no security other than my word. My first purchase was a quart of molasses for a dollar, and a slice of salt pork as large as my hand, for the same price. That pork, by-the-by, was an experience. When it went into the pan it was as innocent looking pork as I ever saw, but no sooner did it touch the fire than it pranced, it sizzled, frothed over the pan, sputtered, crackled, and acted as if possessed. When finally it subsided, there was left a shaving size of a dollar, and my pork had vanished into smoke. I found afterward that many of our purchases were as deceptive, for the long trip around the "Horn" was not calculated to improve an article which was probably inferior in quality when it left New York. The flour we used was often soured and from a single sieve-full I have sifted out at one time a handful of long black worms. The butter was brown from age and had spent a year on the way out to California. I once endeavored to freshen some of this butter

[152]

by washing it first in chloride of lime, and afterwards churning it with fresh milk. I improved it in a measure, for it became white, but still it retained its strength. It was, however, such a superior article to the original "Boston" butter, that my boarders ate it as a luxury. Strange to say, in a country overrun with cattle as California was in early days, fresh milk and butter were unheard of, and I sold what little milk was left from my children's meals for the enormous price of a dollar a pint. Many a sick man has come to me for a little porridge, half milk, half water, and thickened with flour, and paid me a dollar and a half a bowl full. The beans and dried fruits from Chile, and the yams and onions from the Sandwich Islands, were the best articles for table use we had for months. The New York warehouses were cleared of the provisions they had held for years, and after a twelve-months' sea voyage, they fed the hungry Californians.

Half the inhabitants kept stores; a few barrels of flour, a sack or two of yams, a keg of molasses, a barrel of salt pork, another of corned beef (like redwood in texture) some gulls' eggs from the Farallones, a sack of onions, a few picks and shovels, and a barrel of whisky, served for a stock in trade, while a board laid across the head of a barrel answered for a counter. On many counters were scales, for coin was rare, and all debts were paid in gold dust at sixteen dollars per ounce. In the absence of scales a pinch of dust was accepted as a dollar, and you may well imagine the size of the pinch very often varied from the real standard. Nothing sold for less than a dollar; it was the smallest fractional currency. A dollar each for onions, a dollar each for eggs, beef a dollar a pound, whisky a dollar a drink, flour fifty dollars a barrel. One morning an official of the town stopped at my fire, and said in his pompous way, "Madame, I want a good substantial breakfast, cooked by a woman." I asked him what he would have, and he gave his order, "Two onions, two eggs, a beef-steak and a cup of coffee." He ate it, thanked me, and gave me five dollars. The sum seems large now for such a meal, but then it was not much above cost, and if I had asked ten dollars he would have paid it.

After two or three days in Sacramento we sold our oxen, and with the proceeds, six hundred dollars, we bought an interest in the hotel kept in one of the wooden houses, a story-and-a-half building which stood on what is now known as K Street, near

Sixth, close to what was then the Commercial Exchange, Board of Trade, and Chamber of Commerce, all in one "The Horse Market". The hotel we bought consisted of two rooms, the kitchen, which was my special province, and the general living room, the first room I had entered in Sacramento. I thought I had already grown accustomed to the queer scenes around me, but that first glimpse into a Sacramento hotel was a picture which only loss of memory can efface. Imagine a long room, dimly lighted by dripping tallow candles stuck into whisky bottles, with bunks built from floor to ceiling on either side. A bar with rows of bottles and glasses was in one corner, and two or three miners were drinking; the barkeeper dressed in half sailor, half vaquero fashion, with a blue shirt rolled far back at the collar to display the snowy linen beneath, and his waist encircled by a flaming scarlet sash, was in commanding tones subduing their noisy demands, for the barkeeper, next to the stage-driver, was in early days the most important man in camp. In the opposite corner of the room some men were having a wordy dispute over a game of cards; a cracked fiddle was, under the manipulation of rather clumsy fingers, furnishing music for some half dozen others to dance to the tune of "Moneymusk". One young man was reading a letter by a sputtering candle, and the tears rolling down his yet unbearded face told of the homesickness in his heart. Some of the men lay sick in their bunks, some lay asleep, and out from another bunk, upon this curous mingling of merriment and sadness stared the white face of a corpse. They had forgotten even to cover the still features with the edge of a blanket, and he lay there, in his rigid calmness, a silent unheeded witness to the acquired insensibility of the early settlers. What was one dead man, more or less! Nobody missed him. They would bury him tomorrow to make room for a new applicant for his bunk. The music and the dancing, the card-playing, drinking, and swearing went on unchecked by the hideous presence of Death. His face grew too familiar in those days to be a terror.

It was a motley crowd that gathered every day at my table but always at my coming the loud voices were hushed, the swearing ceased, the quarrels stopped, and deference and respect were as readily and as heartily tendered me as if I had been a queen. I was a queen. Any woman who had a womanly heart, who spoke a kindly sympathetic word to the lonely, homesick men, was a queen, and lacked no honor which a subject could bestow. Women were scarce in those days. I lived six months in Sacramento and saw only two. There may have been others, but I never saw them. There was no time for visiting or gossiping; it was hard work from daylight till dark, and sometimes long after, and I nodded to my neighbor and called out "Good morning" as each of us hung the clothes out to dry on the lines. Yes, we worked; we did things that our high-toned servants would now look at aghast, and say it was impossible for a woman to do. But the one who did not work in '49 went to the wall. It was a hand to hand fight with starvation at the first; later the "flush" times came, when the mines had given out their golden store, and every one had money.

Many a miserable unfortunate, stricken down by the horrors of scurvy or Panama fever, died in his lonely, deserted tent, and waited days for the hurrying crowd to bestow the rites of burial. It has been a life-long source of regret to me that I grew hard-hearted like the rest. I was hard-worked, hurried all day, and tired out, but I might have stopped sometimes for a minute to heed the moans which caught my ears from the canvas house next to me. I knew a young man lived there, for he had often stopped to say "Good morning", but I thought he had friends in the town; and when I heard his weak calls for water I never thought but some one gave it. One day the moans ceased, and, on looking in, I found him lying dead with not even a friendly hand to close his eyes. Many a time since, when my own boys have been wandering in new countries have I wept for the sore heart of that poor boy's mother, and I have prayed that if ever want and sickness came to mine, some other woman would be more tender than I had been, and give them at least a glass of cold water.

We lived two months in the "Trumbow House", then sold our interest in it for a thousand dollars in dust, and left it, moving a few doors below on K Street. The street was always full of pack-mules; five hundred would often pass in a day packed heavily with picks, shovels, camp-kettles, gum-boots, and provisions for the miners. A fleet of schooners and sloops anchored at the river bank was always unloading the freight from San Francisco. Steam-vessels had not yet plowed the muddy waters of the Sacramento. When one of these slow-moving schooners brought the Eastern mails there was excitement in the town. For the hour all work was suspended, and every man dropped into line to ask in turn for letters from home. Sometimes the letters came; more often the poor fellows turned away with pale faces and sick disappointment in their hearts. Even the fortunate recipients of the precious sheets seemed often not less sad, for the closely written lines brought with their loving words a host of tender memories, and many a man whose daily life was one long battle faced with fortitude and courage, succumbed at the gentle touch of the home letters and wept like a woman. There was never a jeer at these sacred tears, for each man respected, nay, honored the feelings of his neighbor. Brave, honest, noble men! The World will never see the like again of those "pioneers of '49". They were, as a rule, upright, energetic, and hard-working, many of them men of education and culture whom the misfotune of poverty had forced into the ranks of labor in this strange country. The rough days which earned for California its name for recklessness had not begun. There was no shooting, little gambling, and less theft in those first months. The necessities of hard work left no leisure for the indulgence even of one's temper, and the "rough" element which comes to every mining country with the first flush times had not yet begun to crowd the West.

One of the institutions of '49, which more than filled the place of our present local telegraphic and telephonic systems, was the "Town Crier". Every pioneer must remember his gaunt form, unshaven face, and long, unkempt hair, and his thin bobtailed sorrel Mexican pony, and the clang of his bell as he rode through the streets and cried his news. Sometimes he announced a "preaching", or a "show", "mail in", an "auction", or a "stray". Another of the features of the city was the horse market to which I have already alluded. A platform was built facing what was only by courtesy called the street, and from his elevation every day rang out the voice of the auctioneer and around it gathered the men who came to buy or sell. The largest trade of the day was in live stock. The miners who came down with dust exchanged it here for horses and mules to carry back their supplies, and vaqueros brought in their cattle to sell to the city butchers. Here, too, were sold the hay and grain, which almost brought their weight in gold.

The population of Sacramento was largely a floating one. Today there might be ten thousand people in the town, and tomorrow four thousand of them might be on their way to the gold fields. The immigrants came pouring in every day from the plains, and the schooners from San Francisco brought a living freight, eager to be away to the mountains.

From the brow of a steep mountain we caught the first glimpse of a mining camp. Nevada City, a row of canvas tents lining each of the two ravines, which, joining, emptied into Deer Creek, lay at our feet, flooded with the glory of the spring sunshine. The gulches seemed alive with moving men. Great, brawny miners wielded the pick and shovel, while others stood knee deep in the icy water, and washed the soil from the gold. Every one seemed impelled by the frenzy of fever as men hurried here and there, so intent upon their work they had scarcely time to breathe. Our entrance into the busy camp could not be called a triumphal one, and had there been a "back way" we should certainly have selected it. Our wagon wheels looked like solid blocks; the color of the oxen was indistinguishable, and we were mud from head to foot. I remember filling my wash-basin three times with fresh water before I had made the slightest change apparent in the color of my face; and I am sure I scrubbed till my arms ached, before I got the children back to their natural hue. We were not rich enough to indulge in the luxury of a canvas home; so a few pine boughs and branches of the undergrowth were cut and thrown into a rude shelter for the present, and my husband hurried away up the mountain to begin to split out "shakes" for a house. Since our experience of rain in Sacramento, we were inclined to think that rain was one of the daily or at least weekly occurrences of a California spring, and the first precaution was to secure a water-tight shelter. Our bedding was placed inside the little brush house, my cook stove set up near it under the shade of a great pine tree, and I was established, without further preparation, in my new home. When I was left alone in the afternoon—it was noon when we arrived—I cast my thoughts about me for some plan to assist in the recuperation of the family finances. As always occurs to the mind of a woman, I thought of taking boarders. There was already a thriving establishment of the kind just down the road, under the shelter of a canvas roof, as was set forth by its sign in lamp-black on a piece of cloth: "Wamac's Hotel. Meals $1.00."

I determined to set up a rival hotel. So I brought two boards from a precious pile belonging to a man who was building the second wooden house in town. With my own hands I chopped stakes, drove them into the ground, and set up my table. I bought provisions at a neighboring store, and when my husband came back at night he found, mid the weird light of the pine torches, twenty miners eating at my table. Each man as he rose put a dollar in my hand and said I might count him as a permanent customer. I called my hotel "El Dorado".

From the first day it was well patronized, and I shortly after took my husband into partnership. The miners were glad to get something to eat, and were always willing to pay for it. As in Sacramento, goods of all kinds sold at enormous figures, but, as no one ever hesitated to buy on that account, dealers made huge profits. The most rare and costly articles of luxury were fruits and vegetables. One day that summer an enterprising pioneer of agricultural tastes brought in a wagon load of watermelons and sold them all for an ounce (sixteen dollars) each. I bought one for the children and thought no more of the price than one does now of buying a dish of ice-cream. Peaches sold at from one to two dollars each and were miserable apologies for fruit at that. Potatoes were a dollar a pound and for a time even higher. As the days progressed we prospered. In six weeks we had saved money enough to pay the man who brought us up from Sacramento the seven hundred dollars we owed him. In a little time, the frame of a house grew up around me, and presently my cook stove and brush house were enclosed under a roof. This house was gradually enlarged room by room, to afford accommodation for our increasing business. One Sunday afternoon as a great recreation, I took a walk along the mountainside above the town, now grown to be of some size. Looking down I found it necessary to ask which was my own house, for I had never before seen the outside of it at any considerable distance. We had then from seventy-five to two hundred boarders at twenty-five dollars a week. I became luxurious and hired a cook and waiters. Maintaining only my position as managing housekeeper, I retired from active business in the kitchen.

The "Coyote Diggings", for that was the early name of the Nevada City placer mines, were very rich in coarse gold, and money came pouring into the town. Everybody had money, and everybody spent it. Money ran through one's fingers like water through a sieve. The most profitable employment of the time was gambling, and fifty or sixty of the men who pursued the profession were guests at my table. Many of them made fortunes and retired into a quieter and less notorious life. Of them all I can now remember only one—Billy Briggs, who has grown to prominence in San Francisco. I see him now, portly, swarthy, and complacent, and wonder what has become of the slender, fair-complexioned, smooth-faced, gentlemanly young man, who came and went so quietly, who carried my little boys away on his shoulders and sent them back to me happy with a handful of bright, new silver half-dollars. The "knights of the green table" were the aristocracy of the town. They were always the best-dressed men, had full pockets, lived well, were generous, respectful, and kind-hearted. They were in that day much what the stockbroking fraternity was here in San Francisco in the palmy days of the Comstock. The great gambling house of Smith & Barker was the central point of interest. At night, under a glow of tallow candles, fifteen faro tables were surrounded by an eager, restless, reckless crowd. Stakes ran high into the thousands. Fortunes were won or lost on the turning of a card. Great piles of coin and bags of dust lay heaped on every table, and changed hands every minute. Men plunged wildly into every mode of dissipation to drown the homesickness so often gnawing at their hearts. They sang, danced, drank and caroused all night, and worked all day. They were possessed of the demon of recklessness, which always haunted the early mining camps. Blood was often shed, for a continual war raged between the miners and the gamblers. Nearly every man carried in his belt either knife or pistol, and one or the other flashed out on small provocation to do its deadly work.

It was such a circumstance as this which raised the first mob in Nevada City. So far as I ever learned, I was their only victim. One night I was sitting quietly by the kitchen fire, alone. My husband was away at Marysville, attending court. Suddenly I heard low knocks on the boards all round the house. Then I heard from threatening voices the cry, "Burn the house." I looked out of the window and saw a crowd of men at the back of the house. I picked up the candle and went into the dining room. At every window I caught sight of faces pressed against the glass. I hurried to the front, where the knocking was loudest and the voices were most uproarious. Terrified almost to death, I opened the door, just enough to see the host of angry, excited faces and hear the cries, "Search for him" and "No, no, burn him out". I attempted to shut the door, but could not. Some one spoke to me, called himself my friend, and tried to tell me that they meant me no harm. But I could not understand, and answered, "I have no friends; what do you want?" The sheriff, a kindly gentleman, whom I knew well and who lived in my house, tried vainly to calm my fears. He explained that a gambler named Tom Collins had been killed at a card table by one of his associates who lived in our house and that they were searching for him. Finally my old friend, Mr. Nick Turner, came pushing through the crowd and he, with the sheriff, succeeded in allaying my fright and making me understand. I then let them search the house but the man was not there. Had he been caught they would have made short work of him. The next night, or rather in the morning, my husband came home. He had seen the fugitive, who had ridden into Marysville to tell him of the shooting and of my fright. In disguise he had stood in the crowd, not ten feet from me, had watched them search, and heard the raging of the infuriated crowd. He said it was hard work to keep from betraying himself when he saw how I was suffering from terror. His friends had provided a fleet mule, which they had tied somewhere across the ravine, and when the mob dispersed he made fast time out of the camp. Many years afterwards he came to see me and told me that the greatest regret he felt in regard to the affair was that he had not come forward and given himself up and saved me such pain.

The doctors were busy then, for there were hundreds of men sick and dying from cold and exposure. Indeed, every profession found employment, except the clerical, for it was not yet settled enought at the "Coyote" to require the services of a pastor. Every man was too busy thinking of the preservation of his body to think of saving his soul; and the unfortunates who did not succeed in keeping their heads above water were buried "without benefit of the clergy". Like all California mining towns, Nevada City grew up in almost the twinkling of an eye. There were ten thousand men in the Coyote Diggings, and the streets were lined with drinking saloons and gambling tables. Money came in in thousands of dollars from the mines. New parties came pouring into the town from Sacramento and fitted out here for further prospecting in the mountains. The country was full of men crazed on the subject of "deep diggings", and the future seemed to promise a succession of greater good fortune. These were indeed "flush times". We made money fast. In six months we had ten thousand dollars invested in the hotel and store and we owned a stock of goods worth perhaps ten thousand more. The buildings were of the roughest possible description, but they were to Nevada City what the Palace Hotel is to this city today.

There was no place of deposit for money, and the men living in the house dropped into the habit of leaving their dust with me for safe keeping. At times I have had a larger amount of money in my charge than would furnish capital for a country bank. Many a night have I shut my oven door on two milk-pans filled high with bags of gold dust, and I have often slept with my mattress literally lined with the precious metal. At one time I must have had more than two hundred thousand dollars lying unprotected in my bedroom, and it never entered my head that it might be stolen. The house had neither locks nor bolts, but, as there were no thieves, precautions were unnecessary. I had a large, old-fashioned reticule hung behind my kitchen stove, where I put the money I had made by doing little pieces of sewing for the men. In a month or two I had four or five hundred dollars saved and was thinking of lending it, for interest was very high. But one day I missed the bag. Of course there was a general search, and I found, at last, that my youngest son had taken it down, dragged it out into the sand in the street, and was building houses with the coins. He had been there an hour or more, some of the men told me, and no one had thought of stealing even a solitary half-dollar from the little fellow. I loaned the money, but at such an extravagant rate of interest that I might have foreseen that my man must fail and run away, which he finally did. I believe the rate of interest at which I loaned it was ten per cent a month. The only case of theft I can remember to have occurred during the time I lived in Nevada City, was that of a man who appropriated a mule, and he received so aggravated a punishment that I shiver when I recollect that I was an involuntary looker-on. They tied the miserable man to a tree, and lashed his bare back with a leather whip, until he was cut and striped in a hundred places, and the blood ran down from his shoulders to the ground in a perfect stream.

My wardrobe was still a simple one. For several years my best dress was a clean calico. The first installments of genuine finery which came into the interior were crepe shawls and scarfs from the Chinese vessels which came to San Francisco. But the feminine portion of the population was so small that there was no rivalry in dress or fashion, and every man thought every woman in that day a beauty. Even I have had men come forty miles over the mountains, just to look at me, and I never was called a handsome woman, in my best days, even by my most ardent admirers.


After we had been in the town of Nevada City three or four months, the first ball was given. There were twelve ladies present and about three hundred men. The costumes were eccentric, or would be now. At that time it was the prevailing fashion for the gentlemen to attend social gatherings in blue woolen shirts, and with trousers stuffed into boot-tops. Every man was "heeled" with revolver and bowie-knife. My own elaborate toilet for the occasion was a freshly ironed calico and a plaid shawl. The dresses of the other ladies were similar. A few days before the ball, word came into the town that a family of immigrants, including several grown young ladies had moved into Grass Valley. The news was hailed with rapture by the young men, and two of them, Messrs. Frinx and Blackman, prominent merchants, procured horses and rode over, with testimonials in hand, to engage the presence of the young ladies, if possible, for the forthcoming ball. There were cordially received, and their request gracefully accorded. On the day of the ball, they procured what they could in the form of vehicles, and drove over the mountains to bring back their prizes. It was already dark when they arrived at the little log house, and a knock at the door ushered them into the one room of the residence.

The old lady answered their inquiries for the young ladies by saying, "Not much. If your ball had been in the daytime, and the gals 'ud be home by dark, I wouldn't mind; but my gals don't go traipsing 'round in the night with no young men. No siree."

There was nothing left for the discomfited beaux but to come back alone. When they returned, they gave us a mournful description of their wild-goose chase. They told us how, as they stepped into the room, the clothing on two beds gave a sudden jerk and exposed the symmetry of two pairs of feet. They were at first mystified by the strange sight, but afterwards concluded that these were the dainty pedal extremities of their missing in-amoratas. However, the ball went on, notwithstanding the lessening in number of the expected ladies. A number of the men tied handkerchiefs around their arms and airily assumed the character of ball-room belles. Every lady was overwhelmed with attentions, and there was probably more enjoyment that night, on the rough pine floor and under the flickering gleam of tallow candles, than one often finds in our society drawing-rooms, where the rich silks trail over velvet carpets, where the air is heavy with the perfume of exotics, and where night is turned into a brighter day under the glare of countless gas-jets.

We had lived eighteen months in Nevada City when fire cut us adrift again, as water had done in Sacramento. Some careless hand had set fire to a pile of pine shavings lying at the side of a house in course of construction, and while we slept, unconscious of danger, the flames caught and spread, and in a short half hour the whole town was in a blaze. We were roused from sleep by the cry of "Fire, fire" and the clang of bells. Snatching each a garment, we hurried out through blinding smoke and darting flames, not daring even to make an effort to collect our effects. There were no means for stopping such a conflagration. Bells clanged and gongs sounded, but all to no purpose save to wake the sleeping people, for neither engines nor firemen were at hand. So we stood with bated breath, and watched the fiery monster crush in his great red jaws the homes we had toiled to build. The tinder-like pine houses ignited with a spark, and the fire raged and roared over the fated town. The red glare fell far back into the pine woods and lighted them like day; it wrapped the moving human creatures in a fiendish glow, and cast their giant shadows far along the ground.

The fire howled and moaned like a giant in an agony of pain, and the buildings crashed and fell as if he were striking them down in his writhings. When the slow dawn broke, and the sun came riding up so calm and smiling, he looked down upon a smouldering bed of ashes; and in place of the cheerful, happy faces, which were wont to greet his appearance in the busy rushing town of yesterday his beams lighted sad countenances, reflecting the utter ruin of their fortunes. The eight thousand inhabitants were homeless, for in the principal part of the town every house was swept away; and most of them were penniless as well as homeless. Like ourselves most of them had invested their money in buildings and goods, and scarcely anything was saved. The remnant of our fortune consisted of five hundred dollars, which my husband had in his pockets and had neglected to put away, and with that sum we were to start again. For months my health had been failing, and when this blow came in the shape of the fire, my strength failed and I fell sick. Some generous man offered us the shelter of his cabin in the edge of the woods. For weeks I was a prisoner there, bound in the fetters of fever. When, at last, my returning health and strength permitted it, we moved from Nevada City nearer to the valley.

*One of Luzena Stanley Wilson's most interesting traits is perhaps her ability to assert herself and her confidence in her capacity to achieve what she had set out to do. She was keenly aware of the possibilities which were open to women in California. At a time when most women were taught to be obedient and had to depend upon the good will of others, she managed to make the best use of her talents and decided upon a certain course of action: she opened a boarding house and took her husband as a partner! Through the various turns their lives took, and despite the various obstacles which had to be surmounted, she never stopped believing that her industry, her thrift, her energy would help her overcome any type of misfortune. And eventually the family's circumstances improved and they shared in the development and prosperity of Vacaville. Luzena Stanley Wilson's descriptions of*

*the wonderful changes which occurred in the town and the
country, in the appearance of the people and in the quality of the
entertainments, are presented in a most entertaining manner.*

1. This information has been gathered from the introduction written by
Francis Farquhar, *op. cit.*, no p.
2. *Luzena Stanley Wilson, '49er*, p. 1.

# Active Footsteps

Caroline N. Churchill

(Colorado Springs: Mrs. C.N. Churchill Printer) 1909.

*Mrs. Churchill's strong personality comes out forcefully in her writings and constitutes their main interest. She was a most unusual woman, who cared nothing for housekeeping and seemed uninfluenced by the sentimental effusions about the "home" which are so characteristic of 19th century popular writings in America. Her ideas concerning women's place in society were extremely advanced for the times; she was constantly fighting against traditional ideas and rebelled at the existing conditions.*

*She was born in Canada in 1833 to a family of small means, and had to help with the work and accept certain duties and responsibilities very early in her life. At 14, she started teaching and describes this activity as one of her most successful in life. She was married in the early fifties and explains this event in the following manner:*

> *People did not know what else to do with girls, as there were few avenues of employment for them. A husband was selected, and, however inappropriate, the girl was expected to conform to the condition.[1]*

*Her husband died in the early sixties; she was left with one daughter, which she later trusted to her sister. She found it hard to support herself; in the summer, she taught school, and in the winter, she did some sewing. In 1870, she moved to California for health reasons primarily, and stayed there until 1876.*

*Her book is hard to describe as it does not belong to a well-defined genre. It is partly an autobiography, partly a travel-book; it contains many pronouncements on life in general and on the condition of women in particular, which are interspersed here and there, and are always striking by their sharp and pithy character. Mrs. Churchill was particularly interested in journalism and tried to launch several newspapers. She found it hard to make a place for herself in a man's world, and never lost a chance to hit at the "master class" that "seldom lose a chance to insult a woman who has the ability for something besides service to his lordship,"[2] and always stressed the progress made by women in recent years, announcing that they would eventually surpass men. There is no particular order or progression in the book, only a vaguely chronological arrangement. Mrs. Churchill jumps from one subject to the next without any transition; her descriptions are not especially compelling, her stories and anecdotes are not frequently arresting, but her ideas concerning the condition of women are so provocative that they make the book well worth reading. The preface is a good summary of her views; the second passage selected shows the difficulties encountered by women who tried to set up their own businesses:*

This book is biographical: is written to portray the career of the author. The style preferred is of the third person, that, as much as possible, the ego might be hidden. The statements are facts, as they have occurred in most original methods of conducting business. No method of doing business by man would be considered original; as he is in possession of all the avenues of influence, he can exploit land and sea, and practice most doubtful methods of procuring a livelihood, without question so far as a matter of taste is concerned, and all too frequently without regard to principle. The brainiest woman living is supposed to do nothing only what she is expected to do, as her training has been in the interests of a dominant class. For the flattering of man's vanities it is reiterated, time without end, that any woman who will conduct herself properly can travel anywhere in the United States of America without molestation. As the poor darkey said to the judge, "The *facts* in this case are not true." Women need to give this subject attention in the interest of their own sex. Learn what it means to be constantly coached in the interests of a dominant class. Women of sense will not become the tools of the vicious, but a fool can be coached without knowing the object of the schemer.

If men had to do their vile work without the assistance of woman and the stimulant of strong drink they would be obliged to be more divine and less brutal. The question of the servant girl would be three-fourths settled if woman would give the servant the protection to which even the nurse girl is entitled. Slavery of any character is a most pitiable condition: that of woman keeps the entire race at a low standard. Man has done more for humanity in the last hundred years, since woman began to have influence from the fact of being educated, than has been accomplished in two thousand years previously. The race would be vastly benefited if women were better protected in their enterprises, as she is the unselfish dispenser of all earthly gifts to the race; and, with her advancement in educational matters, man is bound to produce a civilization embracing the brotherhood of the entire race, which will result in causing the wants of one the care of all. May the unseen forces speed the day when man shall not be an unmitigated falsifier that he may live by wronging his fellows. This is an epitome of the earnest prayer of every mother living who has sufficient spirituality to make a prayer.

The author of this work has been obliged to do a traveling business for half a century, because of the physical necessity of being as much as possible in the open air. The work has been made doubly hard from the fact that women have no legal protection when in a strange community, and because women are so easily influenced to help in her degradation. The feminine sex are improving in this respect, beginning to see the necessity of defending their own. Woman in a strange community is supposed to be guilty until proved innocent, while man is supposed to be innocent until proven guilty. That a woman's virtue must depend upon her having a chaperone is too absurd for contemplation. The work performed by nuns may be accomplished in the presence of a tag, but man or woman who has anything to do in the way of legitimate business must give undivided attention to the same for success. I kept a record of my whereabouts for twelve years before establishing a paper in Denver; in case there should be malicious talk from responsible parties a rational defense might be made. Crows are liable to fly over anyone's head, with crow talk. The only remedy for this is to kill the crows. Unless the crops are in danger a crow is not worth killing.

STARTING A PAPER

In 1876 Mrs. Churchill went East for the purpose of getting out her little book, entitled "Over the Purple Hills." This work was descriptive of California. It was Centennial year, and it was difficult to get publishers interested in a new book maker, especially one whose reputation as a novice was centered entirely in the "Wild and Fleecy West." Mrs. Churchill had her book printed in Chicago, and reviewed by the "Tribune," the "Times" and "Post." Two of these publications mentioned the book as being a sprightly written little work, with some description surpassing any previous production on those points, "The Yosemite Valley, Lake Tahoe and Monte Diablo." With this she visited Texas, where she traveled for two years, making a generous sale of her work. Missouri, Kansas and Indian Territory assisted in filling the time until 1879. Mrs. Churchill, desiring to make a permanent home for herself, was returning to California, when she visited Denver, Colorado. She had no idea of remaining in Denver, but found in the course of a few weeks that she had never been in a climate where she could accomplish the work she could perform in Colorado. A high altitude, inland from large bodies of water, whether salt or fresh, was the physical condition needed for Mrs. Churchill's health. The pioneer settlers of Colorado well know that for industrial effort, or rather endeavor, this woman could never be surpassed. For physical strength she might have been outdone, but never in plucky effort to overcome almost insurmountable obstacles and difficulties. Where one can do the most work is where one has the best health. She concluded that Denver was the point from which to radiate in attending to her business. Here was where she would buy some lots and try to make a permanent home. One may have a good traveling business, but if they do not tie up somewhere, and get something together, after the lapse of many years of work they will have little to show for the effort.

Expenses will take everything unless in the case of men with good salaries who have the thrift to invest, and in that way accumulate until ready to leave the road. Mrs. Churchill had for years contemplated publishing a paper. The fact that men hold in supreme selfishness all the great avenues of influence, the pulpit and the press, with the learned professions, rankled in her mind until to get even with the arch enemy of the race became the prime object of existence. Men of sense have generally admired her earnest endeavor, and have shown a disposition to give her assistance, frequently saying it were better for humanity if women would generally spend more time upon the condition of public affairs and less upon dress, frivolity and household display. Chaucer, Ruskin, John Stuart Mill and May, with many other distinguished individuals of both sexes, have delivered the same opinions. The beauty of Mrs. Churchill's great work is that she never sought preferment for herself. Self-aggrandizement never formed any part of her policy. To do the work for which so few women are fitted by nature or experience was the height of her ambition. Her support financially must come from her endeavors, whatever they might be. Susan B. Anthony was liberally endowed for the work she did in behalf of her sex. Lucy Stone also received half the sum, sixty thousand dollars. Those women did noble work in the East, but did not accomplish the political emancipation of a single State. Mrs. Churchill has performed a wonderful work under most difficult circumstances. It is not at all likely that another woman on the continent could under the same conditions accomplish as much. The simple, earnest plaint of the colored people carried an echo of woman's condition more or less pathetic. Those people say why do the ex-slave holders hate us? Did we not help to make their wealth? Did we not as servants give them a chance to educate their children and bestow upon them the best of opportunities? Why should they now hate us that we are trying to do something for ourselves? If we are ignorant and coarse, what have those people who make fun of us done to make us otherwise?

There is a note in this simple statement that strikes to the quick when woman is belittled by the press published in the interests of men exclusively. She has been man's slave. He has been educated at her expense. If he bought the ice cream, she was expected to pay for all his luxuries in reduced wages. She has done the drudgery and borne the insults of those who wronged her, assuming to be her protector. As woman becomes educated and influential this state of things to some extent disappears. The foregoing causes was the incentive for establishing the little monthly paper called "The Antelope." Mrs. Churchill is a dear lover of animals, and knowing an order called after the Elk, not a delicately handsome beasty, thought Antelope rather better than Ursula, Bovine, Equine, Leonine, Feline, Canine or Porcine, she concluded Antelope would do. The paper was a monthly and very well edited. The facilities for getting out a paper in Denver thirty years ago were very poor, as the publishers had only the material for getting out their own productions. At length a firm of lithographers consented to get out the first edition. It produced June, 1879. Mrs. Churchill called for the edition next day. A conceited little printer was to be at the office Sunday morning to deliver the edition to Mrs. Churchill herself, as it must be sold immediately. The printer took especial pains to let her know that he was a married man, so that there should be no serious misunderstanding. Mrs. Churchill was then in her forty-seventh year, and fool proof as well as man proof. She, however, thought that frankness of this stupid piece of humanity was a great novelty to say the least, as most Western men were always bachelors whenever a new woman appeared upon the scene. The edition of a thousand copies was all sold by twelve o'clock, at ten cents a copy, and the demand remained brisk after the last copy was sold. The type not being distributed, another edition was struck off, but not so hastily disposed of, as the first had been read at the rate of about ten persons to the copy. The lithographers can vouch for Mrs. Churchill's promptness in meeting all financial obligations as well as getting out her paper on time.

The little paper soon had a very fair subscription list, and some advertising. The expense of the paper was very high; the cost of living and rents was much in advance of what they were in more Eastern cities. In 1879 Denver had a population of about thirty thousand. Most of the population had not come to stay, so longed to get back to what they called God's country. This may have been a peculiar phrase of pious slang, but people all through the ages have been taught that their own God was a very partial individual, bestowing blessings for the believers' special benefit. The common ear was, and always has been, deaf and blind to the smacking of commercialism in his Gods requiring belief. Faith is a part of nature's requirement in the success of anything undertaken in life, whether good, bad or indifferent. People had no faith in the future of the city of the plains. It was supposed to be just a good atmosphere for weak lungs, and in some cases a good place to come in order to escape the mother-in-law, or any phantom from which the wicked flee. The population was very transient, and withal very democratic, in the dictionary sense of the term. "The New Rich of the West" found that they really needed a residence city in a climate and among people where they had labored the early part of their lives to acquire their fortunes. They wanted the social freedom to wear a cowboy's hat without giving mortal offense, and the Eastern nabob occasionally wanted to go a-fishing accompanied by his housemaid, and there was no reason that he should fear being mobbed in the quiet city of the plains. And Colorado is certainly the place to fish and hunt and have a good time for an outing, as there is so much sunshine and clear weather—nothing to interfere. In the early days of Denver's history the people were very sociable. Mrs. Churchill says many times she was obliged to leave the city for outside towns in order to raise money to pay her bills, because of being interrupted so frequently on the street for a social chat; women especially seem to have very little idea of the importance of business time. It is queer to contemplate how many people there are in any community who labor under the hallucination that if one is engaged in any occupation different from their own, that they are just having a good time, with no possible hardships to encounter. Especially does this idea prevail in regard to people who have a traveling business, by those who have only taken travel in pleasantly small doses for visiting or entertaining.

In publishing the monthly paper there were men entirely incredulous as to a paper succeeding published by a woman. There were those who would buy and read the paper and steadily oppose its publication. There was one man who said to Mrs. Churchill that if she would get out the second edition he would subscribe for the paper. When asked to make his word good, he declined, but suffered the disappointment of his wishes for three years and then went off and died. He was not permitted to live until the weekly paper called the "Queen Bee" was established. There were so many protests coming from the East against the name Antelope that when it was changed to a weekly it was thought best to change the name. "Queen Bee" became the popular name for Mrs. Churchill, many persons knowing her only as by the name of her paper, not knowing her real name. The greatest grievance the editor has to complain of is the habit of the mass of the people to confuse her publication with the Omaha paper called "The Omaha Bee." The Omaha paper is one of Nebraska's leading dailies, a Democratic paper opposed to every sentiment promulgated by the Denver "Queen Bee," or rather the Colorado paper of that name. The owner of this paper seems to have been born with the ability to transact business with men, and with a class of men worth calling upon. Women were not, generally speaking, so easily reached, and were not as liable to be provided with ready cash, and many had prejudices which were not worth the time to combat. It would seem that men in Denver in ye old time were afflicted with woman on the brain. Men have always been afflicted this way more or less, according to the scarcity of woman. It is strong evidence that she is of much more importance in man's economy than most men are willing to admit. In communities where women are in the ascendency men are fondled and favored in every way. All his faults are covered with the mantle of charity, methods right contrary to those practiced on the woman. This is in accord with natural law. An elderly woman who kept a candy store heard so many silly remarks about the editor of the woman's paper, she ventured to ask the cause. The answer was characteristic! More men in the country than women. This is the only reason known, continued she, unless it may be that I am considered more worthy of attention than some others. In the course of six months from the first appearance of the paper Mrs. Churchill thought it best to get an office of her own and keep her own help. A batch of good second-hand type was found, and a printer out of a job, with great effort and many promises, kept sober long enough to get the thing in shape. In 1881 the Chinese riot occurred in Denver. The foreign laborer, without cause or provocation, attacked those people and tried to annihilate them.

Mrs. Churchill was out on a subscription trip when this took place. The Chinaman's greatest crime seems to be his superior industry, sobriety and living within his income. The same objection is frequently mooted in the case of woman. A distinguished Norwegian editor once said the only objection he had to a certain female relative was that she never "gave cause for fault finding." There is a world of human nature expressed in that simple sounding sentence. Really, too much perfection of character has a reflex action on the fellow who thinks he cannot get anything out of life worth while without playing some forbidden game. Mrs. Churchill's employes made themselves useful in caring for the wounded Chinamen, one of whom died upon the floor where her office was located. Mrs. Churchill was obliged to keep her office and home together, partly from the necessity of being away in the interests of her publication, and because the business was not sufficiently remunerative to keep up another establishment. The position was an easy one for the printer; he could take his own time and be really his own boss. There were always enough meddlesome people to make disparaging remarks about being employed and bossed by a woman.

Mrs. Churchill says if "help" need bossing they are not worth having around. She would never keep people for work who had to be called in the morning. If one cannot take sufficient interest in what one is paid to do, to get up in the morning, they had better be sent home to mother, who has so sadly neglected their education. A high-priced man was never employed, as there was not work enough to keep one busy, as there was no job work. At first a young printer was secured who with another aspirant had been trying to make a living by printing cards and doing odd jobs. The time came when they could not pay their rent and had nothing to eat. One of the young men appealed to his home folks and secured money enough to take him to his friends; the other had no such recourse, so applied to a kind-hearted old gentleman whose popular title was "Colonel Sellers," one of the kind who substituted hope for every real want that came to hand. The job was secured for the young fellow, who proved to be excellent help. The young man was a Hebrew and been well brought up. He had left home determined to make his own way without calling on his people. He proved to be respectful, trustworthy, polite and sober, very important qualities in an employe. When he came to the office he was without means, or clothing suitable for cold weather. As this became known, efforts were made to fit out the printer with little regard to waiting for wages to accrue. In the early days of mining camps there is always reckless prodigality as to material things. Denver was no exception to this rule. Mrs. Churchill noticed when E's washing was sent in that there were no drawers. In going out to business she saw something floating from a boarding house window, which she turned over with her umbrella stick and found to be a new pair of drawers, which had been discarded because too small for the original owner. These were taken to the needy and received with a thankful heart. Everybody who knows anything about a mining camp or the new distributing centers thereof knows how men make things fly when away from their natural guardians, wife, mother, sisters, cousins and aunts.

Good clothing could be picked up in sufficient quantity to have clothed a small army if there were no demand for uniforms. Unless the country is in the toils of a panic, Denver is always crowded. One night Mrs. Churchill returned from a month's trip outside in the interest of her publication, and made her presence known at the fastened door. The printer appeared carrying a lighted lamp, apparently greatly embarrassed; with apologies in bashful confusion, the young man stammered: "These boys had no place to sleep, so I let them lie down here, not expecting you home." The editor took in the situation good-naturedly, saying, "Do not disturb yourself; as the boys are here, let them rest," at the same time stepping over the prostrate forms of from four to six youngsters, each of whom was trying to get a foothold in the West. Mrs. Churchill reached her own apartment, and the incident was soon forgotten in a sound sleep. When morning came the coast was cleared, not a boy in sight; "they had folded their tents, like the Arab, and silently stole away." The question was asked, where will they get breakfast? They will scatter to different boarding houses and make their wants known. No woman ever forgets that she is the mother of the race. The substantial, sensible, practicable women should be asked into every important council held by man in the interests of the common good.

Boys need not go hungry in the West who can wash dishes. Good, reliable help is always in demand. Brisben Walker, a brainy little man with a big head, was publishing a paper called the "InterOcean" on the same floor of the building where Mrs. Churchill's paper was gotten out. Mr. Walker reminded Mrs. Churchill of Henry George, the philanthropist, whom Mrs. Churchill knew when he was editor of the San Francisco Post. Mr. George used to have a comic valentine in his office which resembled him more than any picture she ever saw of that distinguished individual. This picture had a Brodigan head, with a small body; it may have been a real picture of Mr. George. The editorial quill was stuck over his ear. It is to be hoped that the picture has been preserved.

*Mrs. Churchill wrote other books, including* Little Sheaves gathered while gleaning after reapers. *Being letters of travel commencing in 1870 and ending in 1873 (San Francisco, 1874) and* Over the Purple Hills, or Sketches of Travel in California *(Denver: Mrs. Caroline N. Churchill Publisher, 1884). In my opinion, they are interesting primarily because, among the mass of information about scenes, manners and customs, lie seminal thoughts on women and their position in society.*

1. Caroline Churchill, *Active Steps*, p. 19.
2. Mrs. Churchill, p. 77. Her grammar is not always very good!

# Ten Years in Nevada, or, Life on the Pacific Coast

Mary Mathews

(Buffalo: Baker, Jones & Co.) 1880


*The circumstances of Mrs. Mathews's departure to Nevada were rather uncommon and deserve special mention. She was a widow with a small child, a boy by the name of Charley, and left her home near Buffalo, New York, in 1869, to try and get hold of the property owned there by her deceased brother Charles who had left twelve years earlier to make a fortune. She spent about ten years in Nevada, attempting to sort out her brother's affairs, and was involved in several legal actions. After having returned East, she set down her experiences in a rather long volume. Her preface gives a good idea of the kind of woman she was and of the life she led while in Nevada:*


I have been frequently requested by my Eastern and Western friends to write up my life in Nevada, and tell them how I managed to sustain myself and child, carry on law, and lay up property. They wish to know something of Pacific life; the manners and customs of the people; all about the Chinamen, the Piutes, and the mines of the Comstock. They wish to know all I can tell them of the Pacific Coast after a ten years' sojourn in California and Nevada.

All have persuaded me that such a book would be very interesting, and have an extensive circulation.

I shall endeavor to write nothing but facts gathered from my own observation and experience, or from other reliable sources.

My readers will see I had but one purpose in going to Nevada—
that of ascertaining the facts concerning my brother's death and
his business affairs, and, if possible, to bring his murderer to
justice, and to prove to his friends that he did not die a beggar, as
was represented by Mr. G. G. Waters, the man who took charge of
his papers.

They will also see with what tenacity I clung to my purpose,
never allowing any obstacle to hinder, or fear deter me. They will
see that while accomplishing it we had to endure a great deal of
sickness, privations, trials, and hard work. We did not shrink from
honest labors, but engaged in anything that would further our
purpose, regardless of the opinion of the *high-toned*. We took
*Conscience* for our guide, and left the rest to God.

Our vocations were as checkered and numerous as those of
P. T. Barnum; for we have been seamstress, nurse, laundress,
school-teacher, and letterwriter; have kept a lodging-house, and
been our own chamber-maid; kept boarders, and did our own
cooking.

My son shared privations and trials with me without a
murmur, and did his part of the work; for, besides attending
school and keeping up with all his classes, he carried the *Evening
Chronicle*, and had a route of his own, consisting of several of the
best New York and San Francisco papers. He had also been an
employee in the N. P. Telegraph Office; had played for benefits,
and finally went on the stage as an actor, and has continued to
follow the business ever since.

Although we engaged in so many kinds of business, endured
privations, hardships, losses; though we were swindled and
robbed, our life on the Pacific Coast has been far from unpleasant;
for few people ever enjoyed life more than we did. Few ever
made more true and lasting friends than we did in the same length
of time. We took life as it came—enduring its trials, and enjoying
its pleasures.

*After she had arrived, she spent some time trying to locate the
claims her brother had in Storey and Lyons counties. She lived for
a while in Dayton, and mentions the reputation it had for easy
divorce. She finally settled down in Virginia City. The account she*

*has left of her various residences and occupations provides information on conditions in cities at that time and on the shape daily life took for a working woman. The following pages show how she earned her living and strived to solve the various problems she had to face:*

I got a little sewing of several, but not enough to pay rent and keep us in food. And the little money I had left of my journey, with the $4 Charlie had earned carrying mail for the boarders while at Mrs. Osborne's, was all I had. He had also bought himself a pair of boots, and a nice worsted dress for a Christmas present for me.

With the $4 I now bought provisions to start on; but, as I said, the money was running low.

The tubs suggested the idea of taking in washing, for the prospects were a hard winter.

Business became dull, and everybody tried to do their own sewing.

I asked Mr. French to give me his washing to do.

He did so, and also got his clerk to send his.

Mrs. Beck got some of her roomers for me, and an old gentleman of the name of French, to whom I had first talked of getting a house, brought me his.

In all I had twelve to wash for, and it brought me about $8 a week. This, with my sewing, just about supported me, for provisions were very high.

Butter $1 a roll—the rolls containing one pound, or a pound and a quarter. Beans were 10 cents a pound. A pound would just fill a coffee-cup. Onions were 6 and 7 cents a pound, and about three would make a pound. Potatoes were 5 cents a pound, and apples the same. In fact, everything sold by the pound.

I have paid $3 and $4 for as many apples as I have seen sold in the East for 25 cents, and have paid 25 cents for no more than four apples, and not large ones either.

Flour was the cheapest article of produce in the market, being $5 and $6 per hundred weight.

I have bought 25 cent's worth of cherries, and found I had paid a penny apiece for them, and plums in the same proportion.

Peaches were 10 cents apiece, unless you bought them by the box.

The Nevadans are no penny-mites.

The smallest change is one dime, which they call a "short bit"—12 cents being a "bit," 15 cents a "long bit," 25 cents "two bits," 50 cents "four bits," and 75 cents "six bits." A dollar is a dollar.

So you see if you just want an apple, peach, or pear, you have to pay 10 cents.

If you want anything that is just 10 cents, and should give 25 cents, they will give you back ten cents, and keep the 15 cents— giving you the "short bit," and they keeping the "long bit."

On the other hand, if you want anything that is worth 15 cents, and should have but 10 cents, they will take it just as readily. For instance, you wish for a yard of cloth that is 15 cents a yard, you will offer 10 cents, and they will take it. But if you give them 25 cents, they will give you back 10 cents.

At these high figures I had hard work to keep up rent. And wood was from $12 to $25 a cord, and coal $25 a ton.

I did a good deal of sewing. I did some for Mrs. Judge Rising, and before I got it finished I took a severe cold. I sent Charlie home with the work that was finished, and when she learned I was sick she sent me a basket of jellies and canned fruit, pickles, and other knick-knacks, as much as the child could carry.

I considered it very kind of her, for I was an entire stranger to her, only having done a little sewing for her. She also paid a good price for it.

The first night that I got settled in our new quarters was the happiest I had seen in three months, and we enjoyed our supper more than any we had eaten in the same time.

One cold day Mrs. Beck came down to see me. She went away, but soon returned, bringing me some jelly, pie, cake, and a pail of hot soup, although the weather was very cold, and I lived several streets from her. Charlie did not have to cook much that day.

I was now very careful, and in a few days got around again; but the washing was too much for me, and wore me out very fast, but I could not give it up just yet.

About three weeks after I had got settled, the water collector called, and while there I made inquiries of him, as I did of everybody; to see if he had known my brother, in hopes to learn something new of him.

He said he did not know him, but he did know Frank McNair, on the Divide.

"Is he a relative of yours?" he asked.

I told him I had a cousin somewhere by that name.

I requested him to let Mr. McNair know where I was stopping. He did so.

The next day he called.

I was not at home, but had left word with a neighbor that if he called, to tell him I would be there at night, for I had to go to Silver City on business.

He called again on Sunday, took dinner with me, and from that time forth I saw him nearly every day.

This took away a great deal of our home-sickness.

One day I sent Charlie to get some milk. When he came home he said: "Mamma, I guess I have spoilt your pail!" I looked at the pail. It looked as if he had used it for a football.

I asked him how he did it—if he played foot-ball with it.

"Worse than that," said he; "I whipped a boy with it, and made him run, too. I know you told me not to fight, but I could not help it. A little boy threw me down and choked me, but some other boys put him up to it. I tried to get away, but they surrounded me, and he took me down and choked me. When I got up I was so mad that I did not care for my finger, whether I hurt it or not. I took my pail, and went for the whole crowd. They all ran, but I caught the boy and thrashed him with the pail until he cried."

I asked the boy's name, and found out where his parents lived.

The next morning I called on the lady. She was a very pleasant person, and quick-spoken.

I told her I had simply called to see if she would be kind enough to keep her boy from stopping Charlie on the street and hurting him, as Charlie had a sore finger, for if he got it hurt, he was liable to have the lock-jaw.

She said: "I am very sorry my boy has hurt your child, but he shall not touch him again."

She was very lady-like, and invited me in, but, being in a hurry, I declined. She then said: "Mrs. Mathews, I am going to move next door to you to-day, and I hope this will not be your last call. I hope that we shall be good friends, and the children, too." And she called Sammie to her, and told him he must never hurt Charlie again.

I thanked her, and said that I presumed we should be friends.
I liked her appearance from the first.

She said: "Do not wait for me to get settled, but come right
along."

I will, said I, and did call on her the same week that she
moved; and from that time the most intimate friendship sprang up
between us.

We often laughed over our first introduction, and I think we
have even been glad the children had the little spat which brought
about our acquaintance.


We spent many happy evenings together that winter.

After I had sent Charlie to school about three weeks, he
caught a severe cold from the window at the school-house being
open on his back. I sent word to the teacher, asking if she would
not seat him somewhere else, and she told him he might as well sit
there as anybody.

When I heard this I took him from school, and taught him
myself, as I always had.

Mrs. Calvin came in one day, and after hearing me instruct
Charlie in his lesson, asked me why I would not start a select
school. I said I would if I could get scholars enough.

"Will twelve do?" said she.

I said it would.

"Well, just keep my baby for me, and I will get you some,"
said Mrs. Calvin.

She was gone about two hours, and when she came back she
had twelve names. The children would commence on the following Monday. This was Thursday. I was to have 50 cents apiece per
week.

But one, Mrs. Babcock, always sent me $1.50 a week for her
two girls, because she said 50 cents was not enough.

Monday came, and with it twelve as bright-looking children
as you would wish to see. They were very smart, and learned very
fast.

In time my school numbered twenty. I now was able to lay up
a little every week till I had $35 laid by to fee a lawyer, for I had
tried nearly every lawyer in the city, but no one would take my

case on contingent fee—all wanted money. I could also afford to buy a few knick-knacks for my child, who seemed to have a poor appetite, and pined for such things; but I always had to share, or pretend to share, them with him or they did him no good.

I always had plenty of hearty, substantial food, for I knew I could not do hard work without it.

But Charlie was a dainty child, and could no more go without dainties than I could substantial food.

One day a gentleman, from whom I had rented the first house when I landed in Virginia City, came and brought me a half-barrel of flour, a large twelve-quart can of raisins, a pail of different kinds of spices, a chopping bowl and knife, a rolling-pin, a ham, and a variety of other things.

Their dwelling was just opposite me, and his wife and myself had become very intimate.

She had just had a little boy killed by the cars, and was nearly insane with grief. But I had done all I could to soothe her aching heart.

She spent many hours at my house, and I suppose he felt grateful to me.

They were now going below for her health, and also to get her away from the scene of the accident, and having a good deal of provisions on hand, was giving it to his neighbors.

Among the things he brought us were two bottles of California wine. Well, I was very much obliged for this little wind-fall, for it was very hard times just then, yet it was very unexpected to me.

With my school, washing, and sewing, I had now laid by $35 towards my law business, but had not yet found a lawyer to take my case on contingent fees, although I had tried eight months nearly every day; had talked with thirty-two lawyers, but all wanted a retaining fee of from $100 to $500, except one, Mr. Elliott.

I was still washing, teaching, and sewing.

Perhaps the reader would like to know how I managed to do it.

I got up early every Monday morning, and got my clothes all washed and boiled and in the rinsing water; then commenced my school at nine. At noon I spent my leisure time sewing; and after school I did the same after I got my supper out of the way. I often sewed till twelve and one o'clock at night. After all was quiet, I could do a great deal of sewing.

Tuesday morning I had my clothes on the line by daylight, and my breakfast ready.

After breakfast my work was soon done up, and I sewed again till nine o'clock.

At noon I starched all my clothes. After school I ironed as many of them as I could, and at night finished the rest of them. Then I had the rest of the week to sew in; but I could not lay up money very fast.

My friend, Mrs. Beck, was very anxious for me to get started in my law business, for she did not like to see me work so hard; so she proposed to me to raffle a large oil painting I had. It was one my sister gave me to sell should I get out of money. She said: "You will not get half what it is worth if you sell it; but we will get out some tickets, and sell all we can before the raffle comes off."

We got out three hundred, and sold them at $1 per ticket. We sold two hundred and twenty-five.

The $25 I spent in provisions, which was money to me. I put the $200 on interest.

The painting was raffled off, but no one came for the picture, and it naturally fell to me by right.

But the man who raffled it off refused to let it go for six months after that. He said I could have it, but when the time had expired, he said it belonged to him, and he gave it to Mrs. Beck to square some present or debt.

She gave it back to me, for she said it rightfully belonged to me, and I gave her $10, for I did not like to have her lose the whole of her present.

I called on a lawyer about this time.

He told me, after examining my papers, that I had a splendid case on my fifty shares of Kentucky stock, and he would take the case for one-third of what he got. I agreed to this. His name was Williams.

He said: "Call again in three or four days, and I will look over the case, and tell you what the prospects are."

I called in just four days, and he said: "You can't get anything without a great deal of trouble, and I want $500 to begin with."

I was perfectly astonished, and told him I thought he was to take it for one-third of what he got. . . .


After I went home I commenced my school again, and taught till the first of April. Then I moved to A Street to a house with four rooms. Here I fitted up two rooms to rent, and asked $12 apiece for them. I paid $12 for the house. The rent of the two rooms, with my sewing allowed me to drop my washing and school, although I had not done any washing for five months before I moved, for I found that it was breaking me down too much, and I had got over $300 laid by. Besides, I had a sewing-machine that cost me $30. I could get plenty of sewing. The school confined me so much that I did not have a good chance to attend to my brother's affairs.

I very often had a chance to watch nights with the sick for $3 a night, and this was more profitable than washing, or even the school.

I did the washing just ten months, and taught fifteen months.

Another very lucrative source of income was baby-tending, and it was also very pleasant, unless the baby happened to be a cross one—then I earned my money. But as a general thing, they were pretty good.

Nearly all of my lady friends had small children, or babies, and all wanted me to attend theirs, and one would offer more than the other in order to get me to take care of hers. There were several rooming at one house just over the way from my place, and I found it very profitable to go and take care of them all for $3 apiece. I have had as high as $5 a night for taking care of one baby.

These ladies were very fashionable, and attended all, or nearly all, of the parties and balls given.

There is something every night in the week to which one can go, and the ladies of Virginia City are always ready for any amusement, and I think enjoy it more than any class of people among whom I ever lived.

So it was no uncommon thing for a lady to give me $5 for taking care of her baby, in order to be sure that no one else would get me before her. I have been engaged for two and three weeks ahead. I only did this for my friends.

Every lady, before she went away, would set a nice little table for two, with all the luxuries of the season. The table would fairly groan beneath the food, some of which was piled on the table, enough for two of us to eat through the night, with a strong pot of tea to keep me awake.

Another table would be piled full of magazines and periodicals of the day, and one or two evening papers. All I had to do was to undress the children, and put them to bed. If the little ones wanted feeding, I fed them, and perhaps held them awhile.

I always took Charlie with me, as I would not leave him alone, and we sat and read nearly the whole time, till we got hungry, then we would have our little supper. Then Charlie would lie down and sleep till they came home, which was generally four or five o'clock in the morning.

There was more real profit in this than any work I did. Although nursing the sick was profitable, it was hard on the constitution.

While on A Street, I took all the money and invested it in stock. I bought Chollar stock for $52 a share, and drew $3 a month dividend for three months; then $2 for three months more; then $1 for two months, until at last the dividends stopped, and the stock dropped to $20.

My friends advised me to sell, for fear it would go lower, and I would lose it all; but it was paid for, and I could afford to keep it, and did.

This was in the fall. In January stocks took a big rise, and Chollar went to $89. I sold. She went on up to $99, and I bought it back, losing $10, as my friends said. But two days later she went up to $320. I then sold it again.

I had now made a handsome profit of $231 per share. I had also bought some Sierra Nevada for $24 the same week, and sold it for $44 in three days' time.

I now had a snug little sum, and I determined to stop paying big rents by buying a place of my own, for in the three years that I had been on the coast I had paid out just $400 in rents.

I now went in search of a place to buy. I wanted one in a good business location, and fortune again favored me. I found a nice little place on C Street, which is the principal street of the city.

I got it quite cheap, for property was down, and the lady that owned it was very anxious to get away from Virginia City, she having had some great sorrow there. She asked $500 for the place, and it was a big bargain. Although property was very low, I bought it, paid her the money, and moved the next day.

Now, what I earned I could live on or lay up, the house-rent being stopped. My house had but three rooms and a wood-shed. I lived in it two years, when Mr. French, my brother's friend, offered to put up a lodging-house, with a store underneath, and give me time to pay for it by way of my rents.

The house, he first thought, would not cost over $1,000, but after his partner figured on it, he said it would cost more, but not over $1,500, as the work upon it was to be done by the day.

I gave them the job. A contract was drawn up, and they went to work. The house, they said, would not take them over a month to finish.

Instead of its being finished in a month, as they agreed to, they were three months building it, and it was not yet done.

I got them to give up the contract, and finished it myself.

But they had finished off the store and all the upper part of the house, save the lining and papering, which I did myself.

As fast as I got a room papered, I furnished and rented it, until the whole house was full.

Then I went down stairs, and did the same to the private part of the house, and got it ready to move into myself, for I was then living in my small house, which was moved on the back part of my lot at the time they first commenced working on the place to grade out for the house.

I was lying very sick with inflammation of the lungs. I was quite low for several days, and was so nearly gone one day that they called in the neighbors to see me die. I was choking, gasping for breath. One ran against the other, not knowing what to do. I could not speak. But Charlie saw me looking towards the table. He looked to see what it was I wanted. A bottle of camphor and hartshorn liniment stood there. His senses came to him at once, and he caught it up and emptied a third of its contents on my lungs, took his hand and rubbed it into my lungs, till I breathed as natural as ever.

I relate this little incident to let people who are attacked with this complaint know what to do. I had been using it all the time; but when I was taken so bad I had been asleep, and the girl went through the room, and left both doors open, and this left me in a draught, and I awoke up so bad I could not speak; but for my boy's quickness in reading my thoughts, I must have died. But I soon got better, and sat up.

They now told me they were ready to move the house; if I would go into one of the neighbors, they would move it.

In about three hours I did so, and in fifteen minutes a man came and told me they had commenced moving it, and found they could not, and they were setting the things on the sidewalk, or any place they could find to set them, and that the Piutes and Chinamen were packing them off.

My boy was off to school, and there was no other way but for me to go to work and take the things up to the top of Silver Street to B Street, and pack them in the house of a friend; and they were three days putting up the house again.

As soon as they got it up, I had to go and line and paper it before I could move into it. This took me two days more; and when I got settled, I found that many of my things had been carried off.

I lived here while they were building the new house, then I moved in, and rented the little one for $25 a month.

I rented the stores for good prices, and my house was full at good rents.

I had agreed to pay $125 a month on the house. When they gave up the house, the bill was over $3,000 and the bulkhead was not built, nor the sewer dug. I also had to pay for all the water pipes being put in, and for the pipes on the outside of the house, which cost me an enormous sum. There was no brick chimney in it.

This was a way they had of building on the Comstock—a way I did not like. And after the big fire, I had two nice brick chimneys built from the ground to the top of the house, after my pipes had cost about $75, for I was constantly having them repaired. They never put them up substantially, and every wind blew them down.

I have two receipts in my possession now to show that I paid $25 at one time and $15 at another—both storms occurring in the same month—making $40 a month for pipes. I thought this a pretty heavy tax just for chimneys, when a brick one would only cost $60.

I had $125 to make out every month, besides these extra bills to pay. My paper and lining came to nearly $360, and then I had all the paint for the inside of the house to pay for. I hired a man to do some of the painting, and some of it my son did.

The most—or at least half—of my furniture I paid for in making ticks at "four bits" and "two bits" apiece. The top mattresses were "four bits," while the straw ticks were but "two bits."

Perhaps the reader would like to know how I managed to do it, for I had twenty-six beds to make up, and rooms to take care of, and all the washing and ironing to do. Well, I can tell you, it was pretty hard. I got up early. While many of my neighbors were sleeping, I was doing up the work of those roomers who had gone to work on the six o'clock shift. If it was Monday, I would pick up all of the dirty clothes together, then I would come down and get my breakfast, do up the dishes, and then sit down and make four or five ticks before dinner-time. After dinner I did up the rest of my work up stairs; then, as some of my roomers used to say I would sit down and make half a dozen more ticks, just to rest myself, and after supper would make another half-dozen ticks, sheets, or pillow-slips, just as it happened.

I took one day to washing and ironing. And this was no small job, I assure you, for most of the roomers had to have both sheets taken off the bed every week, and three towels each week to every person.

There were repairs constantly to be made, but I managed to keep up with the whole of it by working nearly every night till twelve and one o'clock.

*Her detailed descriptions of the way in which her days were spent show how many different activities she crowded into them. Despite several setbacks, she managed to improve her situation gradually and to recover some of her brother's property. She was keenly aware of the opportunities for making money which existed in Nevada at that time, and invested in stocks as well as in real estate. In 1877, when she went back East, her income was $200*

*a month, which her agent sent her. But suddenly the shares
dropped, companies stopped paying dividends and her tenants
left. So she went back to Virginia City and endeavored to restore
her finances. She had suffered heavy losses but still owned a mill-
site and a house, which she decided to sell. She then returned back
East to see her mother die. Shortly afterwards, bad news came
again from Nevada:*

A friend wrote to me, saying my broker was about to leave
town, and I had better look immediately after my stock. I sent for
money, but did not get as much as I expected.

This decided me to send Charlie out, but I sent him too late to
save my stock—at least my bonanza stock—for I still own quite a
quantity of other stock, which may in time turn out to be
bonanzas.

I shall long remember the years of '77-'78. The greatest trials
and troubles I have ever been called to endure were in these two
years. May I never have another such a season to endure. After all
we had suffered in Nevada of sickness, toil, privations, and
hardships; being many times swindled and robbed; meeting with
heavy losses in stocks and bad debts; and the long separation from
my friends—all were very hard on us.

When we left Virginia City I thought our trials were over, for I
now had enough for myself and family to live on without ever
lifting our hands to work again. But it seems our cup of sorrow was
not yet filled; for alas! our greatest trials and troubles were yet to
come after we reached home.

But, reader, after all I have suffered in the land of sage, I
would much rather live there than in the East, for several reasons.
First of all, my health was much better there than here; second, if I
dealt with a person, I knew what to expect. I like a person better
who will show his hand than a sneaking hypocrite with whom I do
not know how to deal. Third, if I transact my own business, I can
make more money in three months than I can in the East in a year;
and I never saw the time while there that I could not borrow from
$1,000 to $2,000 on one day's notice; and the parties lending it
would never think of asking me about my indebtedness, or how
much property I owned, if it was a small sum of $200 or $300, or

less. My word was always quite sufficient for them. But I find it a common practice in the East for persons to inquire into your private affairs if you only wish to borrow $5 of them.

As I have said before, there are no misers or penny-mites in Nevada. Even the bonanza men, who are the hardest crowd to get money out of on a small scale, are sometimes princely in their donations for charitable purposes.

And if we live out our money fast, we make it fast.

Now, kind reader, if I have given the Western people a worse name than they deserve, I have done it unintentionally. If I have given any too much credit (which I doubt), it is because my love for them has blinded me to their faults.

If I have seemingly spoken too highly in praise of my son, the reader will pardon a mother's pride in an only child; and though I may never meet again any of my kind Pacific friends, let them ever bear in mind that though absent they are not forgotten; that the garden of my heart has ever been kept green by the blossoms of their love, the memory of each and all their many acts of kindness bestowed on me, a stranger, while sojourning in their land of sage and silver.

And now, in return, may God's choicest blessings rest upon them and theirs forever more.

Kind reader, with many thanks for your patient indulgence in any short-comings in this narrative, we will also bid you a kind good-bye.


*Her narrative bears witness to the ability of a strong-willed woman to weather many storms alone. It shows something of the situation of women who tried to support themselves and to improve their conditions. From her experience, she concluded that conditions were more favorable for women who were interested in business in the West than in the East, a statement which can be found in other narratives by women. She has devoted many pages to descriptions of the atmosphere in Virginia City and of the manners and customs of the inhabitants. She was fascinated by the fast pace of life, the great variety in the entertainments offered, and the intensity people brought to their quest for pleasures. Her account of the emergence of a class of*

[191]

*wealthy people and her depiction of women of leisure are humorous and sometimes sarcastic; here is an example of what she had to say:*

> *The ladies dress so rich and gaudy, and use so much paint and powder, that they are really not themselves when dressed for church or ball, or for the street, but only painted dolls, dressed in silks and satins, decorated with expensive jewelry, and, as Brother Mc Grath used to say, wearing a whole flower garden on the top of their heads.*[1]

*She had many interests, a forceful personality, and strong opinions. Her report is sometimes biased, as in the chapters on the Chinese population, but it is always vigorous and often incisive.*

1. Mary Mathews, pp. 131-132.

# A Child Went Forth: the Autobiography of Dr. Helen MacKnight

Helen Doyle

(New York: Gotham House) 1934.


Helen Doyle was born in Petrolia, a small Pennsylvania town, so far removed from the mainstream of life that the news of the gold discoveries only reached it in 1878. Her father, who was dissatisfied with the living he was making, was immediately tempted and left the rest of the family behind. In the early part of the narrative, pathetic vignettes appear from time to time, showing his wife's sadness and near despair. As the author was still a child at that time, she only had fleeting glimpses of her mother's unhappiness and concentrated on the pleasant aspects of life. She has left an enchanting record of her childhood days at her grandmother's in a pastoral setting, with poetic evocations of the seasons and warm home scenes. After her grandmother's death, there was a difficult time when her mother scraped a bare living working in a factory; her health deteriorated and she died in 1882 from an overdose of laudanum, it was suspected. The child went to live with one of her aunts who gave her a very hard time. She ran away and found shelter at another aunt's, who was kind to her. Her father arranged for her to come to California in 1887.

Her account of her adolescence there contains vivid descriptions of the natural beauties and picturesque portraits of the people she saw and met. The tone, on the whole, is rather sad: her father was very possessive and prevented her from joining other young people in their amusements; yet, he never became really close to her, so that she was often lonely. There is an undercurrent of rebellion at the authority her father wielded over the rest of the *family (he married a second time and made his new wife almost as unhappy as the first). The portrait Helen Doyle drew of him is very critical and stresses his self-centeredness and the suffering it caused around him. She became engrossed in her studies and moved to San Francisco in the early 1890s. The chapters devoted to her years there as a medical student provide interesting insights into the ways in which men tried to discourage women from entering the professions: there were endless vexations caused by the male students and the professors; the opposition to women took various forms, from ribald jokes to straightforward expressions of misogyny. The evocation of the atmosphere of the 1890s adds much charm to the narrative. The emergence of a new type of woman, who dressed differently and participated in many new activities, is described, and sketches of the lives of such prominent women as Lucy Wanzer, Phoebe Hearst and Jane Stanford are added to the narrative. The constant questioning of traditional ideas about women's place in society and their abilities is one of its most interesting features. After receiving her medical degree (she completed her studies before she was 21), Helen Doyle entered a children's hospital and had her first practical experience there. She soon had to leave San Francisco, however, for her stepmother had become ill and wanted her back:*

COUNTRY PRACTICE
I DEFY MY
FATHER

That night I took the ferry. We glided out of the slip. I looked back on the inspiring tower of the new ferry building that had replaced the old brown sheds. My eyes traveled on to the hills of San Francisco. The lines of Bret Harte came back to me:

*Serene, indifferent of Fate,*
*Thou sittest at the Western Gate:*

*Upon thy heights so lately won*

*Still slant the banners of the sun.*

*Thou drawest all things, small or great,*
*To thee beside the Western Gate.*[1]

Again the familiar trip: to Reno, then south on the Virginia and
Truckee to Mound House, on the Carson and Colorado to
Sodaville, and after a night at the Sodaville Hotel and Bar on over
the desert. My heart was heavy. I dreaded to go home. There is no
one to whom my heart goes out in such quick sympathy as to a
child who dreads to go home. I know what a tragic thing it is.

But I soon forgot everything else in my first hand-to-hand,
unaided conflict with death. There were two physicians in the
town. One was an old army doctor, who refused to consult with
me. The other was a man who treated my degree as a rare joke. He
said I might be a good nurse.

My stepmother needed nursing and tenderness more than she
did prescriptions. She had been over-drugged. There were hours
of terrible uncertainty, when it seemed she would slip away from
me, but gradually she gained strength. She recovered.

My father was immensely gratified, not by the fact that his
wife had been spared to him, but by my ability to cure her. He
went about the town, telling everyone whom he saw: "My wife is
getting well. The doctors gave her up, but Nellie came home and
cured her!"

I knew it was useless to ask him to send me back to San
Francisco. My place in the hospital was filled. I fitted up an office
in the front room of the house and put out my shingle—Helen M.
MacKnight, M.D., Physician and Surgeon. My father was proud of
the M.D., but resented the Helen. I had been christened Nellie.
That was my name. But I remembered the words of the Dean, and
the sign was not changed. I put in a small stock of drugs (it would
be necessary to fill my own prescriptions), bought a medicine
case, and started in.

My conveyance was a two-wheeled cart with a jump seat. I
harnessed and unharnessed the horse myself. I would stand at the
back of the cart with the reins in my hand, raise the seat, clamber in
and start off. I used to smile sometimes, wondering what those
professors with their carriages and coachmen would think if they
could see me.

There was little road work done in those days, and the cart would grind through the sand and strike sparks from the boulder-like rocks that were strewn along the way. Then there were the barbed-wire gates in the fences to be reckoned with. One pulls and tugs with might and main to slip the loop of wire over the top and so release the gate. Then when it seems impossible to get it over the last inch, it suddenly lets go, the post springs out of the lower loop and attacks you, winding the strands of barbed wire around you with all the ferocity of inanimate things. Escaping with minor cuts and scratches, you lead your horse through, and then with grim determination you pull and tug at the gate, apparently shrunken several inches in the encounter, to get the post back into the bottom loop and somehow manage to lasso the wire over the top. If your horse stands quietly through this performance, well and good, if not you are plainly out of luck. Fortunately mine was "gate broken."

Patients came to me, mostly chronic cases at first, who had failed to get relief elsewhere and were curious to see what the new woman doctor might do for them. Every man, woman, and child in such an isolated place has a personal interest in the health of the community. If a woman is "expecting," every good wife knows just when, can tell how long her "morning sickness" lasted, and will venture an opinion on the sex of the child by the way the mother is "carrying it." When a woman is known to be in labor a kind of tenseness settles over the whole community until word is passed about that it is all over. Then the length of labor, the sex and weight of the child, whether "they" wanted a boy or a girl, and other important factors connected with the case are reviewed in detail.

Doctors are supposed to be able to bury their mistakes, but if they do not wish to have post-mortem discussions of why and how it happened they had best keep to the cities. A young doctor, fresh from medical college, can pass many embarrassing moments in the presence of the neighborhood midwife. Country people have been through the stress of illness, without trained medical assistance so often that they have an astonishing knowledge of human ills gained in the school of experience.

Their kindness is inexhaustible. They will drop everything to go to the bedside of some neighbor, cook the meals, take care of

the children, do the laundry, so that the sufferer may be kept fresh
and clean. Even when it comes to surgery, they are not the ones to
stand helplessly by. I remember a case that happened at Benton,
near the Wild Rose Mine. Two Indians, in a drunken brawl, carved
each other with knives, with the result that one of them was ripped
open by a cross-shaped incision in the abdominal region. An
observer assured me that "the entralls" protruded from the wound
and were covered with the sand and dirt into which the Indian had
fallen.

An epileptic, glass-eyed, itinerant doctor of my acquaintance
was in Benton at the time and was summoned to the scene. He
shrugged his shoulders and said there was nothing to do about it.
The Indian would die. But the Indian, Johnny Lynch, was a good
Indian when he wasn't drunk, and the citizens of the town did not
want him to die if it was in their power to help him.

So they brought Kelty Jim, bar-tender, from the town's main
saloon. Now Kelty Jim had been a sailor and the knots he learned
to tie and the sails he had mended stood him in good stead when it
came to a bit of surgery. A small stream of clean water, from a hot
mineral spring, ran by the spot where the Indian lay. Kelty Jim
sponged off the sand and dirt with the hot water, replaced the
viscera, sewed up the wound with sail stitches and sailor's knots,
and Johnny Lynch got well.

You can't put up much of a bluff in a country like that and get
away with it.

My father no longer went on surveying trips. It was apparent
that he was ready to retire and draw the interest on the investment
he had made in me. He stayed at home and watched every move I
made with a consuming jealousy. If a man patient came to the
office, he watched to see how long he stayed. If it was a longer
time than he thought necessary, he would question me about it. He
even forced me to ask some of those patients to discontinue their
visits. I worked under a terrific handicap. I was beating my hands
against the wall—the wall of separation that would not allow me to
give myself up to his utter possession.

What trifles may change the course of human destiny! A man
came from Silver Peak, Nevada, to consult me about growing
deafness. He could no longer hear his watch tick. It was a simple
case. The canals of his ears were filled with hardened wax. I put an

emollient in over night to soften the wax. The next morning I syringed out his ears, and lo! he could hear his watch tick. It seemed a miracle to him. He went home, spreading the news of the woman doctor.

Soon a message came summoning me to Silver Peak, a mining camp one hundred and fifty miles away. I took the train to Sodaville and there changed to a spur that ran to the one-mill mining town of Candelaria. A man, who had evidently been warming up for the occasion at a near-by saloon, met me. We went over to a team and buckboard that were waiting to take us across the desert. He told me to throw my bag in the back and climb in. When I saw how the horses were tied, each one to a separate post by a stout halter, I realized we were going to have a wild ride, and thought it safest to hold my medicine case in my lap.

The driver took his seat, another man undid the halters, and we were off. That team ran like scared rabbits for the first ten miles. Sometimes we were in the road, sometimes just hitting the high spots through the sagebrush. But I managed to hold my seat and my bag and we arrived at our destination at dawn.

A desert mining camp, in the clear light of early morning, is not an attractive scene. There are no trees to shelter the nakedness of high sham fronts and shed backs. There is only the whir of machinery to detract from the gaunt ugliness of the stamp mill. There are no signs of life about the doors and windows to draw the eyes from the empty tin cans, that unfailing flora of mining camps. Even the burros drop their ears and look utterly disconsolate.

My patient was the superintendent of the mine. We found him in a bare, board cabin, spotlessly clean. He lay unconscious, a giant of a man, gaunt and unshaven. His head tossed restlessly from side to side on the pillow, while with his big hands he picked aimlessly at the bed covering. On the floor by his bed crouched his Indian wife, like a faithful dog waiting for some sign from its master.

During the drive across the desert I had learned that the patient to whom I had been summoned really belonged to my medical friend who gave me the credit of being a "good nurse." Medical ethics are difficult to live up to on the desert. When people get dissatisfied with one doctor, they send for another, and by the time number two arrives, the emergency does not permit the usual courtesies.

Well, he had said I was a good nurse, and since it was evident that this was a case of typhoid, sadly in need of less medication and more nursing, I forgot ethics and took charge of the case.

I saw that the other doctor had not been at fault. The powders he had left had been emptied on the swollen, parched tongue of the patient at the directed intervals, and a fruitless effort had been made to administer water to wash them down, but they remained to form a thick, glazed deposit, broken like a checkerboard by bleeding cracks. Sordes had settled on the teeth, which the swollen lips failed to cover. The man's beard and hair were matted. Not a pretty picture, but a typical one of the ravages of typhoid in the high altitudes and under the nursing conditions in those inaccessible places.

The Indian wife of this "squaw man" was not to blame. She had done everything she could do. The bed clothes were clean, the cabin was immaculate, but when her man was no longer able to direct her, she sat down to watch him die, according to the "white man's way." In the tribe it would have been managed differently. If any one died in the camp, it became necessary to burn the village and migrate to fresh surroundings. This being a troublesome proceeding, it was much easier to remove the one about to depart for the happy hunting grounds, before he made his exit.

I have driven to a camp to visit a sick Indian, only to find that he was "heap gone." No other information was forthcoming, and it was only by chance that, some distance from the camp, I spied a rude sapling shelter by a tiny stream. Investigating, I found that my patient had been placed there to die. The shelter extended out, like a bridge, across the stream. His equipment for the journey he was about to take consisted of a rabbit's skin blanket, a half sack of pine nuts, and a cup with which, until too weak to move, he could dip water from the stream.

But under my direction this brown-skinned mahala worked untiringly, with a dog-like devotion to her man. No task was too unpleasant, and there were many such, for her to undertake willingly. With the help of the men in camp, we contrived a rude canvas bath-tub, into which the patient could be lowered to reduce the temperature. We took turns sitting by the bed, constantly giving water, a teaspoonful at a time. There was no milk but condensed milk to be had in camp. I learned of a ranch in

Deep Springs Valley, miles across the mountains, where fresh milk could be obtained. The services of a man on the regular pay-roll were placed at my disposal, and every afternoon he rode horse-back to the ranch, so that he could make the return trip at night, when it was cool. I sterilized the milk, and it was kept in an Arizona cooler, a very efficient ice-box, made of mosquito netting, stretched over a board frame and covered with gunny-sacking, kept constantly wet from a coal-oil can with a hole punched in the side. Sun and evaporation did the rest.

That man was busy as a bird dog. I am sure that he found it a real vacation to go back to work with pick and shovel. Between riding for the milk, hauling the water for baths in barrels for miles over the desert, keeping the coal-oil can filled, splitting wood to keep a fire going in the cook stove in the shed lean-to, to boil water for sterilization of laundry, and disposing of excrement so that it would not become a menace to the camp, he had his hands full. But food and water and nursing won the fight, and in a week's time my patient was far on the road to recovery, and the routine was so well established that I felt it was safe to leave him.

I had spent a week and would have traveled three hundred miles when I reached home. My bill was one hundred dollars! It seemed enormous to me. I was surprised when it was promptly paid in five shining twenty-dollar gold pieces.

All the way home I thought of Grandmother, and hoped that in her abode up there by the beautiful river she knew that I had saved my first typhoid patient. I was elated. I looked forward to getting home, telling my father all about it, and giving him the hundred dollars, my first substantial fee.

My father met me at the station. He was white and trembling with rage. A letter had arrived from Paul during my absence. He had opened and read it. The letter began: "My dear Girl." It was an innocent, friendly letter, but my father read all sorts of jealous imaginings between the lines. He was in an uncontrollable rage. He demanded that I sit down and, in his presence and under his supervision, write to Paul and tell him I never wanted to hear from him or see him again!

Although I prized Paul's friendship, it was not the thought of losing it so much as the injustice of the demand that aroused me. I defied my father. I said I would not endure having my letters opened and read, and my relations to others questioned. I flatly refused to do as he demanded. His rage was a terrible thing to see. I wondered if he would kill me. My stepmother was terror-stricken. She pleaded with him. He got his hat and started for town. Beside himself with passion, he told me that I could leave home, or have the letter ready to send when he returned.

For the first time in my life I realized that I could never reach over the wall that had grown between us. I saw my father for what he was—a cruel, selfish man, who deserted his family and sent for me to come to him only when I was old enough to give him a possessive pleasure. His pride in me was only pride in himself through me.

I never could have left the Papa of Mama's memory. I did leave my father's house. When he returned I was gone. My stepmother afterwards told me that he raged like a mad man all through the night.

### THE WILD ROSE MINE
### FREEDOM A HORSE &
### BUGGY COURTSHIP

I rented a front room on the main street of the town and opened an office. When my father found that my decision was final, he offered to sell me the stock of drugs and my medical books. The shining twenty dollar gold pieces were invested that way.

I bought an old counter from a store and had shelves built behind it. In the room there was an air-tight heating stove, a cot where I slept, and a rough table, which I had made for the examination and treatment of patients. It was not a luxurious place, but it was a peaceful refuge where no jealous, suspicious eyes followed me as I came and went. Grace and her husband lived near-by.

Mary Austin was teaching at the old Academy. She had recently written that exquisitely beautiful book in which she christened the valley, "The Land of Little Rain." She would come in the evening and sit with me and recount fragments of stories that afterwards took shape in "The Basket Woman" and "The Flock."

Strange things happened in that office, difficult to picture now when the telephone is at hand to summon the doctor, and, in an emergency, he arrives in his automobile or perhaps in his aeroplane almost before the receiver is back on the hook. I recall one day when a housewife in a kitchen dress, with hair loosening from the hair pins that held it and falling down her back, came running the length of Main Street to my office with her child in convulsions in her arms. By the time I had procured a wash tub of hot water from my landlady (bath tubs were an unknown luxury) and soused the youngster in it, the office held a good part of the population of the town. They were all as relieved as the mother was when the child was restored to her arms, limp and relaxed, but quite himself again.

For a while I hired a "rig" from the livery stable to answer calls in the country. But an accommodating youngster decided to be born about that time, and through officiating at the ceremony I acquired a fine bay horse as recompense for my services. The hardware store "trusted" me for a new, single top-buggy.

About this time my father deserted my stepmother and went away to the mining camps of the South. He drifted in the region of Randsburg and the Yellow Aster Mine for years. When he was no longer able to provide for himself, I helped to make his last days comfortable, as I knew Mama would have wanted me to do. My stepmother was left penniless. I found that she dreamed of having a little shop where she could sell fancy goods and baked beans and brown bread of her own making. I helped her to realize that dream, and she lived, busily happy, for many years.

I faced the future with new responsibilities, willingly assuming the notes that my father had signed to raise the money to send me to college, and debts that he had contracted with the promise that he would pay when I graduated and began to practice medicine.

My practice flourished. Even twins happened along to enhance my reputation. I was engaged to confine a woman whom the Army doctor had warned not to have any more children, or she would probably die in the attempt. She had given birth to three girls and the desire, shared by herself and her husband, for a boy had inspired her with the courage to defy the ultimatum.

She studied *Tautology*, a book widely read by expectant

mothers at that time, and followed its precepts closely. I have never been sure how much of the credit for the successful outcome of that case should be given to *Tautology* and how much to the instruction in prenatal care that I had received in Toland Hall and the Children's Hospital. At any rate, Aesculapius could not have sent me a greater boon than that patient.

I was called. The woman passed through a normal, uneventful labor, and was delivered of—another girl. I had hoped, as ardently as the parents, for a boy, and sympathized with their disappointment. But on examination, I found that the rotundity that disappears so miraculously when the child is born still persisted. I smiled, remembering the interne who had retired too soon. Without doubt there was another baby, and it might be a boy!

I remember going out to the father, sitting by the kitchen stove, holding his new little girl in his arms. "Don't be too disappointed," I said, "we might have a boy yet!" He looked up at me, entirely puzzled.

"What do you mean?"

"There is another baby, and it might be a boy."

I am sure that the father doubted that I knew what I was talking about. He may have experienced a pang of regret that he had placed his wife in the care of a person with such astonishing lack of the knowledge of the processes of nature. But the twin was born, and it was a boy. I needed no press agents. My patient who had been threatened with such dire misfortune if she ever tried to bring another child into the world had borne twins with no difficulty whatever! Everybody in the valley knew about it.

Although my sign read "Helen M MacKnight, M.D." in big gilt letters, Dr. McLean had graduated a Dr. Nellie, in spite of his efforts to the contrary, for I was Dr. Nellie to the whole countryside.

*The last chapters briefly relate the main events in the author's mature life: her marriage to a doctor, their establishment in the small town of Bishop, the growth of their family and their rise to prosperity, which was closely linked to that of the valley where they lived.*

*It is hard to do justice to the wealth of Helen Doyle's narrative. It touches upon many important problems, raises questions concerning the status of women and the way families were organized, and provides information on the emergence of women in the professions. She was not only a talented woman, but also a gifted writer who could command a wide range of literary expressions: the tone is in turns lyrical, pathetic, reflective, humorous, which makes her book both thought-provoking and enjoyable.*

1. Chatto and Windus, 1889.

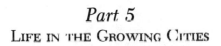

*Part* 5
LIFE IN THE GROWING CITIES

# An Account of My Life's Journey so far: its Prosperity, its Adversity, its Sunshine and its Clouds

Mrs. Nina Churchman Larowe

(Portland: Kilham Stationery and Printing Company) 1917?

*Mrs. Larowe's book is made up by a series of letters which were first printed in the* Oregonian. *They are autobiographical and extend from her childhood in the West to her establishment in Portland in her mature years. It is very hard to reconstruct her life as no dates are provided. Each of the chapters is divided into many sections which offer discussions of widely different topics. Despite the loose arrangement, it is possible to form a general idea about the way in which her life developed, and about her principles and aims. She came from a prominent family (her father was a lawyer) that had its residence in Nevada City, California in the early 1850s. The following excerpt includes both childhood memories and reflections on the times made from the perspective of mature age. It provides glimpses into the life of a well-off family and details on the status of women at that time:*

We had the panorama which was evidently the forerunner of the moving picture. The painted canvas used to unroll and pass over the stage while a man pointed with a long wand and explained meanwhile. Economy prompted the selection of the applicants and they were usually "murderers of the king's English" and ignorant of history. The explainer learned his description by rote. Sometimes the canvas traveled too fast or he was too slow of utterance, and while describing Paris perhaps would find himself with Dublin or some other city in front of him. Consequently he would become confused and would have to stop short and plunge into the description of the city which encroached on the time of the one he had been describing. They used to tell a tale of a Biblical panorama where the interpreter in the scene of Daniel in the lions' den used to say:

"You will distinguish Daniel from the lions by the green cotton umbrella which he carries under his arm." Well, anyhow, we children thought the pictures grand and were entirely satisfied.

We had high post bedsteads with a canopy and curtains to shut out the air. Now we go to the other extreme and have sleeping porches that we may take in all the pure air possible. If children or grown people were at all delicate they were warned against the night air. No windows were allowed to admit it and sometimes rooms were heated all night. The high bedsteads had a miniature ladder of three steps to enable one to get into them. The mattresses were supported by lacings of rope, which were drawn through holes in the woodwork of the bedstead, and every now and then had to be tightened up to prevent sagging. Afterward wooden slats took the place of ropes. The bedsteads were very high to admit beneath the trundle bed, low and on wheels.

The bedsteads had a curtain or valance all around. The trundle bed was pushed under by day and drawn out by night. In it small children slept under the watchful eye of mothers.

In the theatre what we now call the orchestra was the pit, where only men and boys sat. The choice seats were in the first balcony or family circle. Sometimes ladies sat in the circle around the orchestra chairs which is now termed the parquet circle. A curious custom of the time was the throwing of money to stage favorites. At the end of the act would come a tremendous hand-clapping, up would go the curtains and then from all parts of the house would come a shower of silver quarters, half dollars and dollars, which would keep the favorite picking up coin for many minutes. This custom obtained for some years until money was more scarce.

Ladies' shoes had no heels, were made of cloth and were laced on the sides. They were made in drabt, black, blue, green and other colors. The ridiculously high heels of today are an injury to the foot and induce a very ungraceful walk and carriage. The heelless ones, however, made a flat-foot appearance.

The transition of a girl from short skirts to long dresses, though ardently wished for, was a somewhat painful and embarrassing change. Women's dresses trailed on the ground or floor at all times, and when a girl put on a long dress she was an object of universal comment.

"I suppose you think yourself a young lady now," sneered the envious and still unpromoted ones of her own age. If she went on the street or to a party, to church or most anywhere, the older ones had their fun at her expense, and not until her friends had all become used to the situation could her equanimity be restored, her trial be over, and her young ladyhood an assured fact.

No women then were expected to earn their living. People would support their relatives whether or no. The day of general independence had not dawned. Another's bread must be eaten many times in bitter humility. Women did not work in stores, telephones did not exist, women teachers were uncommon, as men largely occupied that field. So it was stay at home, cultivate a delicate look, faint on occasion, until some man was captivated and led the poor relation from the state of dependency to the queenship of a home.

With the customary fine dress for court and office, dress coats and gilt buttons were the fashion among the genteel for day wear as well as evening. In addition went a nice set of good manners. Lawyers of high quality thought the place for their feet was on the floor and they kept them there. They were not elevated to the top of desks or window sills. Father had a student whose feet decorated the office furniture most of the time. Father finally told him that a man whose feet had to be more prominent than his head would not be fitted for the higher walks and fine courtesy of the legal profession of that period.

In every house was a set of candelabra or candlesticks with glass pendants which, like the earrings of the time, had an upper part which hooked onto the candelabra and a long pointed pendant attached by a hook. This pendant could be removed at will. I do not know anything which gave the children of the time more joy. They were forever sneaking into the parlors and taking them off. When the light struck them they reflected all colors of the rainbow. The voices of the mothers were heard in all the land commanding the return of the glittering ornaments.

Chinamen and chickens were greatly respected and treated with great deference in those days. Chinamen were scarce and were objects of great curiosity. They learned our ways quickly, displayed great ingenuity and were able soon to do almost anything that a white man could. They minded their own business, as usual, and were welcomed to the Pacific Coast. We had the first Chinese cook in the town. I do not know who taught him, but he was exceedingly efficient in American cooking. He had learned how to make the things that belonged to the confectioner's art and I used to stand at his elbow and watch him make all varieties of cakes, pies, jellies, etc.

By this time we had got past the dried peach and apple days. The markets were supplying more. Things were costly, of course, but what difference did it make as long as money was so plentiful? Mother at this time was crippled with an attack of inflammatory rheumatism, which arrived suddenly, and, after excruciating agony for six months, departed as suddenly, saying good-bye to her permanently. In all her life afterward there never came another attack. In consequence of mother's sickness, John (we called all Chinese John) took entire charge of our kitchen and dining-room. Father would say:

"John, I shall have dinner company today," would tell him how many guests and leave the rest, marketing and all, to him. John loved company and delighted in showing his skill. His dinners were always a success, so that he was the talk of the town. There were no hoodlums to annoy and persecute the few Chinamen of that day.

Chickens were allowed unusual privileges and carefully watched and cherished, my lady hen being worth $5 at least, and her eggs that much a dozen. There were not many of her family in the whole state. We had a few chickens in our back yard and I soon had them all so tame I could pick one of them up at any time. There was a young pullet that was determined to live in the house and would not take no for an answer, so, being my pet, accommodations were provided for her. She had her own special roost and there she sat till dawn and then came to the foot of my bed and chirped and fluttered her wings until she woke me. She lived to be a full grown hen, but whatever was her end I do not know. She may have been the motive of a stew. I am sure my father was never her executioner. He was a great lover of animals and could never have been persuaded to wring her neck or chop her head off. Probably when we moved she passed into other hands or had lived her life out.

Did you know that many years ago if you drank your tea or coffee from your cup you would be guilty of a breach of etiquette? It was the proper thing to pour coffee into your saucer and sip it from that. Every set of dishes had tiny plates to set the cup in when using the saucer. Thus custom doth tyrannize over us all.

My first long dress was worn to church, and afterward to Sunday school. My self-consciousness and embarrassment were so uppermost as to make me a miserable creature indeed.

Finally we sold the old home in Nevada City and disposed of things in San Francisco. I went the rounds of my pets, watering each and every head with my tears. I had a parrot, a great talker, and a cat which was her firm and staunch friend. They ate together, the parrot perched on the back of a wooden chair, and the cat on the seat. The parrot would come down and get a morsel and then go up and eat it and, turning its head on one side, watch the cat catch the stray crumbs. Harmony flourished between them ever. My father loved animals, and between us the house was pretty well filled. Mother would occasionally rebel and clear out the livestock.

We had to go to Sacramento by stage, which was a long ride. We started on a cold, dreary Autumn morning. (Stages and steamers and cars have a disagreeable habit of starting and making arrivals before daylight.) The roads in this case were always very muddy and the horses would frequently mire and then all the men passengers were ordered out to help. The ladies were privileged and sat up in as much state as possible whenever the jerks and bumps allowed them to preserve their dignity of poise. It had been the custom to go through all the way by stage to Sacramento, but a small piece of the proposed railroad had been finished from Folsom to Sacramento River, so we changed from stage and took the cars. Grown people, before coming to California, had known something of railroads, but I had never been on one. Well, here was a new experience to me—steam cars and trestles, high and long, to go over. My! my! In my innermost heart I was full of fear and grasped the arms of the seat in terror, as do people the dental chair when a rebellious tooth has to come out. We tired travelers from Nevada and all the upper California country welcomed with delight the change from the stage to the deck of the fine steamboats then on the river. We came on board, soiled, travel-stained, apparent tramps (remember we traveled all night on stages), procured a stateroom and emerged ladies and gentlemen in appearance.

The only way to go East was to take steamer from San Francisco. Travelers were still coming across the plains, but you may be sure they did not go back that way. There were some faint whispers of building a railroad clear across the continent, but people laughed and shook their heads at such visionary men as proposed so wild a scheme.

We went to the best hotel, the American Exchange; that and the Oriental were the hotels par excellence. The day of the Russ First, the Grand Second and the Palace had not arrived, and previous to that was the old Rasette House, which was five stories (wonderful height then and was considered dangerous on account of earthquakes. It was built of brick and the others of frame. This hotel stood remote, was in the midst of a large sand lot, which is now in the business heart of the city.

Oh, the wonderful changes in San Francisco! When we lived there we were located on Minna street in a suburb called Happy Valley. There was another suburb called Pleasant Valley, which was separated from us by sand hills. We used to climb to the top and look on the rival valley. These two little valleys were where the United States mint now stands on Fifth street not far from Market. The houses on the residence streets then were brought around the Horn, that is, the frames made ready to set up as soon as they arrived. I suppose that was done on account of the scarcity of sawmills and cut timber.

[212]

*Mrs. Larowe's father was an old friend of President Lincoln's and was appointed Consul to Valparaiso during his tenure. Mrs. Larowe has recorded her reminiscences of the trip and observations on life in the cities in South America in the early 1860s. Her narrative then reverts to customs and mores in California:*

The duel was then in vogue, especially among the Southern "Chivs" of that day. The non-acceptance of a challenge ranked a man as an arrant coward. By means of this unfortunate and heathenish way of settling differences California lost David Broderick, one of her noblest citizens. Mr. Broderick was not a particularly good shot, and his challenger was. Mr. Broderick's friends tried to prevent his acceptance of the challenge, but all in vain, and he, through a mistaken sense of honor, went forth to what proved certain death.

The duelist's pistol and the assassin's bullet sent two of the finest men of that time to a premature grave. David Broderick and James King of William walked the streets no more, but the avenger in the shape of the San Francisco Vigilance Committee did. After their whirlwind campaign came peace and good government.

My father was a Broderick man, hence I heard much of the opinions of the day, not his alone, but those of persons who talked with him.

Fancy a gentleman of the present day being approached in this manner: "Is this Mr. Blank, sah? (Profound bow, hand to heart.) I am, sah, Kunnel Robert Lee Jones, sah (presenting card, with another bow). I am Majah Beauregard Jackson Smith's second, sah. The Majah presents his compliments, sah, and sends this challenge, sah, you to choose weapons, time and place, sah. (Another profound bow.) Awaiting your pleasure, sah, I am, etc., etc." Exit the Colonel with more bowing and another "sah" or two.

There seemed to be but two classes of people at that time, the Abolitionists, pronounced with a sneer always, and the Southern Chivalry, abbreviated "Chivs," also accompanied with sneers. While both sides worked and fought valiantly for their opinions, the despised Yankees and Abolitionists won. The slaves' fetters were broken, the Nation's blot expunged. I think we all realize

now that it was best that the slaves should be free, and thank
heaven, we have all forgotten and have all clasped hands once
more in fraternal love.

Fashions and customs had their peculiarities then as have
those of today. Everybody, men, women and children, used to oil
the hair—more than oil it, literally soak it. It was put on and then
the hair was brushed until it was as straight as an Indian's and
smooth as satin. A bottle of diluted castor oil or jar of pomatum
was on the bureau, not dressing case. Women often made their
own pomatum. Beef marrow, mixed with lard, was melted
together, then beaten until it was like snow and highly perfumed.
As the supply of marrow hardly equaled the demand, the butcher
was in high favor and his good graces equally sought. Sometimes
the marrow had to be "spoken for" weeks ahead.

Curly hair was not valued by either man or woman and no
cunning little tendrils at the neck were allowed. The dandy of the
time wore his hair somewhat long, then parted it at the back and
brushed it forward toward the ears until a path of white scalp was
visible across the room. He brushed the front down in a wave
across the brow. If it did not lie smooth enough it was still further
plastered with stick pomatum.

I think father was almost the only one who did not use hair oil.
He preached against it, but he could not win a victory over
fashion. He had a pretty eloquent tongue, but here it lost its
cunning. He tried to argue mother away from it, but in vain. As for
me, I was the sacrificial victim. I idolized my father. He was
exceptionally fond of me. "Don't" as well as "must" was said to me
many times, and I have always been thankful for it. In the case of
the hair oil I did almost rebel. I wanted to be greased and polished
and plastered down like everybody else.

Another curious article was the nightcap. It was made like a
baby's bonnet, white lawn or cambric tied under the chin with
white strings. It completely covered the head. I presume it was
originated to keep the pillows free from the hair oil. Again father
rebelled. He said it was too heating for the head, and it was. My
mother, I suppose, yielded on the nightcap question because it
was not exposed to public gaze. It did not flaunt itself in the

daytime, it was a thing of the night exclusively. Thereby hangs a tale.

My chum, Kate, always wore a nightcap; so did the rest of her family. Whenever I was allowed to stay all night with my little friend a nightcap was put on me. Kate and I usually had the same boy sweetheart. At this particular period of time the favorite was Charley Hastings, an exceedingly handsome boy, son of an intimate friend of mother.

Charley had large brown eyes and dark hair and was the quintessence of boyhood's grace. We never could tell which he liked the best. We loved each other so we were not jealous and did not quarrel over him. On one fatal night when I stayed at Kate's house we had gone to bed duly nightcapped. A large fire occurred close to us and we sprang up and, dressing completely, went down to the front gate. The whole town was passing and along came Charley. He stayed at the gate with us and laughed and talked till the fire was nearly out. We returned to the house. I passed the mirror. Oh, horrors! I had forgotten to take off my nightcap. My friend, being used to the odious thing, had removed hers as soon as she got out of bed.

Oh, my! What did Charley think? Could I ever face him again? My rival had surely outdistanced me!

Poor Charley, when grown up, just out of college, a credit to his mother's training, went to Virginia City, Nev. That was in the great Comstock mining days, and while visiting a quartz mill, in some way he got entangled in the machinery and had his young life crushed out. He made the last call on me, so that evened up the nightcap escapade.

About this time the hoopskirt began to be seen above the horizon. On it came, like the nightcap and the hair oil, again disgusting my father. Well, then, all the women had them. San Francisco and the other towns were quite small then and everybody knew everybody else. The women had to solve the problem of how to seat themselves gracefully with the hoops. They learned by dear experience that if they sat down too suddenly the hoops would fly up. Woman's ingenuity came to the rescue. She sat down sidewise, as she did so giving a delicate little hitch up behind. Hoops ever afterward were manageable in that respect, but they developed an unpleasant tendency in a new direction. They would occasionally come in contact with the lighter furniture, tipping stands over. But constant use overcame all this; a scarcely perceptible swing and hitch here and there protected most gracefully all intervening obstacles.

Hoop inventors had not considered it worth while to make hoops for growing girls. There was a wail in the air. We girls must have our skirts distended some way. We accomplished it by running a thin wire through the hem of our short white skirt. We procured the wire at a tinner's shop. It was bent into a sort of hook and loop at the ends. We learned this trick through the evolution of the hoopskirt, for it did not arrive all at once. It progressed upwards from four or five starched petticoats, each of great width, worn one over the other. The final dress skirt would be about seven yards in width. All this was weighty.

Then came a skirt of haircloth with a reed run in the hem, afterwards one through the middle, and finally the hoopskirt of many hoops from top to bottom. The desired width could be secured with airy lightness. Finally, oh, rapture! a dry goods store exhibited a girl's hoopskirt. Parents were beseeched and begged until they finally yielded and we also had "evoluted" from our wire, secretly bought at the tinshop, to the top notch of fashion.

Every town there had Indians all about. The squaws saw, admired and adopted the fashion, but with a difference. They always wore a hoopskirt over all their other clothing, nor could they be persuaded to do otherwise. Sometimes they could earn enough to buy one, but they usually depended on the discarded article.

A man's silk hat, plug or stovepipe, and a hoopskirt was the delight of the Indian and the squaw alike. The Indian man greatly delighted in a long linen duster also.

In those days the Empress Eugenie, of France, set the fashions. Frequently a newspaper would announce that hoops were going out, that the Empress had grown tired of them. Men would read this with delight to their womankind, but it had no effect. They would not give up until they knew to a certainty that fashion had struck the hoops a death blow.

Men wore dress suits much like the prevailing style, but they were made of blue broadcloth, always blue, and trimmed with gilt buttons. They also wore black satin stocks around the neck and linen turned-down collars, but always limp, never stiffly starched, ruffled shirts and gray beaver top hats. Trousers were strapped beneath the boots with a lot of waste leather up the leg beneath the trousers. Shoes were almost unknown for street wear.

Men wore to parties boots of the finest calfskin with extremely high heels. In Europe the boot legs were and are worn outside the trousers by the higher military at balls and parties, never beneath them. These boots for balls cost $25 a pair.

The lawyers of that time always went in full dress to try an important case. My father invariably went into court in blue cloth, gilt buttons, satin stock and soft shirt. Lawyers then had to be largely masters of oratory. Fine dress, like good scenery in a theatre, heightened the general effect. Women wore long, trailing dresses in the street. It was not correct to lift them up; in fact, they could not do so because of the hoops beneath. People had not investigated the microbe kingdom then. The microbes found a safe refuge in the folds of sweeping robes. The sidewalks received a good deal of free cleaning.

At the theatre the custom of the time made all villains recognizable by a black cloak of voluminous folds and a scarlet lining. It was thrown carelessly across the left shoulder. The entrance was to staccato music, stride, 1, 2, 3, pause; stride, 1, 2, 3, pause, across stage. Villains always had black hair and heavy black eyebrows. Blonde villains were unknown, just as black-haired angels do not find favor with the artist. Today our villains may be either dark or light haired and are known by the cigar or cigarette and the frequency with which they puff it in extremely perilous situations. It gives an appearance of great coolness and courage and is supposed to frighten the enemy to a finish. It takes the place of the long and jerky stride and is equally effective.

Music to "come on," music to "go off," music to "die with," have become old-fashioned. Let us hope music through dialogue, by fashion's decree, will soon take its departure also. How often the accompanying music kills the actor's lines in Shakespearean parts. The music reaches our ears and the text is lost while we fume and fret. Music in operas, yes; music with the words of drama, no. They are two distinct fields; let them each keep within their boundaries.

If ever we are compelled to have accompanying music, why under the sun cannot musicians learn to play softly? Recently in the play of "Every Woman" the character Nobody would begin to speak, then crash! boom! the orchestra would come in and completely drown the lines, notwithstanding the actor who spoke them had a deep voice and especially fine enunciation. If his facial expression was read aright, the responses of the orchestra were most irritating.

It was the fashion for women to be delicate. Lord Byron thought women should have no appetite, so, as Byron was much read, there was little eating in public and much satisfying of appetites secretly from the pantry shelves. To faint on the slightest excuse and to have a fit of hysterics or the vapors once a month, an idea gained from the reading of the "Children of the Abbey," implied high birth and delicate breeding. Oh, how I used to rebel at my robust health! Many of my little friends were at times ill. How I envied them their hours in bed, the dainty dishes prepared for them, the flowers sent and the many attentions! Was there ever a piece of toast that was browned so delicately or looked so delicious as the one that fell to the invalid's share, or was there ever a piece of chicken so juicy and tender as the one that found its way to the sick chamber? No, decidedly not. None that my eyes ever beheld before or since.

As with the stage so also the magnificent steamboats on the Sacramento River have yielded to the superior speed of the railway trains. Good old mining days, good old stage days, good old steamboat days, good old hearty hand-grasp days, good old Golden Rule days! Is there a Californian living now who would not leave everything behind and travel miles and miles could another such land under such conditions be found?

There has always been a wrong impression conveyed through pioneer stories and plays as to early social life in California. The idea has somehow taken root that every man went around with a knife in his boot, a pistol on his hip, a big sombrero on his head and ready at any instant to shoot any and everybody. Although at first people lived in small houses on account of the scarcity of building materials, there has never been a time since when society itself was more cultured and elegant. The rough element had its quarters of the town and it was not necessary to rub elbows with them any more than we do here today with the denizens of the North End. But to make fiction I suppose there must be allowed exaggeration just as we allow poetic license.

We had one church in town which was attended by all denominations. We had a young minister, J. H. Warren, just from an Eastern college. He was extraordinarily solemn and extremely orthodox; about every two or three months he preached, as did most preachers of that time, an extremely ferocious sermon picturing the burning lake where we poor mortals would languish and writhe on red coals and in blue flames, never consumed totally, but eternally roasting and sizzling. It was all very real to us children; we went home frightened and stayed thoroughly frightened until the time came for another such sermon. However, the ministers all grew out of it and if I am not mistaken, none of them now believe in an actual ever-roaring pit.

Rev. Mr. Warren became quite famous and lived to celebrate his golden wedding day and came near reaching the diamond period, 75 years, of married life.

When I was about 9 years old a little girl friend, Kate Overton, who had crossed the plains when I did, joined the Sunday school with me. We had a Sunday school superintendent, Mr. Harrison, whom none of the children liked. He was very homely, poor fellow, he could not help his looks, and very prosaic. He had served one term, whatever that was, and was to be voted in again. I became a sort of politician, got the girls together, talked it over and they all promised to vote against Mr. Harrison. When the day of the election came they asked all those in favor of Mr. Harrison to stand up. Then they asked for those opposed. I rose, supposing my flock would rise with me, but, alas, I stood there alone. But as I always had the courage of my convictions I did not flinch.

Mr. Harrison was having his house raised, and on Monday

following, before the workmen came, went under to inspect. While he was under there the screws gave way, killing him instantly. Those of us children who had been against Mr. Harrison's re-election and who had so expressed ourselves to each other beforehand were very remorseful. We considered ourselves responsible in some way for his death. The rest had only their consciences to reproach them, but the whole school knew that I had voted against the man and knew nothing of the treachery of my little companions.

Placer digging had to be supplied with water, so ditches or miniature canals were constructed to carry water from a large stream to the places where it was needed. These ditches were expensive to build, but yielded a handsome income on the money invested. Father owned very largely in one of them. That, with the fees from his profession, enabled us to live in as fine style as was possible at the time. The water was sold at $1 an inch. That was measured by the size of the aperture through which it flowed from the main ditch; if 20 inches square; then 20 inches a day or so many hours as required.

We lived alternately in Nevada City and San Francisco. We had a good theater in Nevada City and the best talent used to come to us. There I attended my first play, the old drama called "Pizzaro," a great favorite with heavy tragedians. My mother, not wishing to go, some friend at the hotel where we lived volunteered to take me. Poor martyr, she had her hands full. The first scene had a fierce combat with swords. The fight frightened me and also the loud applause at the end which I did not understand. I bawled and had to be taken out. But that was the last of it. I loved the theater ever afterwards, and whenever I was lucky enough to get there I was in a most blissful state of rapture and was ever crying for more and more, like Oliver Twist.

There were no matinees then nor till many years afterward. It would have been impossible to darken a theater sufficiently and then illuminate it satisfactorily with the crude lighting of that day. To go to the theater when I was a child was an education in itself. We had Shakespeare's plays the most of the time and Shakespearean knowledge was widely diffused. The gallery boys even knew their Shakespeare thoroughly and their applause was most judicious. This was the case at the old Bowery Theater in New York City also. People often went there to see the enthusiasm of the acting and to accept the play judgment of that intelligent Bowery gallery. We had fine tragedy, brilliant farce, exquisitely elevating romantic plays and fine comic operas.

Musical comedy, chiefly made up of rough buffoonery and horseplay, devoid of plot and full of inane songs, filled with vulgar suggestions, sly winks and a multiplicity of uncovered legs and arms, did not then exist.

It is common for people, as they are growing old, to condemn the present and boast of the past. Too much of it is probably done, but really it is a fact that young people of today, contrasted with those of yesterday, do not compare favorably from a literary standpoint. I know that when I was from 12 to 15 years old I had read all the Shakespearean plays, knew the novels of Sir Walter Scott, Bulwer and Dickens; had read Agnes Strickland's "Lives of the Queens of England," could recite Scott's and Byron's poems. I was not precocious, all my playmates, both boys and girls, had this knowledge at their fingers' ends.

Our literary culture was further increased by the class of plays we attended. I also think that parents made it a point to cultivate good literature in their children more than they do now. I am quite certain I should have loved to read anyhow, because I came from a literary family, but my mother did not trust to that. My father was a polished orator and my mother a great lover of books. I was a very healthy, romping child, but ever and anon my mother would say to my companions, "Run home now, my little girl has to come in and read with me." Then she would read from a well-selected book and if it was a little ahead of me she generally managed to make me understand some of it, anyway. Mother being greatly interested then in Lamartine's French Revolution, read it aloud to me when I was 12 years old. I have never read it since, but can remember much of it. This was followed by historical and poetical readings and novels of the highest order and I firmly believe that had I had no other education this would have been a pretty good foundation with which to start me out in the world.

We had a full measure pressed down and running over when

we went to the play. All plays had five acts. Then came some kind of dancing and singing between and a one-act farce at the close so we might go home in good humor. The programme was never long enough for me and what caused me great anguish was that grown people, the most stylish and fastidious sometimes, thought it was not quite fashionable to stay for the farce. I always feared I would have to go home before the final piece. I did hope that whoever took me would be democratic enough to stay.

Between the first play and the farce the bill for the next evening's performance was tacked on the side of the proscenium arch. It was a fearful tantalizer. I began immediately to wish I could go the next night.

The theaters all had green baize curtains with a weighty pole at the bottom to weigh them down. This curtain always fell with a thud and woe to the unlucky wight who did not die far enough up stage. Stage people have been killed by this same heavy pole. A tinkling bell announced the rising of the curtain. Oh, how eagerly I listened for the bell and when that green curtain—we had no painted ones—rose, I rose myself to the seventh heaven of happiness.

Great artists visited California in those early days, among those that I remember being Edwin Forrest, Edwin Booth, James Stark, James Anderson, Matilda Heron, Jean Davenport, Fanny Morant, Julia Dean Hayne.

Among the first plays I saw was the "Marble Heart," a beautiful romantic play with Booth as Raphael and Katherine Sinclair as Marco. Katherine Sinclair had been the wife of Edwin Forrest, but was divorced. The great Forrest divorce case had agitated the whole United States, as it was previous to the time when divorce was so customary. Now it is so common as to hardly receive comment.

Edwin Booth was at that time a very young actor and was traveling mostly on his father's, the Great Junius Brutus Booth's reputation.

My chum was a little girl my own age, named Kate Overton. My Kate and I went together almost everywhere. We knew a nice boy of whom we were both fond—we shared our sweethearts. This boy had an aunt, a great actress, Mrs. Potter, so he was on the free list. He secured a box and we, duly chaperoned, were allowed to go with him. Oh, the joys of anticipation, and oh, the joys of realization! Was there ever such a night as that? Sometimes I went to the theater without my Kate, and she without me, and then we would meet and tell each other all about the plays which we had attended. We would describe the entire play from the first act to the fifth and then compare notes on the farces that followed, and when we had finished there was nothing more to be said.

Kate was the daughter of a noted physician. Her family was Southern and mine was Northern; my father was an "abolitionist," hers a "secessionist"; I was very robust, she delicate. But with all these differences we were entirely harmonious and our love endured till the end of her life, many years afterward.

We lived in very stirring times. The North and the South were restless, impending calamity was in the air. The death knell of slavery could be frequently heard in the distance, but was growing louder and ever louder.

Julia Dean Hayne came to play an engagement. She was in the height of her beauty and fame. It was the custom in those days for professionals, when off duty, to hide themselves as much as possible from the public gaze. They took their meals in their rooms and scarcely ever walked the streets. In this way they wrapped themselves in a sort of mystery. Curiosity was excited, everyone wondered how they looked off the stage. They seemed beings apart. It was indeed hard on them to keep so aloof; however, it added largely to their receipts. Today stage people show themselves in the street and around hotels over much. People no longer regard them as out of the ordinary. They see them as just common men and women and all the illusion is gone.

Once the beautiful Julia came out of her hotel and ventured to a drygoods store. I happened to have been sent down town on an errand. I forgot everything; a fair-haired angel had seemingly dropped down from the clouds, all other things had shrunk into insignificance. I followed her from store to store, I gazed up into her face with eager curiosity and admiration. She did not seem conscious of my presence. I went wherever she did and only ceased following her when the hotel doors closed on her.

I was late home and had utterly forgotten what I went for. When I next met my companions I felt very superior and boastful. Had I not walked behind an actress? Had I not heard her talk? Then they all sighed and wished they had come across such an opportunity.

We had gone to San Francisco to live permanently, but father's water-ditch property and his legal business called us back again and we rented a house that had a garden, the only flower garden in the town. The owner had taken valuable time to make it. It was filled with the commonest kind of old-fashioned flowers, Sweet Williams and pinks. I presume no better seed was to be had. Beneath the house was a basement and in the basement treasures—old play books, discarded theatrical costumes, including an old gorgeous red plumed hat, an old velvet cloak and one or two faded satin dresses. Where they came from I do not know. My chum Kate and myself reveled in these bewildering things; we dressed up every time she came to see me. The wonderful hat was worn alternately. The one whose turn it was would array herself in an old skirt and, whip in hand, mount the back fence and, imagining it was a steed, would ride until the impatience of the other party would demand her turn. We passed many agreeable hours in this way.

On one occasion when my father went to Downieville, an adjacent town, to try a very important case, the house was shut up and mother went with him. I was left with the Overton family until they should return. My Kate and I were to have three or four weeks together and we danced and clapped our hands with joy. As I have said before they were a Southern family. They brought a slave boy and girl with them to California. The slaves did not wish to leave "Mars Charles" and Miss Mary Ellen, and so they lived with the family and served them. The boy's name was Jacob Esau Napoleon Bonaparte, usually boiled down to plain Jacob. Colored people revel in long names for their children.

While mother was gone somehow or other, I could not tell how, with Jacob's assistance I embarked in a business enterprise. I think I must have been prompted by the wish to have a pair of slippers I had seen. Up to that time nobody wore heels on their shoes and heels had just come in fashion. July 4 was near at hand

and flowers were in great demand. So I made a bargain with Jacob to sell them. I went down to the house and made the bouquets, two sizes, one very small, which sold for 50 cents, and one a little larger for $1. Jacob peddled them about the streets and sold them all; there could not have been a great supply. I went every day until there was nothing left growing. We divided the profits. As I remember it we worked secretly until our speculation was brought to a successful culmination. I bought the slippers with heels.

When mother came home and heard of the commercial instincts I had developed she was disgusted. She herself would have given the flowers away. Her pride was mortified to think that her little girl had stooped so low, had gone into partnership with a colored boy and had actually made money and sold flowers when there was no necessity for it.

In those days we used to have wonderful May Day parties with a queen and maids of honor, courtiers, pages, etc. The crowning of the queen with fine speeches and always the Maypole dance to finish. It was a lovely custom which seems to have sunk into utter disuse. The election of the queen, maids of honor, crowner, etc., was a very important proceeding. Regular nominations were made and there was much electioneering. My friend Kate and myself were nominated for queen on one occasion. The election was hotly contested. Our minister and Sunday school superintendent counted the votes. My little friend beat me by one vote. I was awfully disappointed, but was consoled with the next best royal office.

Just after my parents' return from Downieville father went immediately to Sacramento. Mother was rejoicing over her return. I was in my room making my doll a dress. We were talking from room to room and I had been looking in the mirror when I said to mother:

"I am not very good looking so I will have to know a great deal when I am grown up."

Just then I heard shouting, went to the door and the whole town seemed to be on fire at once. What fire apparatus we had was drawn by men and they did not get started very speedily. It was a hot July day and some way the water had been shut off. By evening what had been the town was just a mass of burning coals. Everything was lost, provisions were scarce, nobody saved any clothes except those they were wearing, people slept outdoors.

Those early-day fires were terrible. Buildings were all of frame, many of them only lined and papered. I wept and wept over my doll, the grand riding hat and feather, and the beautiful treasures in the cellar. They were all the world to me then.

Mother had sent to Sacramento for a bonnet for me. It came the day after the fire. It was a blue crepe with straw buttons and I had nothing to wear with it. I used to take out the box and admire it. I did so until I had something to wear with it.

Father was at Sacramento at a great political convention. He was one of the organizers of the Republican party in California and used to make political speeches in the midst of great danger. The Southern element was then very strong and everything was leading up to the vigilance committee days of San Francisco which avenged many outrages of which the shooting of James King of William was the climax. I could not comprehend that name. I thought he must be a king. There were so many men with the name of James King that Mr. King attached the name of his birthplace and so became James King of William.

Father was one of the rare politicians who worked for the good of the party without office reward. When it was tendered him he said:

"No, I want no office. My profession is enough for me."

His voice could always be heard when needed and his speeches were considered eloquent and convincing. He was followed to Sacramento after a powerful speech and fired on from behind in the office of the old Old Orleans Hotel of Sacramento. The bullet just grazed his temple, passed by him and wounded another man. Thus, while his family was being burned out in Nevada City, he was in danger of his life from an assassin's pistol.

Frank Pixley, of the San Francisco Argonaut, in speaking of those stirring times, referred to James Churchman, my father, as "an exceptional politician, a man working heartily, unwearyingly and unselfishly for the good of the party."

The great political fight on then was between D. Broderick and William Gwin. My father was a Broderick man.

The family moved to Austin, Nevada at the time of the mining booms. Conditions were still primitive, and society had not yet become stratified:

> There was no distinction between a mansion and a cottage, all houses were alike, stockade poles on end close together and filled in with mud. . . . We had dirt packed hard for floors. . . . Equality killed envy, so we were gay and happy.[1]

While in Nevada, the author got married to a lawyer who was then elected State Senator, so they moved to Carson City. Conditions were highly favorable at that time, money kept flooding into the cities from the mines, and the inhabitants were swept up in a continual swirl of excitement and entertainments:

> Conditions were almost the same in Carson and Virginia City as they had been in the early days of California. Money was plentiful, stocks were booming, politics seething, cordiality and good fellowship at the top notch. Velvets, silks, satins and jewels were in evidence on all great occasions contrary to the usual outside impression of things. No place on the Pacific Coast entertained more noted visitors than Virginia City in her great and glorious bonanza days.[2]

The rest of the book contains an account of Mrs. Larowe's move to New York, of her travels to Europe and in the West, and of her thwarted attempts to build up a theatrical career for herself. She explains that the situation of women had changed and that they could no longer depend on relatives, but had to find a way to survive when left to their own resources. After various ups and downs, Mrs. Larowe finally gave dancing lessons and achieved moderate success. She found much satisfaction in being able to buy her own house and expressed contentment with her circumstances.

Mrs. Larowe's book constitutes an interesting testimony on life in the cities and contains many details concerning social life, *entertainments, fashions, and artistic matters. The story of her life deserves attention too, as it shows the efforts made by a woman to overcome traditional prejudices and stand on her own feet.*

1. Mrs. Larowe, p. 29.
2. Ibid.

# Crossing the Plains and Early Days in California: Memories of Girlhood in California's Golden Age.

Mrs. Mary E. Ackley

(Privately Printed for the Author) 1928.

*Mary Ackley's account of her childhood experiences is dedicated to her grandchildren and great grandchildren, and was thus written late in life. It starts with a description of her parents' prosperous farm in Missouri (she mentions the presence of slaves) in a beautiful location; the tone is lyrical, and the narrative features descriptions of the seasons, of the agricultural activities and of the guests who were entertained. She tells of the gold fever, of the preparations for the trip and of the parting, in April 1852 (she was ten), from her grandmother, whom she never saw again. The family travelled in a large train, to be better protected against the Indians. Mary Ackley gives a sense of the way life went on during the trip, and of the hardships which marked their way: cholera struck, her mother died, and was buried on the prairie. When they finally reached California, the participants were in a state of near exhaustion:*

After crossing the plains in 1852 and our arrival in California, September 20, our first home was a two-story frame house on the Marysville road, four miles from Sacramento City. As the house was on low ground and likely to be flooded in winter, as soon as we took possession it was moved to a high knoll.

The house contained six large rooms, a living room, a dining room and kitchen on the first floor, and three bedrooms on the second floor. One large room had bunks built around it, like a stateroom on a steamer. The partitions between the rooms were of canvas, and the house was lined with the same material.

Our nearest neighbors lived on a ranch a mile away—a man, his wife and two children, and two bachelors. Further away were several shanties, occupied by bachelors.

Late in the fall Sacramento was almost destroyed by fire. Canvas houses and tents were immediately put up, and Sacramento was called "Canvas Town."

We had several heavy rainstorms in November. The Sacramento and American Rivers overflowed their banks in December, flooding Sacramento and the lowlands on the Marysville road. Our house, high up on the knoll, was entirely surrounded by water, but was not flooded.

Bachelors from the shanties in the neighborhood came to us for shelter. We took them in. One was a physician and one a large man called Uncle Tom, who was well known and a favorite among the men. The refugees, with our family of six, made the number a dozen.

No board was charged, but each man contributed to providing the provisions, and the men did the cooking. The kitchen stove was moved into the dining room, for it was the only stove in the house.

The food in the house was getting scarce; a storm was raging, but someone had to go to the city for supplies. A small skiff was the only mode of conveyance, and it was a dangerous undertaking. Who was to go? Uncle Tom volunteered, and another large man consented to accompany him. They expected to be gone a day and a night.

The second day they had not returned, nor the third, and all we had for dinner the third day was bean soup.

We were alarmed for their safety, but in the middle of the third night they returned with a boatload of provisions. They were completely exhausted with such a strenuous trip in the storm. The men who remained at home arose and cooked a big meal, which they all enjoyed very much.

Several days after Uncle Tom was taken sick. My sister

Margaret (thirteen years old) took his breakfast up to him. She noticed that a rash had broken out on his face. The physician in the house went up to see him and pronounced his case smallpox.

Five young people in the house had never been vaccinated, so the physician vaccinated all of us that day except Brother John (eight years old), who was very ill. We had to remain in the house, as there was no other place for us.

Uncle Tom recovered, and a short time afterward another man was stricken. Uncle Tom nursed him. The man was very sick, but recovered. The rest of the household escaped the disease.

The flood receded and all the refugees left the home except Uncle Tom. He was about the same age as our father (forty-three years). His family was in the East, he said; he had two little daughters the same age as my sister Margaret and myself, so he felt at home with us.

After the flood had subsided, the man who had charge of our father's stock brought home a cow with a young calf. The cow had supplied us with milk during the trip across the plains the previous year.

The only butter in market was firkin butter that came around the Horn and was very salty. We did not like to use that kind. Sister Margaret sent for a churn, and for several months made enough butter to supply the family.

Our eldest sister took care of our brother, who was sick, and seldom came downstairs. Sister Margaret and I (eleven years old) were the housekeepers. Our father was handicapped, having lost his wife on the plains the previous year, so did not leave his family day or night all winter.

Teaming was profitable in early days—hauling goods to mining towns. Our father hired out the teams we used to cross the plains, and received quite an income.

As there was such a demand for hay, in 1853 father bought some beautiful meadow land about two miles from the Marysville road and built a canvas house. We moved in as soon as my brother John recovered from his illness. The meadows were covered with beautiful wild flowers, and the only amusements we children had were picking flowers and playing with the calf.

We had heavy rain storms in April, and the weather being warm, the snow on the Sierra Nevada Mountains was melted, which caused the Sacramento and American Rivers again to overflow their banks, flooding Sacramento City, and the backwater from the rivers flooded the lowlands in the meadows and our canvas home. With the assistance of our neighbors the house was moved to higher ground.

About that time, I noticed a young man was coming frequently to see us. I soon discovered sister Annie (eighteen years old) was the attraction. This young man wanted to marry her. She said she could not leave her father. He said he would help her take care of her young sisters and brothers. He was building a two-story house on his farm. In June they were married and we all moved to his house.

At Lisle's Bridge, on the American River, lived a doctor and his wife. The wife had a canvas house erected under a grove of trees near her home and taught a private school for four months, having seven pupils. Sister Margaret and I attended. We enjoyed school and were much benefited. Our walk to school was three miles.

We liked our new home and were very happy.

The latter part of September, in 1853, brother John came running to me, very much excited. He said some people were camping near by who had just crossed the plains. He saw children and a little girl. We went immediately to the camp; on a log sat a beautiful black-eyed girl, nine years old. I introduced myself and had a pleasant call. On leaving, I invited her to visit me. Her father was a well-to-do farmer from Missouri. He bought a farm and settled in the neighborhood, and we found the family an agreeable addition to our small community.

From the first time I met the little girl until her death recently, a period of a little over seventy years, we were friends.

She was the dearest and truest friend I ever had. She was married to a worthy young man when she was sixteen years of age, and later became the mother of eight children. More than thirty years ago she founded the "Tuesday Club" of Sacramento. Her husband was three times elected state senator.

It was customary in early days for girls to marry at fourteen, fifteen and sixteen years of age.

My sister Margaret was married to a farmer just before Christmas, 1854. A little while later her husband and my father went about ten miles from Sacramento to a beautiful little valley on the American River. They believed it had been government land, and bought a farm from a man who claimed he owned it.

We moved over, leaving sister Annie, her husband, and their baby daughter in their home. In 1855 I attended school in Sacramento, which had a most excellent school for that time.

The valley was soon settled up. Father was appointed school trustee and had a schoolhouse built on the hill overlooking the valley, where we had school in the summer. Church was held in this little schoolhouse, and parties occasionally.

Father was elected justice of the peace in that township and held court in the schoolhouse. Before the schoolhouse was built, father held court in our home.

Court day was quite an event; the living room was full of men, and the women of the family found it a pleasure to visit the neighbors on that day.

Just across the American River, opposite our farm, was situated Patterson's Station, a hotel and pleasure resort. A plank road was built from Sacramento City to the station, a distance of ten miles. A ballroom was connected with the hotel, where grand balls were frequently given, and many persons went there from the city. The ladies were beautifully gowned and the men always wore white kid gloves when they danced.

The midnight suppers were very elaborate. The guests danced all night, the roads being too dark to travel.

Mr. Patterson had four lovely daughters. One of them was my age, and sometimes I was invited to these balls, and I gladly accepted the invitations. Father rowed me over the river in a skiff and called for me in the morning.

In 1856 a camp meeting was held near Lisle's Bridge, in a grove of trees on the American River. One Sunday afternoon a party of friends attended the meeting, which was very interesting. Our only conveyance at that time was a wagon with a high seat in front, with two low seats in the back. The bottom of the wagon was covered with straw.

Going home, it commenced to rain. We covered the two lower seats with blankets that we had with us, then sat down on the straw in the bottom of the wagon and were as comfortable and happy as if we had been in a grand carriage.

Not long after this ride a supply of buggies came to Sacramento around the Horn. We were a happy neighborhood. But alas! Word came to us in 1857 that we were on Norris' Spanish grant and we must vacate. It was a hard blow to the people in the little valley. Some friends of ours who lived at Oak Grove, eight miles from Sacramento, on a beautiful farm, raised cattle, horses and grain. They built a $5,000 barn. After the husband's death, Norris ordered the widow to vacate, and they went to law about it, and he remarked to her, "I will law you as long as you have a bonnet." She afterward told me she lost her farm and all her stock.

Before our family left the valley I was married (June 1857) to a man from Sacramento. I had a pretty trousseau. My bridal costume was of white organdie, made with an overskirt, very wide, with a train, over a hoop skirt, orange blossoms in my hair, white kid shoes and a white tulle veil, which fell to the bottom of my dress. My traveling dress was a lavender silk, a silk mantle, and a white lace bonnet with three pink roses on one side.

We were married at high noon, with the family and a few friends present. At two o'clock p. m. we boarded the steamer on the Sacramento River for San Francisco. The steamer was very elaborately furnished, and an elaborate dinner was served on the way. We arrived at San Francisco at eleven o'clock that night.

We stayed at the International Hotel while in San Francisco— the best in town. Montgomery street was then the principal street.

I did not like San Francisco at all. Houses were built over gullies, and the wind blew the sand in our faces, which almost blinded us. I loved the ocean, but the sand dunes were not pleasant to see.

We visited the Ocean House, taking two of our friends with us. My husband hired a two-seated carriage. The ride was not pleasant, as the roads to the ocean were so sandy. I enjoyed the Ocean House and thought the ocean a grand sight. The Cliff House had not been built at the time.

San Francisco at that time (1857) was not a pleasant place to live in.

After returning to Sacramento we boarded with friends until November, when we went to housekeeping in our own home, a two-story brick house with six rooms. Thanksgiving Day we had a turkey dinner and invited four friends to take dinner with us.

People dressed well in those days. Money was plentiful and living was cheap compared to what it is now. Twenty-five-cent pieces were the smallest coins in circulation. A dollar gold piece and a $50 gold piece, called a slug, were also in circulation.

Church attendance was good. For amusements we had theaters, lectures, operas, parties, etc. Theater and opera tickets were $1, and we had excellent dramas, tragedies with fine actors and actresses. One drama, "Marble Hearts," was played several nights in succession in Sacramento. J. Wilkes Booth took the leading part—a most excellent actor and a handsome man.

In those days a woman or girl would not think of going to the theater, opera, or downtown in the evening, without a man as escort. We were not afraid of being molested, but of our reputations. It was not the custom for women to go about alone.

*This brief sketch, which covers about five years, gives an idea of the hard life the motherless girls led during their first years in California. They had to contend with sickness, had to assume all the tasks of the household, and for a while were exposed to adverse weather conditions. There were several moves in the area just around Sacramento. From the descriptions of the houses at the time they arrived, it is possible to form an idea of the immediate surroundings of the city. Fires and floods were major obstacles to its development. After the family moved to a valley at a short distance from Sacramento, their circumstances improved and they became part of its development. Gradually, their life became more than just a struggle for survival; social amusements were organized. Descriptions of clothes make their appearance in the narrative, and the word "elaborate" starts cropping up from time to time. According to Mary Ackley, life in San Francisco held no particular attraction in 1857. The short passage concerning Sacramento, on the other hand, contains only positive remarks.*

*The narrative moves on, giving scanty details about life in the late 1850s. Floods occured in December 1861 and January 1862, and many people left the city. Mrs. Ackley then suggested to her husband that they should buy some real estate while the prices were low. He refused, and started to make preparations to go to Aurora, Nevada. They moved there in 1864. The narrator de-*

*scribes a lively town of about 7,000 inhabitants, featuring good schools and churches, and a very active social life. But as the mining excitement died down, people started to leave. Mary Ackley spent six and a half years there with her husband and family; then, they went to Carson City in 1870, and back to Sacramento, which they found much improved. Her husband died in 1871, leaving her a widow with four children before she was thirty. She lived there until she had educated all her children and then moved to San Francisco.*

*Mrs. Ackley's book offers some interesting details about life and customs at that time (the item concerning early marriages, in particular, is noteworthy). It can be used to draw comparisons with or to supplement other accounts. One of its most remarkable aspects is the insight it provides into her relationship with her husband: it appears that he was used to making the decisions concerning the family alone, and was not open to her influence. Yet it is clear that she was shrewd, and was well able to manage: she was quite successful in meeting her responsibilities toward her family after his death. She helped in founding an Association of Pioneers in San Francisco in 1891. It is such a pity that her testimony is so skimpy, as she was certainly a most interesting woman, who suffered many hardships in her adolescence and early maturity, but overcame them all.*

# Five Years within the Golden Gate

Isabelle Saxon

(London: Chapman & Hall) 1868.

*Isabelle Saxon was an Englishwoman who first went to California in 1861, and lived in San Francisco. She returned to Europe to visit her family, and came back to the City toward the end of 1866. She then set down in writing her observations of life there, relying heavily on impressions from her earlier stay. The book contains notations on practically all aspects of life in San Francisco and accounts of trips in the surrounding area. There is no specific arrangement; the narrative just moves on according to the author's whim. Most of the observations are general and concern manners and customs, daily life, entertainments; few specific examples are given, and when a person's life is used to illustrate a point, no name is provided, and the story is related in a rather vague manner. The book covers too many subjects, and says too little about each. But here and there it is possible to find interesting observations, comparisons with life in England, and vivid descriptions. The following passage concerns celebrations in San Francisco and contains some information on the life of women from the upper classes:*

America has her annual "Thanksgiving Day," which, being an occasion for unlimited feasting and jollity, is generally observed. It occurs upon the 24th of November, and is the season for that annual gathering of familiar faces at the festive board which in England belongs exclusively to "merrie Christmas." New Year's

Day is observed much as the French keep it. The ladies remain at home, receiving the calls of all their gentleman friends. Refreshments are served, varying from the *recherché* champagne and exquisite French conserves, crystallised fruits, delicate and elegant trifles offered with good taste by the *haut monde* on such occasions, to the loaded tables of the *parvenus* or *nouveaux riches*, which literally groan under the weight of turkeys, poultry, and food of every description, as the unhappy callers inwardly also groan at being compelled to partake of these collations at every house of the kind they enter where madam's whole soul is absorbed in making them devour more than they wish to do, and afterwards perilling her wits to discover whether Mrs. B. over the way "set a better table" than she did.

"Such is life," at least New Year's life, in San Francisco, and New York parallels it in this respect. Sensible people there are who are so disgusted with the custom, resulting often in actual inebriation among the men, that they significantly hang out a basket at their hall doors to receive the cards of callers, as a hint that they are not at home. Others, who really desire to keep up a sociable custom in its pristine simplicity, risk the innuendoes of Mrs. Grundy by daring to offer nothing more than a glass of wine and a slice of cake to those who pay them the compliment of calling at that season. The ladies of many families at such times indulge in considerable gaiety of the toilette. I remember one lady, the wife of a gentleman who possessed a comfortable competence, but only kept one servant, presiding over the luncheon spread in her dining-room, on a New Year's morning, in a superb crimson velvet dress which would assuredly not have been unsuited to a reception at St. James's! Yet her taste in ordinary dress was quiet. As before remarked, American women generally are fonder of showy toilettes in the street than either their French or English sisters. In the ball-room, at evening parties, or on any full-dress occasion, the English lady is not an unworthy rival of the French belle. The tenor of her education, to the credit of her country, is usually such as to give a higher tone to her ambition than an overwhelming devotion to dress, such as is undoubtedly too generally the failing of the French and American ladies. They show it not only on the dress occasions where the English women especially shine, but on all possible opportunities for exhibiting the splendour of their costume, be it ball or promenade, or, as far as the American is concerned, the street, where she invariably decks herself in the utmost amount of jewellery she can wear. It is true that custom in America deprives her of the privilege of full dress at the theatre and opera, it being usual there to appear in bonnets. Madame l'Américaine, however, compensates herself for this by wearing the most airy or brilliant toilette possibly compatible with the bonnet; and if graceful necks and rounded arms are veiled from public gaze, the glories and gaieties of Epsom and Ascot toilettes, at least, are rivalled by them at those places of public resort. Since the Prince of Wales's visit, however, on which occasion, in compliment to him, full dress was worn at the opera, there has been a sprinkling of fair dames with hardihood sufficient to attempt an innovation on the long-existing mode. They wear "Nubias," or woollen coverings for the head, of which, in consequence of the want of cloak-rooms in American theatres, they are compelled to disencumber themselves in the dress-circle itself. Gentlemen rarely take the trouble to make any alteration in their daily toilette for the theatres in San Francisco, unless it be for the opera, and then white gloves on their part are the exception rather than the rule. White waistcoats, one would suppose, are at a premium, for they are very rarely seen.

One of the most salient features of American life is their patronage, not merely of large hotels, but of fashionable boarding-houses. It is in San Francisco as in New York. Newly-married couples, averse to the anxieties of housekeeping, caring nothing for that sweet domestic retirement which to the English mind constitutes so much of the prospective enjoyment at such an era in life, commonly take up their abode, at least for the earlier years of marriage, at some fashionable hotel or boarding-house. Others of less influence, importance, or means, take furnished rooms at a stylish lodging-house, and eat at some of the restaurants with which the cities abound. The motive is obvious. While it deprives them of much of the pleasures of society, it enables them to make a much better appearance socially than they could do, with the expenses of hospitality to maintain, in a house whose rent would cost them no more than their rooms at the lodging-house. It is grievous to see such a strong love for ostentation pervading every

class of society as even republican America undeniably presents to
the stranger. The chief evil of the midde class of English society is,
that it displays the same anxiety to "keep up appearances." But, to
do England justice, it is chiefly evidenced in discharging the duties
of an exaggerated housekeeping hospitality, not in the avoidance
of them. Americans are notoriously a very generous people, and it
is saddening to see their love of display darkening the pristine
simplicity of a noble republicanism, and that to the extent it
assuredly does at the present day. Moreover, this same system of
restaurant and lodging-house or hotel life, as the case may be,
coupled with the passion for dress of the women, who are among
the most beautiful in the world, goes far towards rendering them
the mere puppets of society. With none of the thousand delightful
home duties, which are the pride and pleasure of every true
woman, devolving upon them—usually educated, or rather half-
educated, in those hotbeds of frivolity and superficiality, large
seminaries (the larger the more fashionable)—thrown entirely
upon their own resources for pleasure or occupation during the
husband's daily engagements in the duties of his profession or
business—they but too often trifle away the precious hours of
existence to an extent inconceivable by the English matron, who is
absorbed either in family duties or those of hospitality, and even in
the highest and most fashionable ranks will occupy leisure hours in
unostentatious cares for the poor of the immediate neighbour-
hood, with too high a sense of moral accountability to spend an
undue portion of the time which can never be recalled upon mere
personal adornment. The daughters of the highest aristocracy, it is
notorious in England, are no way to be distinguished in the street
from those inferior in rank, unless it be by the exceeding plainness
of their attire. It has been the habit of many newspaper correspon-
dents and others, particularly those writing from Paris, to contrast
unfavourably the toilettes of Englishwomen there with those of
their American and French friends. Let the former rather receive it
as a credit than otherwise that they rely more on the qualities of
head and heart than on the face, beautiful as even these critics
usually admit them to be, or on the skill of their milliners, for the
influence they wield in society. It is absurd to suppose, were the
energies of the cultivated classes of Englishwomen directed that
way, or more, were they willing to cramp the incomes of their

husbands to the necessary extent, that they could not as easily attain the art of perfection in dress as in the varied accomplishments in which they usually excel. The real truth is, they do not estimate fashion so highly, and it is to be hoped they never will. The higher ranks feel that mere dress cannot elevate them. To be elegantly and becomingly dressed is a duty every woman owes to society. To worship dress is the abuse of that duty. To so great an extreme does this proceed among American women, that the wife, possibly of a mechanic or small tradesman, whose husband can afford but one servant, supposing them to "keep house," is unhappy without a "point-lace set," diamond rings and earrings, and a costly set of furs, the latter alone ranging in value from £50 to £100!

I am not in the slightest degree afraid of incurring the animosity of sensible American women by these remarks. Their opinion on these points, I am satisfied, will coincide with mine, having frequently heard the subject discussed and deplored by women whose merits are not surpassed anywhere else in the world.

England can discover much worthy of imitation in the noble institutions and aids to human progress which are so liberally put forth by America. In the matter of social refinement, so far at least as the middle and upper classes are concerned, America can find much excelling theirs in the life and habits of their English cousins, if not as far as regards what is termed the lower class. The American, in point of politeness, especially towards women, in information, and general good breeding (always excepting the use of the spittoon), is far superior to the Englishman. If a group of men in America stand on the pavement and in San Francico the name of the groups that thus stand there is "legion"—and a lady, no matter how poorly dressed, passes along, the group instantaneously retires on one side to give her room to pass. In London no notice whatever would be taken of her. Again, when a mail steamer arrives, as it does only semi-monthly in San Francisco, there is naturally a great rush to the post-office, letters not being delivered at the door by postmen, as in England. It is true there is a window exclusively for ladies, which might account for husbands or fathers who call for their relatives' letters feeling bound to give ladies the precedence there; but, *vice versa,* let a lady approach the gentleman's window, and not a man will press forward till she is served. I remember being greatly struck with the contrast in cases presented to my notice in this respect on my arrival in England. Advancing to secure my ticket at the railway depot, I found only two persons, who doubtless considered themselves eminently entitled to the name of "gentlemen," before me at the window. There was ample time, and certainly no excuse possible for the rude manner in which they determinedly excluded me from a precedence, which, seeing no necessity for haste, I had not the smallest intention of taking. A matter of life or death, at the latest possible moment for securing tickets in a crowd, might have excused such a breach of good manners, but here no ground for it existed.

This chivalrous feeling of deference towards women is greatly abused in San Francisco. The street cars are not limited to carrying only a certain number of passengers, as they are in England. The conductors make a constant practice of taking up more passengers than they can seat, well knowing that a female is secure of a seat so long as one gentleman remains sitting; and frequently not until every gentleman in the vehicle has so resigned his place does the conductor cease to take up female passengers. On wet days especially is this nuisance carried on. As the practice simply suffices to fill the pockets of the omnibus proprietors, it struck me that gentlemen should make a more decided stand against it. At late hours on a wet night only is it excusable, for ladies themselves do not like to feel, in entering a public conveyance, that they will probably cause some gentleman to lose the seat for which he has paid, and of which his courtesy ought not to be suffered to deprive him, as it assuredly will, rather than he will be content to lie under the imputation of a deficiency in politeness towards a woman. Of course the law ought to put an end to the practice by making it illegal for public carriages to carry more than a specific number of passengers. I am obliged to admit also that women are too apt to lose sight of courtesy in the custom, and omit even an expression of thanks to those who so unselfishly promote their comfort.

The restaurants, as before suggested, form a striking feature in San Francisco economy. There are several first-class French restaurants where a good breakfast, claret included, may be obtained for half a crown. Some of no mean pretensions are to be found in Montgomery Street, kept by Americans and others. These have a large room for gentlemen, and a separate apartment of spacious dimensions for the accommodation of ladies and their attendants. These rooms are always handsomely carpeted and fitted with two or more large mirrors. Tables accommodating from two to four persons are thickly scattered about, ready prepared for dining. Here, from 6 A.M. till noon, breakfast, consisting of food served *à l'Américaine*, may be had in the shape of coffee, tea, or chocolate, with fitting accompaniments of steaks, cutlets, broiled fowl, fried fish, and those *chef-d'oeuvres* of American culinary art, "buckwheat," "corn-batter," or "flannel" cakes. These cakes resemble the pancake in size and shape. Buckwheat cakes are made from a peculiar kind of flour. They are common in Germany as well as in America, but I never ate them in England. Corn-batter cakes are prepared from the flour of the Indian corn, and the flannel cake resembles the Shropshire "pikelet." The favourite dish called "waffles" by the Americans is similar to the English "gauffres." Dinner, consisting of soups, joints, poultry, game, fish, and pastry, can be obtained at these restaurants any time from noon till 6 or 7 P.M. From that hour till twelve supper is served, and coffee, tea, chocolate, eggs, chops, and steaks are to be had at any hour of the night.

The visitor to these restaurants calls for any dish he pleases,— roast or boiled meats, or chops. He is charged at the moderate rate of sixpence each plate, potatoes, boiled or mashed, and bread and butter, being added without extra charge. For any extra vegetable he pays an extra sixpence. Poultry varies from one to two and three shillings a plate. Fish is generally sixpence per plate, and pastry the same price, as are also tea, coffee, and chocolate.

By this it will be seen that a very fair dinner may be obtained for the small sum of one shilling by a poor man. Ices are one shilling each, and fruit is sometimes dear, because of its scarcity.

*Isabelle Saxon's book never goes very deep; it is an evocation of the surface appearance of things which is supplemented by a certain number of concrete details concerning daily life, institutions and events; it includes descriptions of specific customs of the times (one noteworthy passage concerns hotel life in California). It restores some of the atmosphere of the epoch depicted, and is interesting in its attempt to picture life in all its variety.*

*Part 6*
CHILDHOOD AND ADOLESCENCE IN THE WEST

# Adobe Days

Sarah Bixby-Smith

(Cedar Rapids, Iowa: The Torch Press) 1925.


*In a foreword, Sarah Bixby-Smith explains that her book is an expanded version of a shorter account of her childhood memories, and that she has used new material concerning her family to supplement them. Her early days were spent on a sheep ranch near San Juan Bautista, an old mission town, in the 1870s. Her family had its roots in New England, and her mother had the traditional principles of her time: she expected obedience from the small girl. At the same time, she expressed a less common concern for making her childhood happy. It seems that she was successful in achieving these two aims. For Sarah Bixby-Smith's account of her early years is an idyllic narration of life close to a bountiful nature which offered all kinds of delights:*


Our home was in a little valley, with no other houses in sight, but a mile and a half away, down a hill and across a bridge, lay the old town of San Juan Bautista, with its post-office, store, adobe inn and its homes, a medley of Spanish and American types. The old mission church with its long corridor, arched and tile-paved, and its garden, where peacocks used to walk and drop their shining feathers for a little girl to pick up, was the dominating feature of the place, its very cause for being. Inside was dim silence; there were strange dark pictures on the walls, and burning candles, a very large music book with big square notes, and a great Bible, chained to its desk.

There was another church in San Juan, one that was wooden, light, bare and small, where I learned from a tiny flowered card, "Blessed are the peacemakers," which, being interpreted for my benefit, meant, "Sallie mus'n't quarrel with little sister." I ate up a rosebud and wriggled in my seat during the long sermon and wondered about the lady who brushed her hair smooth and low on one side and high on the other. Had she only one ear?

I have been told that my church attendance involved certain distractions for my fellow worshippers, and that my presence was tolerated only because of the desirability of training me in correct Sunday habits. On one occasion my restlessness led me into disaster. My parents had gone to the chancel, carrying my little sister Anne for her christening, leaving me in the pew. It was a strange performance. The minister took the baby in his arms, and then put something from a silver bowl on her forehead, and began to pray. I must know what was in the bowl! Everybody had shut-eyes, so there was a good chance for me to find out without troubling anyone. I darted forward and managed to discover that the mysterious something was water, for I spilled it over myself.

The trip to church was made in a two-seated, low carriage, with a span of horses, while my every day rides with Papa, were in a single buggy, but with two horses, also, for we had far to go and liked going fast. Sometimes we went to Gilroy, and sometimes to Hollister, often just about the ranch to the various sheep camps, which were widely separated.

I began these business trips almost as soon as I was old enough to sit up alone. When we started I would be very erect and alert at Papa's side, but before long I would droop and be retired to the bottom of the buggy, where, wrapped in a robe, and with his foot for a pillow, I would sleep contentedly for hours. I remember my disgust when I had grown so long that I must change my habit and put my legs back under the seat, instead of lying across in the correct way. I objected to change, but was persuaded that it would be inconvenient for me to get tangled, during some pleasant dream, in the actualities of the spokes of a moving wheel.

At one time Papa and I were very much occupied clearing a field, a piece of work which he must have reserved for himself, since there were no other men about. He also enjoyed chopping wood and this may have been his "daily dozen." We cut down several large oak trees, cleared out underbrush, and, piling it up against the great stumps, built fires that roared for a time and then smouldered for days.

Sometimes I walked with Mamma on the hills back of the house, and when we were tired we would sit down under a tree and she would tell me a story and make me a chaplet of oak leaves, folding and fastening each leaf to the next in a most ingenious way. If our walk took us into the lower lands she made bewitching little baskets from the rushes that grew near the water's edge. I also found the strange equisitum, that I sometimes called "horse tail," and sometimes "stove-pipe," which latter I preferred, because none of the horses that I knew had disjointable tails, while the little hollow tubes of stem that fitted into each other so well must serve the fairies most excellently for their chimneys.

Several spring mornings as I grew older, I got up at dawn with Mamma, went to the early empty kitchen for a drink of milk, and then went out with her for a horseback ride, she in her long broadcloth habit and stiff silk hat, and I, a tiny timid girl, perched on a side-saddle atop a great horse. From the point of view of horsemanship I was not a great success, but the joy of the dawn air, the rising sun, the wildflowers, the companionship of my mother is mine forever.

It was on one of these morning expeditions when we were comparing notes about our tastes in colors, that I found she liked a strange shade of red that to me looked unattractive. I was overwhelmed by the thought that perhaps it did not look the same to both of us, and that if I saw it as she did I might like it also; but there was no way for either of us to know how it actually looked to the other! I realized the essential isolation of every human being. However, I forgot the loneliness when Papa joined us on the road beside the pond, where the wild lilac scattered its blue-violet lace on the over-hanging bank, and cut for me a willow whistle that sounded the shrill joy of being alive.

On the Sunday afternoon walks when we all went up into the hills together I learned, among other classics:

> "Little drops of water,
>     Little grains of sand,
>   Make a mighty ocean
>     And the wondrous land."

But it was at night when I was safely put in my bed that I heard through the open door, Mamma, at the parlor piano, singing to me:

> "I want to be an angel,
>     And with the angels stand,
> A crown upon my head,
>     A harp within my hand."

I suppose that neither she nor I were really in immediate haste for the fulfillment of that wish, but it made a good bed-time song. Another favorite was, *Shall we gather at the River?*, and there was occasionally a somber one called *Pass under the Rod*.

My bed was a very safe place, for did not angels guard it, "two at the foot, and two at the head"? I knew who my angels were,— my very own grandmother, who had died when my mother was a new baby, the aunt for whom I had been named, little Cousin Mary who really should have been guarding her brother Harry, and a fourth whom I have now forgotten.

The songs were not gay, but my life was not troubled by thoughts of death. Heaven seemed a nice place, somewhere, and angels and fairies were normal parts of my universe.

I did have a few minor troubles. My language was criticized. "You bet your boots" did not meet with maternal approval. Then, if I carelessly put my sunbonnet strings into my mouth, I got my tongue burned from the vinegar and cayenne pepper into which they had been dipped for the express purpose of making the process disagreeable. Those sunbonnets, with which my head was sheathed every time I started out into the airy out-of-doors, were my chief pests. I usually compromised my integrity by untying the strings as soon as I was out of sight. I would double back the corners of the bonnet, making it into a sort of cocked hat with a bow on top, made from the hated strings, thus letting my poor scratched ears out of captivity.

Papa and I went to the circus on every possible occasion. Once, at Hollister, I saw General and Mrs. Tom Thumb, Minnie Warren and Commodore Nutt, whose photograph—with Mr. Barnum—I have preserved. Minnie Warren was supposed to be the size of a six-year-old, but the standard for six-year-olds must have come out of the East. I was several inches taller than she.

A pretty lady, dressed in pink tarleton skirts, who rode several horses at a time, and jumped through tissue paper hoops, was my first heroine. Dick and I kept her picture for months on a ledge under the office desk, and there rendered her frequent homage.

The mention of this desk calls to mind other activities centering in that office. On one occasion, when I was suitably young, the spirit moved me to carry a shovelful of live coals out through the door to the porch, and there coax up a fire by the addition of kindling wood. The same spirit, or another, however, suggested a compensating action. I summoned my mother to see my "nice fire," to the salvation of the house.

Fire, candles, matches, revolvers, all held a fascination. It is evident that neither my cousin Harry nor I were intended for a violent death, for it was our custom to investigate from time to time his father's loaded revolver, turning the chambers about and removing and replacing the cartridges. Our faith in our ability to handle the dangerous weapon safely seems to have been justified by our success.

It was deemed wise to keep me occupied, so far as possible, in order to thwart Satan, ever on the lookout for idle hands. So I was taught to sew patchwork and to knit, to read and to spell. There were short periods when I had to stay in the house, but like most California children, I spent out-of-doors most of the time not given over to eating and sleeping. Now-a-days even those duties are attended to upon porches.

Under Mamma's guidance I once laboriously and secretly sewed "over and over" a gray and striped "comfort bag" for a birthday gift to Papa. It was modelled on the bags made for the soldiers in the Union army when my mother was a girl. We made a special trip to Hollister to buy its contents, black and white thread, coarse needles, buttons, wax, blunt scissors, and to top off, pink and white sugary peppermint drops. That bag remained in service for twenty years, going always in father's satchel whenever he went away. It came to my rescue once when I had torn my skirt from hem to band. As he sewed up the rent for me with nice big stitches, first on one side and then on the other, he told me it was a shoemaker's stitch and had the advantage of bringing the edges together just as they had been originally, without puckering the cloth. Mamma used the same stitch to mend the torn pages of books and sheet music, in those days before Mr. Dennison invented his transparent tape.

Time went by slowly, slowly, as it does when one is young. All day there was play, except for the occasional stint of patchwork, or the reading lesson,—every day but Sunday, with its church in the forenoon and stories and walks in the afternoon. Mamma would say, "When I was a little girl in Maine," until to me Maine meant Paradise. In that country there was a brook where one could wade, and the great river, on whose banks in the woods children could picnic and hunt for wild berries,—what a charm in the words, "going berrying!" Even the nest of angry hornets with their sharp stings did not lessen my enthusiasm. At San Justo there were no Martha and Susan, no Julia and Ella for me to play with,— just boys, (who seemed to answer very well for little tom-boy Sallie when Maine was not in mind).

When I heard of snow and sleighs and sleds and the wonderful attic with its cunning low curtained windows and the doll colony who lived there, I forgot the charms of the ranch and the boy play. It was nothing to me that there were horses and cows, ducks, geese and chickens. It was nothing to me that Dick and I could make figure-four traps, and, walking beyond the wool-barn, set them on the hill side for quail; that once we had the excitement of finding our trap upset, our captives gone, and great bear tracks all about. The long sunny days of freedom with the boys, the great herds of sheep that came up for shearing, the many rides with my father through the lovely valleys and over the hills were commonplace, just what I had always known. No, life in California was very tame compared with the imagined joys of Maine.

*A huge part of the book is devoted to the history of the development of the ranch which belonged to Sarah Bixby-Smith's family and of the establishment of the firm of Flint, Bixby and Co.; it was based primarily on stock-raising, but its owners were very enterprising and branched out into many other lines. The concern was extremely prosperous and at one time a communal arrangement was worked out: the families of the three partners lived on the ranch and each wife took the responsibility for running the household and the servants in turn for a month. It lasted for fifteen years; many trips were interspersed to relieve the strain. Tragedies occurred, which darkened the atmosphere: Mr. Bixby's first wife, with whom he had no children, died six years after coming out West. His second wife died after eleven years of marriage, just after the family was moved to Los Angeles, when she could at last have her own home. She left three small children, and one of her sisters came to replace her. From this point on, a double strain runs through the narrative, which provides detailed information on conditions in Los Angeles in the 1880s and also descriptions of the various activities on the ranch at San Justo:*

Our home in Los Angeles became the headquarters for the out-of-town relatives, and several times a week we had some of them for luncheon guests. On the other hand we of the town grasped every chance to spend a day, a week, or the long summer vacation at one of the adobes. All the festival days were shared. Cerritos claimed the Fourth of July most often, for its bare court yard offered a spot free from fire hazard. What a satisfying supply of fire-works our combined resources offered! There were torpedoes, safe for babies, fire-crackers of all sizes, double-headed Dutchmen, Chinese bombs,—to make the day glorious,— and, for the exciting evening (one of the two yearly occasions when I was permitted to stay up beyond bird-time) there were pinwheels that flung out beauty from the top of the hitching post, there were dozens of roman candles with their streams of enveloping fire, and luscious shooting stars and sky-rockets, that rose majestically with a disdainful shriek, as they spurned the earth and took a golden road to the sky.

Inter-family feasting at the three homes in turn marked Thanksgiving, Christmas and New Years Day. It was the laden tree on Christmas Eve that offered the second annual escape from early bed-time rules, in itself enough to key one up to ecstacy, without the added intense joy of mysterious expectation and satisfied possession of the largesse of Santa Claus. A Christmas celebration at Cerritos when I was four stands out distinctly in my memory,—a tall, tall tree, as much as twenty feet high, judged by present standards, stood in the upper chamber whose ceiling, unlifted by an excited imagination, is about eight feet. From that tree came Isabel, my most beloved doll, a small bottle of Hoyt's German Cologne,—how I delighted in perfume,—a small iron stove. The latter was put to a use not contemplated by the patron saint, for I am sure he did not want me to spend the whole of the following morning in duress vile in my bed, because of that stove. This was what happened. After breakfast my almost-twin cousin Harry and I, while our mothers chatted at table, re-visited the scene of the past evening's festivities and wished to bring back some of the joy of it. Drawn curtains gave semi-darkness, candles stolen from the closet under the stairs and placed lighted in the wide window-sills gave a subdued light, and many little stubs of the gay Christmas tapers from the tree made a wonderful illumination under the bed and in the tent made by the turned-back bed clothes.

But it was the escaping fire from the paper-stuffed toy stove which stood on the sheet about the foot of the tree that made us decide to hear the clamoring for admittance of the suspicious mothers,—we had sense enough to summon help when conditions arose with which we were unable to cope. But Harry was cannier than I, for he sent me to open the door where the worried women stood, while he escaped from the far end, going down a ladder from the flat roof of the wing to the tall weeds beyond the huge wood-pile. I was apprehended and punished. He wasn't, not being subject to the same administration of discipline as was I. Then it was that I learned that justice does not always prevail in this world.

This Christmas visit affords my earliest memories of Cerritos, although I know I had been there several times before. It was the long blissful summer when I was seven that packed my mind with vivid pictures and remembrance of joyful activity. Is not seven a peak in childhood,—old enough for self direction, young enough for thrills?

After this visit was over and we departed for nearby Los Angeles to make ourselves a new home my life went on in parallel lines, school days in town, vacation days at the ranches. I should tell of them both at the same time to be truly realistic, but the exigencies of narration make it seem better to write of the two experiences as if they were separate. So first, the ranches.

I have told at length of my birthplace, the San Justo. Although it, as well as the southern ranches, was devoted to sheep raising, there were many differences between them. The houses and gardens at San Justo were of New England type, built and developed according to the early associations of the young men. At the other ranches the homes were of adobe, old ones, handed down from an earlier period.

The locations and surrounding country also differed greatly. In the north the house stood in a valley between wooded hills, with no wide outlook. The southern houses were each placed on the brow of a mesa, with a view across a characteristic California river which might be a dangerous torrent or a strip of dry sand, according to the season of the year. The eyes could follow across flat lands, treeless, except for a few low-growing willows, to far, blue, mysterious mountains. It was a very empty land, empty of people and towns, of trees and cultivated lands.

The people on the northern ranch were but two miles from a village, with friends, a post office and a church, and San Francisco, a real city, not far away nor hard to reach. When Aunt Margaret came to Los Cerritos there was not a railroad nor a street car within five hundred miles, and Los Angeles, the small village, was sixteen miles away—by horse power, not gasoline or electricity.

However, distance did not prevent the making of good friends, and the isolation of the frontier life was broken by an occasional visit to San Francisco, one or two trips to distant Maine (Aunt Margaret traveled East on the first through sleeper to go over the new railroad), and by the coming of visitors from neighboring ranches or from away.

On one occasion the ranch welcomed for a week the officers of the flag-ship, Pensacola, anchored at San Pedro, including Admiral Thatcher, an old friend of the family, who was in command of the Pacific squadron.

Often there was unexpected company in this land of great distances and few inns. Even after my day wayfarers used occasionally to drop in, so that it was necessary to be prepared to double a meal on short notice. Liebig's Extract of Beef many a time counteracted in soup the weakening effect of quantity-extending water. Locked up in a large tin box a ripening fruit cake awaited an emergency call for dessert, and there was always an unlimited supply of mutton and chickens.

The young people did not have time to be lonely. Uncle Jotham was engaged in building up a large sheep business and Aunt Margaret had her sister for company; she had her children and sufficient help so that she did not suffer any of the hardships that are usually associated with pioneer life. I have observed that if a woman is occupied with a young family, and of a reasonably contented disposition it makes no great difference whether the people outside her home are near or far, few or many;—there are books for spare minutes.

This foggy morning Uncle John was driving and as it was April there was a pearly light over everything. Every hair of his beard and eyebrows was strung with tiny drops of water; we had a most happy hour, drawn by Thunderbolt and Lightfoot. The next day came word of sudden sickness. In ten days my merry young uncle was dead. It did not seem possible. It was my first realization of death. And childhood ended. When my mother had gone I was ten, and while it seemed strange, it did not stand out from all the strangeness of the world as did this later coming face to face with the mystery. In the case of my mother I missed her more as years went by than I did at the time of the actual separation.

Aunt Martha was distressed when after mother's death she came to us, to find how often we children played that our dolls had died. We held a funeral service and buried them under the sofa in the parlor after a solemn procession through the long hall. We wore towels over our heads for mourning veils, copied not from any used in our family, but from those of two tall, dark sisters who sat in front of us in church, whose crepe-covered dresses and veils that reached the floor were a source of unfailing wonder.

As I look back it does not seem to me that the playing of funerals involved any disrespect or lack of love for our mother, but was, rather, a transference into our daily activities of a strange experience that had come to us.

We had another play that was connected with a death, but at the time I did not recognize the relationship. Just before we came south for the long visit, Harry's five year old sister Margaret had died of diphtheria and was buried in the ranch garden. Soon after our arrival a mason came and set up a gravestone for her. Beside her grave were those of an older sister, and of a little unnamed baby. The ranch had been robbed of its children and the heart of the young mother sorrowed. Harry had been devoted to Maggie and was disconsolate without her, so that I must have been a most welcome visitor for the lonely small boy. Taking our cue from the mason we spent many hours in the making of mud tombstones, (I modelling and he polishing them and putting on the inscriptions), for our bird and animal burial plot over near the graves of the children.

We wandered about day after day, in the cool summer sunshine,—so near the ocean that oppressive heat was rare. As soon as breakfast was over, away we went. I was clad in a daily clean blue-and-white checked gingham apron, Harry, although but seven, in long trousers, "like the men." We romped in barn or garden, visited the corrals or gathered the eggs, we played in the old stage left in the weeds outside the fence, or worked with the tools in the blacksmith shop. When the long tin horn sounded at noon the call for the men's dinner we returned to the house to be scrubbed. I was put into a white apron for meal time, but back into my regimentals as soon as it was over. A second whitening occurred for supper and lasted until bedtime.

Sometimes we went down to the orchard, where all summer long we could pick ripe apples and pears; and occasionally, as a rare treat, we were allowed to go barefoot and play in the river, reduced to its summer safe level. One day, after having built elaborate sand houses and laid out rival gardens, planted with bits of every shrub and water weed we could find, we went to a place deep enough for us to sit down in water up to our necks, where, grinning over the top of the water, we enjoyed an impromptu bath. We hung our clothes on a willow until they were dry and then wondered what uncanny power made our mothers know that we had been wet.

A half mile or so beyond this ford lived Uncle Marcellus and Aunt Adelaide, and their boys, Edward and Herbert, who used to come over to help at shearing time. Just inside their front door they had a barometer shaped like a little house where a woman came out and stood most of the time, but if it were going to rain the gallant husband sent her inside and stood guard himself.

The largest and loveliest hyacinths I have ever known grew for this aunt, and she had tame fish in her pond that would come and eat breadcrumbs which we gave them. Aunt Adelaide was a very short woman with the shiniest, smooth, dark hair that never turned gray. It went in big waves down the side of her face. Once she showed mother a number of large new books and told her about a way to study at home and learn just as if you were going to college, and a long time afterwards she showed us a big piece of paper that she said was a chatauqua diploma and meant that she had studied all those books.

Every time we went over to the station on the railroad, or came back, or went to Compton to church or camp meeting, or came back, we always saw the old house that had been the first ranch house, belonging to the Cotas, but which had now only pigeons, many, many shining lovely pigeons living in it,—and so many fleas that we called it the "Flea House" and knew better than ever to go into it.

But we were not afraid to go into the deserted coyote hole that we found in a bank down on the side of the hill below the house. Luckily we did not find a rattlesnake sharing it with us.

The sum of child happiness cannot be told. How good it is to wander in the sun, smelling wild celery, or the cottonwood leaves, nibbling yellow, pungent mustard blossoms while pushing through the tangle; how good to feel a pulled tule give as the crisp, white end comes up from the mud and water, or to bury one's face in the flowing sulphur well for a queer tasting drink, or to cut unnumbered jack-o-lanterns while sitting high on a great pile of pumpkins of every pretty shape and color, and singing in the salty air; how good to wander in the sun, to be young and tireless, to have cousins and ranches!

*The development of southern California is then outlined. The narrative next turns to Sarah Bixby-Smith's education and to the way schools functioned in Los Angeles: the primitive conditions added to the enjoyment of the pupils but made the teachers' task more difficult. Sarah Bixby-Smith spent some time at Pomona College and went on to Wellesley, then returned to Los Angeles to keep her father's house. She pursued various intellectual and artistic activities. The home was broken up after her father's death in 1896; the rest of her life was spent outside California, but she made frequent visits to the state.*

*Sarah Bixby-Smith's recreation of her childhood on a ranch is made endearing by her openness to the beauty of nature, her diversified interests, her ability to convey the freshness and sense of wonder which characterize a child's perceptions. It covers a wide range of expressions, from extreme delight to a pathetic kind of sadness verging on the morbid at times. The dominant note is one of bliss, however. The warm family environment in which she lived, as well as the pastoral setting, helped this particular child to emerge relatively unscarred from the loss of her mother, which could have been a traumatic experience.*

# Life among the Piutes; their wrongs and claims

Sarah Winnemucca Hopkins

Edit. by Mrs. Horace Mann. (Boston: For Sale by Cupples, Upham and Co., G.P. Putnam's Sons, New York, and by the author) 1883

*In the preface, the editor states that Mrs. Hopkins came East to inform people about the Indians' misfortunes and sufferings, and that her dominant aim in her book was to give the truth about them. It starts as an autobiography (the author indicates that she was born around 1844) and dwells on childhood experiences. There is a constant attempt to embrace the whole of the tribe in the account, and to give expression to the ideals which governed the way of life of the Piutes. The following passage is a good example of the way in which the narrative moves back and forth, from the particular to the general, from the presentations of the principles which controlled the education of children to the author's own individual reactions:*

Our children are very carefully taught to be good. Their parents tell them stories, traditions of old times, even of the first mother of the human race; and love stories, stories of giants, and fables; and when they ask if these last stories are true, they answer, "Oh, it is only coyote," which means that they are make-believe stories. Coyote is the name of a mean, crafty little animal, half wolf, half dog, and stands for everything low. It is the greatest term of reproach one Indian has for another. Indians do not swear,—they have no words for swearing till they learn them of

white men. The worst they call each is bad or coyote; but they are
very sincere with one another, and if they think each other in the
wrong they say so.

We are taught to love everybody. We don't need to be taught
to love our fathers and mothers. We love them without being told
to. Our tenth cousin is as near to us as our first cousin; and we don't
marry into our relations. Our young women are not allowed to talk
to any young man that is not their cousin, except at the festive
dances, when both are dressed in their best clothes, adorned with
beads, feathers or shells, and stand alternately in the ring and take
hold of hands. These are very pleasant occasions to all the young
people.

Many years ago, when my people were happier than they are
now, they used to celebrate the Festival of Flowers in the spring. I
have been to three of them only in the course of my life.

Oh, with what eagerness we girls used to watch every spring
for the time when we could meet with our hearts' delight, the
young men, whom in civilized life you call beaux. We would all go
in company to see if the flowers we were named for were yet in
bloom, for almost all the girls are named for flowers. We talked
about them in our wigwams, as if we were the flowers, saying,
"Oh, I saw myself today in full bloom!" We would talk all the
evening in this way in our families with such delight, and such
beautiful thoughts of the happy day when we should meet with
those who admired us and would help us to sing our flower-songs
which we made up as we sang. But we were always sorry for those
that were not named after some flower, because we knew they
could not join in the flower-songs like ourselves, who were named
for flowers of all kinds.

At last one evening came a beautiful voice, which made every
girl's heart throb with happiness. It was the chief, and every one
hushed to hear what he said to-day.

"My dear daughters, we are told that you have seen your-
selves in the hills and in the valleys, in full bloom. Five days from
to-day your festival day will come. I know every young man's
heart stops beating while I am talking. I know how it was with me
many years ago. I used to wish the Flower Festival would come
every day. Dear young men and young women, you are saying,
'Why put it off five days?' But you all know that is our rule. It gives
you time to think, and to show your sweetheart your flower."

All the girls who have flower-names dance along together, and those who have not go together also. Our fathers and mothers and grandfathers and grandmothers make a place for us where we can dance. Each one gathers the flower she is named for, and then all weave them into wreaths and crowns and scarfs, and dress up in them.

Some girls are named for rocks and are called rock-girls, and they find some pretty rocks which they carry; each one such a rock as she is named for, or whatever she is named for. If she cannot, she can take a branch of sage-brush, or a bunch of rye-grass, which have no flower.

They all go marching along, each girl in turn singing of herself; but she is not a girl any more,—she is a flower singing. She sings of herself, and her sweetheart, dancing along by her side, helps her sing the song she makes.

I will repeat what we say of ourselves. "I, Sarah Winnemucca, am a shell-flower, such as I wear on my dress. My name is Thocmetony. I am so beautiful! Who will come and dance with me while I am so beautiful? Oh, come and be happy with me! I shall be beautiful while the earth lasts. Somebody will always admire me; and who will come and be happy with me in the Spirit-land? I shall be beautiful forever there. Yes, I shall be more beautiful than my shell-flower, my Thocmetony! Then, come, oh come, and dance and be happy with me!" The young men sing with us as they dance beside us.

Our parents are waiting for us somewhere to welcome us home. And then we praise the sage-brush and the rye-grass that have no flower, and the pretty rocks that some are named for; and then we present our beautiful flowers to these companions who could carry none. And so all are happy; and that closes the beautiful day.

My people have been so unhappy for a long time they wish now to *disincrease*, instead of multiply. The mothers are afraid to have more children, for fear they shall have daughters, who are not safe even in their mother's presence.

The grandmothers have the special care of the daughters just before and after they come to womanhood. The girls are not allowed to get married until they have come to womanhood; and that period is recognized as a very sacred thing, and is the subject of a festival, and has peculiar customs. The young woman is set apart under the care of two of her friends, somewhat older, and a little wigwam, called a teepee, just big enough for the three, is made for them, to which they retire. She goes through certain labors which are thought to be strengthening, and these last twenty-five days. Every day, three times a day, she must gather, and pile up as high as she can, five stacks of wood. This makes fifteen stacks a day. At the end of every five days the attendants take her to a river to bathe. She fasts from all flesh-meat during these twenty-five days, and continues to do this for five days in every month all her life. At the end of the twenty-five days she returns to the family lodge, and gives all her clothing to her attendants in payment for their care. Sometimes the wardrobe is quite extensive.

It is thus publicly known that there is another marriageable woman, and any young man interested in her, or wishing to form an alliance, comes forward. But the courting is very different from the courting of the white people. He never speaks to her, or visits the family, but endeavors to attract her attention by showing his horsemanship, etc. As he knows that she sleeps next to her grandmother in the lodge, he enters in full dress after the family has retired for the night, and seats himself at her feet. If she is not awake, her grandmother wakes her. He does not speak to either young woman or grandmother, but when the young woman wishes him to go away, she rises and goes and lies down by the side of her mother. He then leaves as silently as he came in. This goes on sometimes for a year or longer, if the young woman has not made up her mind. She is never forced by her parents to marry against her wishes. When she knows her own mind, she makes a confidant of her grandmother, and then the young man is summoned by the father of the girl, who asks him in her presence, if he really loves his daughter, and reminds him, if he says he does, of all the duties of a husband. He then asks his daughter the same question, and sets before her minutely all her duties. And these duties are not slight. She is to dress the game, prepare the food, clean the buckskins, make his moccasins, dress his hair, bring all the wood,—in short, do all the household work. She promises to "be himself," and she fulfils her promise. Then he is invited to a feast and all his relatives with him. But after the betrothal, a teepee is erected for the presents that pour in from both sides.

At the wedding feast, all the food is prepared in baskets. The young woman sits by the young man, and hands him the basket of food prepared for him with her own hands. He does not take it with his right hand; but seizes her wrist, and takes it with the left hand. This constitutes the marriage ceremony, and the father pronounces them man and wife. They go to a wigwam of their own, where they live till the first child is born. This event also is celebrated. Both father and mother fast from all flesh, and the father goes through the labor of piling the wood for twenty-five days, and assumes all his wife's household work during that time. If he does not do his part in the care of the child, he is considered an outcast. Every five days his child's basket is changed for a new one, and the five are all carefully put away at the end of the days, the last one containing the navel-string, carefully wrapped up, and all are put up into a tree, and the child put into a new and ornamented basket. All this respect shown to the mother and child makes the parents feel their responsibility, and makes the tie between parents and children very strong. The young mothers often get together and exchange their experiences about the attentions of their husbands; and inquire of each other if the fathers did their duty to their children, and were careful of their wives' health. When they are married they give away all the clothing they have ever worn, and dress themselves anew. The poor people have the same ceremonies, but do not make a feast of it, for want of means.

Our boys are introduced to manhood by their hunting of deer and mountain-sheep. Before they are fifteen or sixteen, they hunt only small game, like rabbits, hares, fowls, etc. They never eat what they kill themselves, but only what their father or elder brothers kill. When a boy becomes strong enough to use larger bows made of sinew, and arrows that are ornamented with eagle-feathers, for the first time, he kills game that is large, a deer or an antelope, or a mountain-sheep. Then he brings home the hide, and his father cuts it into a long coil which is wound into a loop, and the boy takes his quiver and throws it on his back as if he was going on a hunt, and takes his bow and arrows in his hand. Then his father throws the loop over him, and he jumps through it. This he does five times. Now for the first time he eats the flesh of the animal he has killed, and from that time he eats whatever he kills but he has always been faithful to his parents' command not to eat what he has killed before. He can now do whatever he likes, for now he is a man, and no longer considered a boy. If there is a war he can go to it; but the Piutes, and other tribes west of the Rocky Mountains, are not fond of going to war. I never saw a war-dance but once. It is always the whites that begin the wars, for their own selfish purposes. The government does not take care to send the good men; there are a plenty who would take pains to see and understand the chiefs and learn their characters, and their good will to the whites. But the whites have not waited to find out how good the Indians were, and what ideas they had of God, just like those of Jesus, who called him Father, just as my people do, and told men to do to others as they would be done by, just as my people teach their children to do. My people teach their children never to make fun of any one, no matter how they look. If you see your brother or sister doing something wrong, look away, or go away from them. If you make fun of bad persons, you make yourself beneath them. Be kind to all, both poor and rich, and feed all that come to your wigwam, and your name can be spoken of by every one far and near. In this way you will make many friends for yourself. Be kind both to bad and good, for you don't know your own heart. This is the way my people teach their children. It was handed down from father to son for many generations. I never in my life saw our children rude as I have seen white children and grown people in the streets.

The chief's tent is the largest tent, and it is the council-tent, where every one goes who wants advice. In the evenings the head men go there to discuss everything, for the chiefs do not rule like tyrants; they discuss everything with their people, as a father would in his family. Often they sit up all night. They discuss the doings of all, if they need to be advised. If a boy is not doing well they talk that over, and if the women are interested they can share in the talks. If there is not room enough inside, they all go out of doors, and make a great circle. The men are in the inner circle, for there would be too much smoke for the women inside. The men never talk without smoking first. The women sit behind them in another circle, and if the children wish to hear, they can be there too. The women know as much as the men do, and their advice is often asked. We have a republic as well as you. The council-tent is our Congress, and anybody can speak who has anything to say, women and all. They are always interested in what their husbands are doing and thinking about. And they take some part even in the wars. They are always near at hand when fighting is going on, ready to snatch their husbands up and carry them off if wounded or killed. One splendid woman that my brother Lee married after his first wife died, went out into the battle-field after her uncle was killed, and went into the front ranks and cheered the men on. Her uncle's horse was dressed in a splendid robe made of eagles' feathers and she snatched it off and swung it in the face of the enemy, who always carry off everything they find, as much as to say, "You can't have that—I have it safe"; and she staid and took her uncle's place, as brave as any of the men. It means something when the women promise their fathers to make their husbands *themselves*. They faithfully keep with them in all the dangers they can share. They not only take care of their children together, but they do everything together; and when they grow blind, which I am sorry to say is very common, for the smoke they live in destroys their eyes at last, they take sweet care of one another. Marriage is a sweet thing when people love each other. If women could go into your Congress I think justice would soon be done to the Indians. I can't tell about all Indians; but I know my own people are kind to everybody that does not do them harm; but they will not be imposed upon, and when people are too bad they rise up and resist them. This seems to me all right. It is different from being revengeful. There is nothing cruel about our people. They never scalped a human being.

The chiefs do not live in idleness. They work with their people, and they are always poor for the following reason. It is the custom with my people to be very hospitable. When people visit them in their tents, they always set before them the best food they have, and if there is not enough for themselves they go without.

The chief's tent is the one always looked for when visitors come, and sometimes many come the same day. But they are all well received. I have often felt sorry for my brother, who is now the chief, when I saw him go without food for this reason. He would say, "We will wait and eat afterwards what is left." Perhaps little would be left, and when the agents did not give supplies and rations, he would have to go hungry.

At the council, one is always appointed to repeat at the time everything that is said on both sides, so that there may be no misunderstanding, and one person at least is present from every lodge, and after it is over, he goes and repeats what is decided upon at the door of the lodge, so all may be understood. For there is never any quarrelling in the tribe, only friendly counsels. The sub-chiefs are appointed by the great chief for special duties. There is no quarrelling about that, for neither sub-chief or great chief has any salary. It is this which makes the tribe so united and attached to each other, and makes it so dreadful to be parted. They would rather all die at once than be parted. They believe that in the Spirit-land those that die still watch over those that are living. When I was a child in California, I heard the Methodist minister say that everybody that did wrong was burned in hell forever. I was so frightened it made me very sick. He said the blessed ones in heaven looked down and saw their friends burning and could not help them. I wanted to be unborn, and cried so that my mother and the others told me it was not so, that it was only here that people did wrong and were in the hell that it made, and that those that were in the Spirit-land saw us here and were sorry for us. But we should go to them when we died, where there was never any wrong-doing, and so no hell. That is our religion.

My people capture antelopes by charming them, but only some of the people are charmers. My father was one of them, and once I went with him on an antelope hunt.

The antelopes move in herds in the winter, and as late in the spring as April. At this time there was said to be a large herd in a certain place, and my father told all his people to come together in ten days to go with him in his hunt. He told them to bring their wives with them, but no small children. When they came, at the end of ten days, he chose two men, who he said were to be his messengers to the antelopes. They were to have two large torches made of sage-brush bark, and after he had found a place for his camp, he marked out a circle around which the wigwams were to be placed, putting his own in the middle of the western side, and leaving an opening directly opposite in the middle of the eastern side, which was towards the antelopes.

The people who were with him in the camp then made another circle to the east of the one where their wigwams were, and made six mounds of sage-brush and stones on the sides of it, with a space of a hundred yards or more from one mound to the next one, but with no fence between the mounds. These mounds were made high, so that they could be seen from far off.

The women and boys and old men who were in the camp, and who were working on the mounds, were told to be very careful not to drop anything and not to stumble over a sage-brush root, or a stone, or anything, and not to have any accident, but to do everything perfectly and to keep thinking about the antelopes all the time, and not to let their thoughts go away to anything else. It took five days to charm the antelopes, and if anybody had an accident he must tell of it.

Every morning early, when the bright morning star could be seen, the people sat around the opening to the circle, with my father sitting in the middle of the opening, and my father lighted his pipe and passed it to his right, and the pipe went round the circle five times. And at night they did the same thing.

After they had smoked the pipe, my father took a kind of drum, which is used in this charming, and made music with it. This is the only kind of musical instrument which my people have, and it is only used for this antelope-charming. It is made of a hide of some large animal, stuffed with grass, so as to make it sound hollow, and then wound around tightly from one end to the other with a cord as large as my finger. One end of this instrument is large, and it tapers down to the other end, which is small, so that it makes a different sound on the different parts. My father took a stick and rubbed this stick from one end of the instrument to the other, making a penetrating, vibrating sound, that could be heard afar off, and he sang, and all his people sang with him.

After that the two men who were messengers went out to see the antelopes. They carried their torches in their right hands, and one of them carried a pipe in his left hand. They started from my father's wigwam and went straight across the camp to the opening; then they crossed, and one went around the second circle to the right and the other went to the left, till they met on the other side of the circle. Then they crossed again, and one went round the herd of antelopes one way and the other went round the other way, but they did not let the antelopes see them. When they met on the other side of the herd of antelopes, they stopped and smoked the pipe, and then they crossed, and each man came back on the track of the other to the camp, and told my father what they saw and what the antelopes were doing.

This was done every day for five days, and after the first day all the men and women and boys followed the messengers, and went around the circle they were to enter. On the fifth day the antelopes were charmed, and the whole herd followed the tracks of my people and entered the circle where the mounds were, coming in at the entrance, bowing and tossing their heads, and looking sleepy and under a powerful spell. They ran round and round inside the circle just as if there was a fence all around it and they could not get out, and they staid there until my people had killed every one. But if anybody had dropped anything, or had stumbled and had not told about it, then when the antelopes came to the place where he had done that, they threw off the spell and rushed wildly out of the circle at that place.

My brother can charm horses in the same way.

The Indian children amuse themselves a great deal by modelling in mud. They make herds of animals, which are modelled exceedingly well, and after setting them up, shoot at them with their little bows and arrows. They also string beads of different colors and show natural good taste.

*This is an idealistic description of Indian customs and mores, and one feels a constant desire to explain the ideas which were behind them in order to draw the reader's sympathy and understanding. Mrs. Hopkins shows how the tribe used to live in close harmony with nature, and implies that there was a time when they were happy. Words connoting beauty, joy, love are used constantly. Detailed descriptions of certain rituals and celebrations are given, and insights are provided into the way the families and the tribe were organized. There is much insistence on such principles as duty and responsibility, on the strong ties which linked the members of the tribe, and on the good will and peacefulness of all. She draws contrasts with the institutions and habits of white people, showing for instance that the Indian conception of religion was much more humane, that love among relatives was instinctive, and that children were taught primarily to be kind to every one.*

*Mrs. Hopkins's personal story is interwoven in the saga of her tribe. Her grandfather was the chief, and they lived near Humbolt Lake, Nevada, at the time whites started coming into the area. She uses quotes from her grandfather's and her father's speeches to prove their good will and implies that the arrival of white immigrants in ever growing numbers disrupted their peaceful life and forced them to move to California.*

*The second part of her book is an account of the trials the Piutes had to bear, of the wars and their causes. She constantly stresses their good intentions and shows that the promises which were made to them were never fulfilled. Her own contribution was to serve as an interpreter, and in an appendix she has included letters which acknowledge her services to the whites and her assistance to her people.*

*Her book is a vindication of her tribe, and her life's aim was to obtain a redress to the wrongs they had suffered; she hoped that her lectures and writings would promote a new and more favorable policy toward her people. It provides a valuable account of events viewed totally from the Indian point of view. The chapters which concern the customs of the Piutes are thought-provoking, and her evocation of their life is both sensitive and delicate. Her very simple words and the constant link established between the people and nature create the impression that an idyllic state of innocence and joy existed at the time when whites had not yet started to invade Nevada. It would be hard to imagine a more moving plea in favor of the Piutes than this very feminine presentation of their traditional way of life and of the ideals upon which it was based.[1]*

---

1. A biographical section on this author can be found in Elinor Rickey, *Eminent Women of the West* (Berkeley: Howell North Books), 1975.

# Memories of Pioneer Childhood and Youth in French Corral and North San Juan, Nevada County, California. With a brief narrative of later life, told by Edith White, emigrant of 1859, to Linnie Marsh Wolfe, 1936

Edith White

*Edith White's* Memories *were written from an oral narrative she made during a series of interviews; in the first of these, an outline was mapped out, which was subsequently filled in; the narrator's own words have been preserved in the written text.[1] She was born in Iowa in 1855. An emigrant company which comprised the family headed by her Grandfather Stanton and some friends was formed, and they set off in 1859. The trip was long and uncomfortable; it involved dangers such as crossing rivers and being attacked by Indians, and was complicated by illnesses. But the family emerged from it unscathed:*

When we reached Washoe, Nevada, my grandparents decided to settle there, and the rest of us went on to California. We landed at Georgetown in Eldorado County. We had no money, only our wagon and oxen. But Father was resourceful. He sold the wagon and oxen and got a job. After a few months we moved to French Corral in Nevada County, where his brother, Lovell White, had already settled and opened a general store. French Corral, a small town of about 500 people, was huddled in a small valley among the hills. It was first settled by French Canadians. Hence the name.

Father never mined. He didn't like the uncertainty of it, and never speculated with his earnings. But he established a stable business by selling picks, spades, and shovels, also other miner's tools; and by manufacturing for sale tinware and hydraulic iron pipe out of raw material hauled up by mule teams from Marysville, thirty miles distant. So while miners 'struck it rich' and sometimes lost, he went on his way, thrifty and industrious, making a good living for his family.

When we first went to French Corral, the town was crowded with miners and their families, and all that we could get to live in was a shabby old cabin that a miner moved out of that we might move in. Father and Mother cleaned it up, and added to it. Then Father, who didn't have any money to buy furniture, made chairs and tables out of drygoods boxes, and Mother covered them with chintz calico. It was my parents' way to improve everything they had to do with, and we soon had a very attractive home. Years later Father used to say, "That little cabin was the prettiest home we ever had!" Some time afterwards Father bought a frame house under a big pine-tree, and we moved to it. Mother planted flowers and father started an orchard, and we had a fine vegetable garden. But we children liked best of all the tall pine-tree that every day during the season, shed a harvest of tiny nuts upon the ground beneath, and we gathered the crop every day.

During the summer solstice of 1861, when the weather was terribly hot, my little brother Nathan was born. I welcomed him with most loving arms. He was a beautiful boy and I helped in the care of him and fairly worshiped him. I think I associate almost every joy of my childhood with this cherished child. The three of us had a happy childhood. It was an ideal town for children to grow up in, democratic and brotherly in spirit, where children didn't get any false ideas of social caste. The nabobs of the town, if there were any, were the mine-superintendents and their families. But they were friendly, and always ready to help. I remember Mr. William Eddy as one of the superintendents, and the wealthiest man in town. His wife was a little aloof, but he was a friendly townsman. My uncle Lovell White was also a man of importance. He was a man of fine intelligence and the sort that would be outstanding in any community.

Strange as it may seem a highly respected citizen of French Corral was the town's only saloon keeper, Mr. George Parshley. He was honest and never one of his own best customers! Everybody felt a good deal of sympathy for him because of his family troubles. His young wife deserted him and left him alone to take care of their little daughter, Lydia. The latter was a pretty blond child, about the age of my sister Olive. Mother took Lydia to board and cared for her like one of her own children. Mr. Parshley never got over being grateful. In hot weather—and it was regularly about 110 degrees on a summer's day—he would bring us cool sherry cobblers, made of light wine, sugar and ice water.

But to get to the happy life of the children, and their share in the simple, pastoral pleasures of the village. The soil was good, and everybody had gardens with roses and oleanders, vegetable gardens, and strawberry vines and every other kind of berry vines, as well as every conceivable variety of temperate zone fruit. It was a land of plenty.

And everyone had chickens and a cow. The cows of the community were pastured out on the hills, and each night one of the villagers—they took turns at it—went after the herd. It was one of my greatest pleasures to go with my father when it was his turn. The hills were lovely, especially in the spring. There were many kinds of trees, pines, oaks, manzanitas, etc. Often as we climbed some high hill after a stray cow, we looked off over the mountains and saw range beyond range in the pale blue distance. As far as the eye could see, there were only mountains. And up there in the clear air we could hear the far-away music of the ten mule teams as they toiled up the narrow winding grades, carrying their loads of freight. Each pair of leaders carried bells suspended from iron frames rising from their collars. The grades were narrow and these bells were warnings for other teams that they might meet, for there were occasionally wide places for teams to pass.

Then we had wonderful picnics on the top of the highest hill. On every Mayday we had a little ceremony and crowned a Mayqueen with a wreath of roses. Children and grownups enjoyed playing games together, and one of the favorites was "Grace-hoop." I don't know where it came from—perhaps from France or Wales or Ireland, for we had lots of Irish and Welsh in the town. The game is unique and I never heard of it being played anywhere else. Barrel hoops were wound with bright strips of muslin, and each player was supplied with a pair of slender sticks. Then all the players, big and little, stood in a circle, and the game was to toss the hoop over the head of some one else. The one who succeeded in this feat received a kiss as reward.

Several hoops would be going at the same time and the game was exciting. There were numerous other games where the forfeit was a kiss, for this sort of thing was all the rage. And there were dancing parties where the grown-ups and children danced together, square dances, waltzes, schotisches, mazurkas and polkas. In those days, up there in the mines the little girls all learned to dance not with little boys, but with friends of our fathers. And there were spelling bees and socials in the homes and, most exciting of all, an occasional "nigger" minstrel show. The performers were always white men blacked-up. They traveled from town to town. As soon as they were ready to open the doors two boys would start out armed with school bell and hotel dinner bell, ringing with all their might and shouting:

"Roll up, tumble up, any way to get up,
Here's a chance to get your money back."

And all the houses would soon be emptied—everyone in town would be sure to be on hand to enjoy the show. The entertainment consisted in banjo-playing, clog-dancing and jokes, as well as songs. The two men on the ends called the "end-men" did most of the dialog, working in a lot of local hits, and getting a great laugh.

It was always a gala day for us children when Peddler Marks came to town. He was a Jew, and he and his wife kept a little store at North San Juan which Mrs. Marks conducted in his absence. At first he carried his pack on his back, and as he became more prosperous he had a mule to carry it. Still later he arose to the dignity of a horse and wagon. It was fun for us children to watch the unrolling of his goods from their big denim wrapper, and display on the floor of our sitting room calicos, woolens and all sorts of 'notions.' The neighbors came in too and it was an afternoon given up exclusively to buying and selling.

Mother always bought needles and thread and dry goods, and put them to good use making clothes for the family, and teaching my sister and me to sew. Before I was five years old I had pieced one side of a quilt, sitting at her knee half an hour a day, and you may be sure she insisted on tiny stitches. I was permitted to have material with which I cut out, fitted, and made on the sewing machine a dress for my sister when I was eleven. Of this I was justly proud.

My parents were ahead of their time in that they worked gymnastics into our play, even if two of us were girls. Father made stilts and swings, rings and poles and we learned how to use them all, dressed in the gym suits that Mother made for us. Perhaps that's why I can still paint pictures at my age, because I was allowed to develop a strong body and steady nerves.

We had good schools in French Corral, better than they had in San Francisco at that time. Most of our teachers were young men who were college graduates out from the East for a chance to make money and go back to take up further studies. One of our best teachers was Marion McCarroll Scott, a young Southerner. The various teachers found a congenial atmosphere in our home and spent many evenings playing cards with my parents. We children were always interested in the fun and in the conversations. But the best part of our education probably was gained in the evenings spent alone with our father and mother. Father read the novels of Charles Dickens aloud to us, and I recall distinctly our delight over *David Copperfield* and *Great Expectations*. Mother's busy hands would be sewing while my sister and I did tatting and crochet, which was all the rage at the time. The books of Dickens are almost sacred to me because of those happy times of the long ago, and because all those dear ones are now in the Silent Land.

The children of French Corral as they grew up, demonstrated the value of a happy wholesome environment and good schools. Nearly every one of them amounted to something in later life. The Welsh families loved music, and several of their children lived to distinguish themselves. In our family my sister was the musical one while I had some talent for painting.

There wasn't any organized church in French Corral. Once a month a Methodist Presiding elder preached in the school-house, and one of our townsmen conducted a Sunday school. Most of the Welsh people were Methodists and rather religious. There were a good many Irish Catholics in the town. When any of them passed away they held a wake and all their friends up and down the ridge attended. They evidently had a good time judging by the way they tore through the town afterwards singing and driving furiously.

But everybody's heart was in the right place when it came to doing something for the family of miners who were unfortunate enough to lose their lives in the mines. Money was plenty and often within an hour $500 would be raised for the bereaved family.

My parents were always ready to help their neighbors in trouble. Mother often spent night after night nursing the sick, especially during those terrible epidemics of dyphtheria in the winter. It cost $10 to get a doctor to come from North San Juan, six miles away, and often the people couldn't well afford this. But they all had confidence in Mother and if she said "Get the doctor" they got him; if she thought that she could handle the case, they trusted in her skill. In those days everybody who died must be wrapped in a shroud to be properly prepared for burial. Mother made many a shroud for her neighbors, and sat up all night doing it. She washed and dressed them and helped to put them into the home-made wood coffins covered with black cloth. Those were sad times for the whole town.

Mother organized many a community Christmas tree. She went around to the storekeepers and miners taking up subscriptions and then rode on horseback to Grass Valley to buy the presents. She had a friend named Mrs. Black who was a rollicking sort of young person, and they went on these excursions together. She kept every person in mind, and tried to get just the right thing. Later the purchases were delivered by stage coach, and Mother would superintend the decoration of the tree and the naming of the presents. No one was forgotten and we were like one big family—this community of 500. But my mother never neglected her family in spite of her services to the community. Her capable hands could turn off work faster than any other person I ever knew.

From my earliest childhood I always tried to draw and paint, and model from clay. Once, my father brought home from Grass Valley a small box of paints—water colors—and I became the wonder and the envy of all the neighbors' children. I remember how I sat in state surrounded by my admiring playmates, while I daubed good white paper, and we all thought it was wonderful. But for the most part I had to depend upon the resources that Nature afforded for my materials.

Sometimes we were allowed to go into the mines. This was always a wonderful experience, because of the beautiful colored chalks that I found there. These were pieces of soft rock in colors of pastel shades, soft grays and tans tinted with green, blue and rose. And in the sluices that ran through the town from the mines on their way to the Yuba river I found fine yellow clay with which I could play at modeling. These were tapped for water to irrigate our gardens and when the water was turned off there was a thick layer of moist clay the next day. This I scraped up and used for modeling-clay. Of course the kitchen oven was always available for my dryings and bakings.

Father was always interested in making an artist of me. It happened that when I was eight years old we moved to San Francisco. Almost immediately an artist named John Brink, whom we had known in Iowa came to see us, with the result that he took a room in our house and established his studio there. I remember him well, with his dark eyes and black curly hair—I still have his photograph. Every day I hurried home from school to watch him paint. I was enraptured with his pictures of sleeping ladies dreaming of angels portrayed upon the atmosphere above them, and especially I was charmed with a painting of a ragged newsboy with a rag tied around his big toe. Father, always on the lookout for art exhibits, one day took me to the County Fair where I beheld for the first time really good paintings. There I beheld Toby Rosenthal's 'Elaine.' That was a great moment when I looked upon the Lily Maid of Astolat, lying dead and black-palled on her barge, floating on the tide to Camelot. I was also deeply impressed by a portrait of Starr King, just then the hero and saint of San Francisco.

After fourteen months we returned to French Corral. But even there in that remote mountain village opportunities came to us, and my parents saw that we made the most of them. When I was about twelve, a charming and gifted lady came to live among the mining camps along the ridge. Her name was Sweetland, and her home was in Sweetland, a town named after her husband. She had come from Virginia, and had married this mining man who was supposed to have wealth. Well, it turned out he hadn't, and that it would be necessary for her to earn their living. Mrs. Sweetland was a proud lady and refused to go back to her home but remained to take care of her husband who became an invalid (a mental case, eventually) and died in an asylum. Mrs. Sweetland was accomplished in music, art, French, and various kinds of crafts and was a great help to families who wished to give their daughters advantages. I loved her very much and I'm sure that she was a refining influence in our life. Every Tuesday we stayed at home from school, and she spent the day with us, taking dinner with us, and giving us piano, drawing and French lessons. My sister was especially talented in music. Lydia Parshley, the saloon keeper's daughter, still making her home with us, also had piano lessons, and we had to get up early in the morning in order get in an hour's piano practice each, every day before school. But my mother was a thorough disciplinarian, so it was always accomplished, and we never for a moment attempted to do otherwise.

I must not leave the happy associations of French Corral without recalling the share that my young uncle, Tom Stanton and the Olsen cousins had in those childhood years. Tom was my bosom friend and playmate. I remember Grandfather had a mule team and carried freight from Marysville. There was only one watering-trough in town and that was in front of the store. It was one of Tom's privileges to lead one of the mules to water, and it was one of my delights to be perched on the back of that animal—I in calico gown and pink sunbonnet, I can see the picture yet.

Tom, many years after this married and lived in Los Angeles, where he was one of the leading photographers. In later years the Stanton family moved to Santa Barbara, where my grandfather passed away. Grandmother lived for a while in Oakland and later in Los Angeles where she died. When I was thirteen and my sister about ten and our little brother seven, we all moved up the Ridge to North San Juan. This was a larger town, having about a thousand people, and it was a little more progressive. We were frightfully homesick nevertheless! Our old dog Fun went with us, and I remember how he used to sit in front of the fireplace and tradition has it that the tears ran down from his eyes. Father and his partner, Billy Menner, bought a two story brick building—quite

the finest store in town—and started a hardware store, fully
equipped with miner's tools, with a shop for the manufacture of
tin-ware and the hydraulic pipe that was used in the mines up
there.

The altitude of San Juan was higher, the climate colder in
winter, and the town all up and down hill. There were only two
spots in the town level enough for a game of croquet. I remember
the schoolhouse was on top of a hill, near the edge of the bank
precipitately leading into one of the mines. I might add that we
never fell over the edge.

When we moved to San Juan the school was so full that there
was not a desk left for one of us. So our parents hired the teacher,
whose name was George Washington Stoddard, to come to the
house every evening to teach us three children. He was a
handsome young man, and soon became quite an intimate friend
of our family. With mother he often played croquet and I was
included in the game, which was one of the diversions of that time.
Incidentally I might mention that he went back to Maine, and after
graduating at a dental college established an office in Belfast. Such
was the way of all our young teachers. Later on we were sent to a
private school kept by a lovely woman named Mrs. Telyea, and
we really learned a lot while there.

North San Juan was a more sophisticated town than French
Corral. It had more stores and hotels and—saloons, by the way—
and a town hall that could be used as a theater, and a church with a
resident minister. The Masons and Eastern Stars, Odd Fellows,
and Good Templars all had lodges there. We had a newspaper too
called *The San Juan Times*. It was edited by Judge Stidger who
was a lawyer as well. We also had a volunteer fire department and
a shed in which was kept a hose cart and over the roof was a bell.
The sound of that bell in the night fills me yet in memory with
palpitation and pallor. The houses were all built largely of pitch
pine and it was no easy job to put out a fire. Wild excitement
prevailed whenever that bell rang out an alarm.

Yes, we were quite civilized in San Juan; every summer a
circus came to town, and its arrival was the excitement of the day.
We couldn't miss seeing it go by with its cages of wild beasts and
monkeys and all else that makes a circus a delight to children even
unto this day. We lived on Main street, the route by which all

traffic entered the town and our opportunities on these occasions were great. Everybody went to the circus. In those days we were blessed with just one tent for our entertainment and the terrible distraction of a three ringed circus was unknown to us. We saw it all with one look. How we reveled in peanuts and pink ice lemonade, "one bit a glass." By the way, a bit was ten cents, our smallest coin. Two bits was a quarter of a dollar and in making change no account was ever taken of the five cents. No matter which one it went to! I well remember, by the way, that a stick of candy or an orange always cost a "bit."

Upon ordinary occasions most of the men, and some of the women, were in the habit of drinking something somewhat stronger than lemonade. The Good Templars didn't, and so fun was poked at them. They were called "Peanuts," and their organization the "Peanut Lodge." The Good Templars Hall stood next to our house, and one night when my father came home late, he found an irate Irishman named Mike McGowan pacing up and down in front of the hall, and getting madder at every turn. His daughter, Mary Ellen, belonged to the lodge and he was there waiting to take her home. Father hailed him and asked him what he was doing there, when Mike exploded: "I'll tell you, Mr. White, shure and next week there'll be one Paynut less." Mother and I belonged to the Good Templars, and we kept our pledges as regards drinks. But when it came to puddings and mince pies— well, it couldn't be done!

Among the stores of North San Juan I remember especially the combined men's clothing store and bank owned by Simon and Dan Furth. The Furths were highly respected and were among the well-to-do people of the town. They lived in one of the best houses. Edwin Furth, son of Dan Furth, in later years became a member of the firm of Capwell, Sullivan and Furth of Oakland.

Amid all the sophistications of North San Juan we were growing up. But our parents watched over us carefully, and kept us at our studies. Father especially didn't propose that any untimely romance should blight the career of any one of his children. There was a certain young stage driver in town whom Father at one time highly approved of, calling him a "Rara avis," and this facetiously because this last word rhymed with his name. But when this young paragon commenced beauing me about he

immediately lost favor with my parent. It was then that I was
bundled off to boarding school, which happened to be Mills
Seminary in Oakland. I was then seventeen.

Dr. Cyrus Taggert Mills and his wife, Susan Tolman Mills,
returned missionaries from Ceylon and the Hawaiian Islands, had
taken over the school when it was Miss Atkins' Young Ladies'
Seminary of Benicia, and had moved it to Oakland in 1871. It was
in the following year that I went there to school. There were about
150 girls in attendance at the time, and we all lived in a large four-
story frame building, since known as Mills Hall. The first floor was
used chiefly for class rooms and general assembly rooms, and the
upper floors were dormitory and piano practice rooms. I went on
with my painting, my teacher being a Mr. Wandesford, an English
artist of the old school. He was one of my dearest friends among
the teachers. I became under his guidance the star painter among
the students, and my pictures were so recognized by the faculty.

*Many different threads are interwoven in this short narrative.
It gives an idea of the way in which the family rose, through work
and thrift, to a level of moderate prosperity, and takes pains to
underline the mother's specific contribution. It provides a great
deal of information on the organization of community life in
developing settlements and on the part women played in it, and
also on the progress civilization made in California and the
changes it brought about. It constitutes a very evocative picture of
childhood in a pastoral setting. The descriptions show great
feeling for and appreciation of the beauties of nature and a deep
enjoyment of outdoor pleasures. Within the home, a variety of
interests was pursued, and the children were encouraged to
engage in artistic and cultural activities. The figures of both
parents emerge vividly; the father, who had many talents and
knew how to do all kinds of work, had an inventive and
enterprising spirit and dreamed of a full life for his daughters as
well as for his sons—a rather uncommon attitude in those times;
the mother, who had a great capacity for work and practised a
variety of manual activities, believed in discipline as far as the
education of her children was concerned, and upheld an ideal of
service to her family and to the community. The links which tied*

*the family together were very strong: they formed a self-sufficient unit within which creativity and self-reliance were constantly stressed. But it was not a self-centered unit, as friendships were made and solidarity with the other pioneers constituted an important aspect of life.*

*Many factors were present which combined to make Edith White's childhood happy and full. The charmed atmosphere of the family circle was disrupted by one of the daughters' death in 1876. Edith White followed her father's advice and chose a career in preference to marriage. She earned her living as an artist and lived with her parents until they died. At 81 she was still working. She felt much pride in her "chosen life-work"[2] and in her success, which she attributed to the influence of her environment, and expressed great satisfaction with the way in which her life had developed.*

1. All this information comes from the preface to the book, p. 4.
2. Edith White, p. 22.

# Pioneering in Arizona: the Reminiscences of Emerson Oliver Stratton and Edith Stratton Kitt

Edith Stratton Kitt

Edited by John Alexander Carrol (Tuscon: Arizona Pioneers' Historical Society) 1964.

*The book which relates Edith Stratton Kitt's memories of her pioneer life, supplemented by those of her father, is divided into two parts, the first of which is presented here. The second, entitled "My Town Life" concerns her school years and later life. She grew up in Arizona at a time when frontier conditions still prevailed:*

My father's family were New Yorkers, my mother's New Englanders. Both came to California in 1850 during the gold rush. Dad's family stayed in California, but Mother's soon became homesick for their beloved Cape Cod and returned to Cotuit, Massachusetts. Dad and Mother knew each other as children in the gold fields. After Dad graduated from business college in San Francisco he came to Cape Cod to claim his bride. They went together to Peru in 1871 and returned to California by way of Panama and New York. In 1874 Dad came to Arizona to take a job as bookkeeper at Maricopa Wells. Maricopa was then a very important stage and freight station on the overland route, the receiving point for mail and freight going north to Phoenix and Prescott as well as east and west across the country. The next year Dad moved to Florence, where Mother joined him in the summer of 1876 after spending almost a week in a stage coach with a small child, my sister Mabel, in her lap.

I was born in Florence, Arizona Territory, on December 15, 1878. My birth was really an experience for my father since I came while he was scouring the town looking for the only doctor, whom he found later drunk and playing cards in the back room of a saloon. The small house in which I was born had dirt walls, a dirt floor, and a dirt roof. There was only one board floor in the village, and that was in the most prosperous saloon. Once in a while the townspeople would clear out the bar and hold their dances in this saloon. All the mothers brought their babies and put them to bed on a long bench. Mother was a New Englander, but she did go to these dances until some man sat on me. After that, she refused to go any more. That may have been the first time I was ever sat upon, but it was far from the last.

The walls, as in most of the other places in Florence in the 1870's, were adobe. It was cool and nice, except when it rained. The ridge pole and rafters were made of rough-hewn timbers. Small branches, brush, and bear grass were laid on these, then finer grass or hay, and finally the dirt—no, last of all were the weeds which grew in the dirt and looked quite gay in the spring. If this roof sprang a leak, it was just too bad. First there would be a drop or two of water. Then the hole would widen—a fine example of erosion—and Mother would grab buckets, tubs, dishpans, anything to catch the muddy stream.

I do not remember this place in Florence, but I do remember the next. When I was a year and a half Dad decided to homestead, and now took up the first ranch on the north side of the Santa Catalina Mountains. It was located about twelve miles north of the present town of Oracle. Dad called it the Pandora Ranch. To start with, we lived in a dugout—a dwelling actually dug out of the side of a hill. It had three walls of "mountain," a dirt floor and roof, and a real door and windows which Dad had brought with him from Florence. Soon, however, our home was a stockade made of cedar posts hewn smooth on one side and stuck up on the ground. These were chinked with mud and covered with a shake roof made from the nearby junipers. The roof sloped toward the back of the house, and in the center of the back wall was a huge fireplace made of flat slate rock. The front room was large, with a bed on either side of the door. I believe that Dad's and Mother's bed was made of lumber, but the children's bed was made of mesquite poles with strips of rawhide laced across them in lieu of springs. I remember Mother's bed because she used to tie me to the bedpost for safety. Dad killed fifty rattlesnakes in our first year at the ranch.

Mother's big trunk stood against one wall. That trunk was a sacred thing. It held the remains of Mother's trousseau and a few keepsakes. I remember a tight-fitting, Kelly-green taffeta basque, trimmed around the collar and down the front with a double ruffle and fringed instead of hemmed, a very short dark brown velveteen jacket, a pair of embroidered white silk stockings, and a huge tortoise-shell comb—all now relics of a past long gone.

While we were living in the stockade my chief playmate, aside from my sister Mabel who was six years older than I, was an Indian boy, the son of Dad's vaquero. Mother would make me divide my playthings with him and then send us out back of the house to play. Soon the boy would be yelling at the top of his voice and I, apparently all unmindful of the sound, would be playing unconcernedly with his toys when Mother arrived on the scene. "You give those things back to Juan this minute," she would say, and I would turn the things over to him cheerfully and keep on playing with my own. I think I always was good at submitting to the inevitable.

Playthings were not very numerous. Usually they consisted of a string of spools or buttons, a few pieces of brightly colored glass from some broken bottle, and some oak balls or red chilicote beans. If I could get hold of a hammer I was happy. Dad would say, "Edie, take the hammer in your other hand"; and I would answer, "I can't. I hits my thumb." About the only thing I did with my right hand in those days was to cut with the scissors. I cut the fringe off the baby's shawl and the hair off the dog. When I announced that I had "banged" my hair, Dad said that if I did it again he would "bang" me.

I do not remember that I was much impressed when my brother Johnny was born in 1881. I was more interested in the colored cook. She had come over from Oracle to help Mother out, and she made most delicious sourdough bread which she set in front of the fireplace to rise. When we children thought of it, we took a peek to see if it was ready to bake. When we didn't think about it we were very apt to run into it.

In 1884 we moved into a new house built of rough lumber from the small sawmill at the Apache Mine in the Santa Catalina Mountains. The house stood on a little sloping flat. About a hundred feet from the house, the ground dipped down sharply into the creek bed. Across the creek was another flat, and then the high mesa beyond. The cattle trail came off the mesa directly in front of the house and led down to the corrals. It was interesting to watch the cattle come down that trail single file, each stepping in the tracks of the one in front. The trail, in fact, was like gradual steps; the bare spots where the animals trod were the steps, surrounded by stones that had been pushed out of the way by the many hoofs. The wagon road from Oracle also topped the mesa in front of the house, but it had to angle down the steep slope and hit the creek about a mile and a half above the house. When we saw company coming, we always had time to get cleaned up before they arrived.

The kitchen corner of our new house rested on the ground and the opposite corner was about four feet above the ground. The kitchen corner was a wonderful place for skunks to make their home. We could hear them squealing and knocking against the floor at night. They did not bother us much, except once when a greenhorn came to the ranch and took a shot at them. Then we had to move out of the house for the night, and I can remember that I cried because even my milk tasted of skunk.

Dad used to say that the only way to handle a skunk was to pick it up by the tail and pack it off. He repeated that advice very often among the neighbors, rather chiding them for their lack of courage. One day I came rushing into the house all excited because I had seen a skunk behind some barley sacks where I was looking for eggs, and a neighbor, who chanced to be at the ranch, said to Dad: "Now, Stratton, here is your chance." Dad took the thing up by the tail all right and paraded it around the yard. Everything went fine as long as he kept giving a little jerk now and then—just enough that the weight of the body kept it and the tail in a straight line. But then he stopped long enough to hit the animal over the head with a small iron bar. That was too long. I forgot to say that Dad had a good-sized beard. For days thereafter he soaked his clothes and he washed and he scrubbed. Two weeks later Dad went into Tucson for supplies, and there he met a friend who usually invited him to have a drink. This was the custom in those days—and therefore it was much easier for a man to get drunk in town than to stay sober if he did not come to town often. But this time Dad's friend sniffed the air and remarked, "Stratton, it seems to me I smell skunk."

I have learned since that if coal-oil is poured on the offending spot it will kill skunk odor. I knew one woman who doused her dog with coal-oil because she was bringing him down from the mountains in a friend's car. It killed the odor, but it nearly killed the dog, too.

By the time we had moved into our new house I was able to hold my own with my sister Mabel and be a real playmate, though a little later she was sent away to school, first to Tucson and then to our aunt's in Massachusetts and to boarding school nearby. One of our favorite pastimes was to play "ranch." We each had our string of stick-horses fashioned from the flower stalks of bear grass. The bloom ends made nice bushy tails. And how some of those horses could buck! Our stables were marked off on the ground, and usually a large bunch of bear grass was the hay stack. Then, too, our horses had to be branded or how could we tell them apart? Our cattle were made from green yucca fruit with sticks inserted for legs. These we could kill and cut up for jerky or sell over the counter. We used small pieces of colored glass for money. Our play meals were very simple and usually consisted of slices of "beef" served on pieces of colored glass.

We often took our stick-horses down to the creek where we waded, planted little patches of barley two or three feet square, and built dams and ditches to irrigate them. If we played at the game long enough for the barley to sprout, a cow usually got into our crop and ate the barley or a flood came along and washed it out. There was one good-sized pool in a hollowed-out rock where we used to bathe. Once we took to "sea" in Mother's wash tub but got shipwrecked and had to go to bed while our clothes dried. We sometimes "rode" our stick-horses down to the corral and sat on the very steep bank, which formed one side of the enclosure, while we watched Dad's men brand the calves. Our play houses were the oak trees on the hillside. Mine was very accessible, with each spreading branch making a separate room. Mabel's was so tall that I could not grasp the lower branches and swing myself up, and so big around that I could not shinny up. When I went there "to call," she had to come down and give me a boost. This was very humiliating.

Mabel had a fine rag doll with a bisque head and many fine clothes which had belonged to our great-grandmother. Dolls did not, however, particularly appeal to me. Once I was given a cloth doll with a china head, but she did not last long. I took her down to the corral to watch the cowboys brand calves, and she got excited and fell off the fence and broke her head. On rainy days, when I had to stay in the house, I made long strings of paper dolls and dressed them up. But my one great love and joy was "Diggie." She was my constant companion for many years. Sometimes she was just a stick, sometimes a handkerchief with a stone tied in one corner for a head; but most often she was, like Harvey, "just there." I could always talk to her and tell her all my troubles, and she was a great comfort.

I guess I could always ride. Dad used to say that at first he carried me in a sling made of an old tablecloth knotted around his neck and shoulder, forming a hammock. By the time we moved out to the ranch, however, I was riding on a pillow in front of him. I can remember the day I graduated from that and he let me ride behind. It was very thrilling, but I held onto his shirt like a leach. My brother Elmer was born while we were in the new house, and in time we four children had our own horse—a small, chunky, flea-bitten gray called Little Bill. Poor patient Little Bill! Sometimes one of us would ride him alone, sometimes all four of us. We usually rode bareback because we could get more of us on that way. First I would cup my hands and form a stirrup to help Mabel up. Then between us we could boost the two boys on. The trick was to get me on without pulling the boys off. The easiest way seemed to be to use the joint of Little Bill's hind leg as the least bit of a toe hold, and let those on his back pull me up over his rump. Oh! the wonderful exploring expeditions we made, wandering farther and farther from the house until we were not quite sure where we were and had to depend on Little Bill to get us home.

Little Bill was one of us. He never hurt us intentionally, but now and then he might step on our toes. He seemed to take an intelligent interest in all that we did. As we grew older we seemed to depend on him more and more. Whenever I tried to bring in an unruly range cow so that Dad could doctor her or her calf, I would let Little Bill have his head and he would plod along slowly behind her, moving from right to left just enough to keep her going in the right direction but never fast enough to get her excited. If she did get wise and try to bolt, he would turn almost as fast as she did. Once we were driving a cow along a fence when she suddenly turned back. Little Bill turned as suddenly as she did —but I kept on going. Then he had to stop and wait for me. When we children went in to Tucson to go to school, we took Little Bill with us. We also took him to Florence when we left the ranch for good. He finally died of old age.

In time we had other horses to go with Little Bill, and many a wild and joyous ride my sister and I took together when we had more than one horse in our care. Each of Dad's cowboys had assigned to him two or more horses for his own use, and he was supposed to look after them. But now and then, and especially at rodeo time when they were ridden hard, one or more of the horses would get a sore back. Usually these were scalds on the small of the back caused by dirty, sweaty saddle blankets under the hot leather. When this happened, the horse would be turned over to us to care for—and to ride if we were careful. We had a nice padded blanket with holes cut in at just the right place over the kidneys, and we would put our saddle on top of that. It was surprising how quickly the horses got to know us and let us do for them what they would make an awful fuss over if a man tried to do. I have fallen off a horse many times, and I do not believe that one ever went off and left me. One horse that we had been doctoring was quite gentle but never could be ridden without a saddle, and it was always a stunt to get some unsuspecting cowboy on him bareback. For some reason I had not heard of the animal's idiosyncrasy, and everybody stood open-mouthed when I rode him up from the pasture one day with nothing on him but a rope.

Mother did not like us to play around the cowboys very much. We were always to remember that they were not in our class. Since reading Mrs. Cleaveland's *No Life for a Lady,* I have realized how many experiences I missed by not being a cowboy among cowboys. Dad used to let me sit on the corral fence and keep tally for each calf branded—one, two, three, four, tally, five calves branded—and one day I dropped my pencil and climbed down after it. A cow objected, but one of the men drove her away. That was only one of the lessons I learned the "hard way."

I learned to shoot at an early age. When I was ten years old my grandfather presented me with a sixteen-gauge, single-barrel shotgun. I learned to shoot fairly well, but nothing fancy. I preferred to shoot with a rest and never learned to shoot on the wing. The reason? I never had the ammunition. Dad did not go to Tucson often for supplies, and shells were expensive. I had only two brass shells, and when I went hunting I would carry a tin pail with powder, shot, wads, caps, and the tools with which to reload my shells. Whenever I used one shell, I would sit down and reload it. I have sat at a water hole for hours waiting for two or more doves to get in line so that I could kill more than one with a single shot. And I have chased Gambel's quail all over the hills trying to get them to huddle before flying. Usually by that time I would be so out of breath that I could not shoot straight. I never got many quail.

Once I shot at three teal duck swimming in a row. I wounded them all, and after thinking that I had successfully wrung their necks I packed them home behind me. When Mother asked me what I was holding behind me, I proudly threw them down in front. One lay still, one ran under the house, and the third started to flutter off but the dog caught it. Mother stuffed all three with onions and we had roast duck for supper.

Of all the predatory animals at which I took pot shots, I think the coyotes were the most aggravating. They had much curiosity and would trot around in a circle, stopping every now and then to look at me but never letting me get within range. Chicken lovers like the fox and lynx seemed to be able to get the chickens no matter how high they roosted in the trees. Someone once told me that they ran around and around the tree until the watching chickens got dizzy and fell off, and I believed him. The badgers preferred staying on the ground, eating both the chickens in the hen house and their eggs. Badgers were great pests but were very hard to kill because of their tough skin. The hides of those I skinned usually looked as if the badger had a case of smallpox. My bird shot just would not penetrate.

Skunks were death on chickens, too, but it produced a much more pleasant atmosphere if they could be trapped rather than shot. They have too much respect for themselves to use their favorite weapon when in the confines of a fox trap. Our traps were homemade, fashioned out of wooden boxes with a trapdoor at one end. The door was held up with a stick, and a string was attached to the stick and run back into the trap through a hole. Here it would be baited, and when the skunk pulled at the bait the string would pull on the stick and the door fall. I would drown the skunks, skin them, and sell the pelts. Skunk skins were worth fifty cents to a dollar, and in one season I made fifteen dollars this way.

I did much of my hunting on Little Bill. He was almost as good as a setter for pointing out game. If anything moved, he would prick up his ears and look in that direction. Game was not as afraid of him as of me, and I could ride quite close to it, slip off my horse on the far side, and use his back as a rest for my gun. He seldom moved when I ran after my game, and always turned to see if I had anything when I returned.

But better than hunting with my own gun was to go with Dad when he went after deer. I would follow close behind, usually with a piece of jerky tied on the back of my saddle because I could never tell when we would get home. Dad had one dog, Fanny, that would stay at heel until told to go. Any other dog was tied to the tail of my horse, and when Dad saw a deer and jumped off his horse it was my duty to grab the animal's reins—which was no easy task if it happened to be gun shy—and wait quietly until he called for the dog. This he did if the deer was wounded and had to be tracked. If Fanny could not pick up the scent, she would look at

Dad and he would motion her in this or that direction. I was a proud youngster if I was able to ride home with a big buck hanging from the back of my saddle.

There were mule deer on the mesas and whitetail deer in the mountains. Deer meat was often sold in the towns. I saw an advertisement not long ago in one of the old newspapers: "Venison 8 cents a pound." Game was plentiful everywhere and the vegetation to feed it lush. As one traveled toward our ranch from Oracle Junction—we called it Walnut Tree—one could look to the left over a wide, beautiful field of undulating grama grass and see one or two large herds of antelope feeding on the plain. Sometimes they would come near and stare at the intruder. Curiosity was their undoing. There are very few left in southern Arizona now. In the mountains there were even some bighorn sheep. I have seen their horns and once one that had been killed, but never a live one. There were also lion and bear, and *javelina* (wild hog) a little lower down. Around the ranch were squirrel, cottontail and small blacktail rabbits, a large rabbit we used to call the antelope rabbit because of the white patch on its rump, and the huge plain jacks. All were edible. If properly dressed, the bear and the wild hog made good eating, too. Bear tastes like a cross between beef and venison, and the wild hog something like pork though I have heard that it is not officially related to the hog family. Mother would not cook the wild hog. I remember once when we had been out of meat for some time Dad brought in one that he had nicely dressed. Mother would not even have it in the house. Dad, in disgust, cut off a hunk of the meat and tossed it to the dogs. They sniffed it and turned their backs.

As Dad went to town only every two or three months, he had to buy food in quantities—three or four hundred-pound sacks of flour, one or two sacks of potatoes and one of onions, big boxes of macaroni and raisins on the stem, cereals, rice, and beans in bulk— no fancy packaging—a small barrel of molasses, canned goods by the case, and lump sugar in hundred-pound sacks. The sack of sugar is what we kept our eye on. Sometimes we would snitch a lump, but mostly Mother would give us a certain number of lumps as a bribe or reward. These we might flavor with a drop of wintergreen and eat, but most often we saved and pooled our resources and then begged Mother to make us candy in payment for chores well done.

Please do not think that we were like Topsy and "just grew." In the mornings we could do pretty much as we liked, but we had a few regular chores. What we disliked most was to fill the coal-oil lamps, trim their wicks, and clean their sooty chimneys. Sometimes we "helped" Mother in the kitchen. I can remember standing on a box beside her when she rolled out her bread. My piece was small, and after I had dropped it on the floor a couple of times you could not tell whether it was white bread or spice cake. Then we might seed raisins and beat eggs for a real cake, and get to lick the cake pan. Once in a great while we had a special treat. One of the Mexican vaqueros would bake a mescal root in the ground, preparing it much as they did their baked cow's head or a Hawaiian does his *kalua*. The finished product was a very sweet, slightly smoky molasses tasting and chewing something like sugar cane.

We seldom lacked for sweets. Many wild bees made their hives in hollow oak trees in the hills. The trick was to find them— and then, of course, to get the honey out. To find the trees was our job. We would put a saucer of sweetened water in some likely place, wait for a bee to come, sprinkle him with flour so that we could follow him more easily when he made a "bee line" for home—that beeline is no joke—and then run to where we saw him last and repeat the process. We would leave it to the men to don mosquito-cloth masks, cut a chunk out of the tree, and get the honey. Bees are no segregationists A cell containing honey would be right next to one containing bee bread of maybe one housing a young bee. Mother would be days getting the honey extracted and ready to put into jars.


Our trips to Tucson were memorable events. We did not go often. Mother was once on the ranch for eight months without seeing another American woman. When we did go to town, it was an undertaking. It took sometimes two, sometimes three days each way, depending on the hour that Dad got started. Ordinarily we went in the big Bain wagon because there was a heavy load of supplies to bring home.

Dad never started anywhere until he was absolutely ready.
Everything had to be packed just so. He had to be sure that he had
some string, some rope, and a piece of baling wire in case of a
breakdown. Then he always had to stop and talk. At the ranch it
was to give final orders to his men; in town it was to say goodbye to
friends whom he would not see again for a long time. On the road
he had to stop and talk with everyone we chanced to meet. Dad
just naturally was never in a hurry. On the return trip we usually
got only as far as the Steam Pump, a few miles out of town, and
stayed there for the night.

The ranch was about thirty miles from Tucson as the crow
flies, but seventy-five miles as the road crawled. To begin with,
we had to go around the point of the mountains. When we got
within eight miles of the ranch, Dad usually changed his mind and
turned toward the San Pedro. He did this, he said, in order to go
across a single wash instead of its many branches. I believe,
however, that he saw the wonderful tints on the Galiuro Mountains
at sunset and something drew him toward that land of mystery. At
any rate, instead of going the eight miles we went twenty-five.

Often we traveled late into the night. I think that I must have
been afraid of the dark, for I would get to whimpering. When
Mother would ask me what was the matter, I would sob, "Edie's a
fraid cat." The worst was when we camped out. If we were in the
light wagon Dad would take out the two seats, place them on the
ground facing each other, pile the harness in between to fill up the
space, and cover all with a canvas. He had to cover every piece of
harness because the hungry coyotes would chew up any leather
left within their reach. (I have heard that a coyote once took a
fancy to the buckskin string on a man's watch and pulled vest and
all out from under his head as he lay asleep.) This was how Dad
made a bed for us children. He and Mother slept in the bed of the
wagon.

It was not the most comforting thing in the world to wake up
in the night and listen to the coyotes calling from one hill to the
other and know that you were sleeping on that harness. Many a
night the blood has absolutely congealed in my veins at the near
and unexpected howl of a coyote which would be answered first
from one hill and then from another until it seemed as if the souls
of the dead were moaning and wailing and closing in on me. I

would lie and sob to myself, but I did not dare to cry out because I feared Dad's scolding worse than the coyotes. But at the end of the second day, as Mother hunted candles and nightgowns and took the clothes from our tired little bodies, we children would all cry together.

Our trips to town during Indian scares were the most exciting. We were living on the ranch during the worst of the Apache troubles in the early 1880's, but we never knew of hostile Indians getting up in the Santa Catalinas as far as our place. That seemed to be out of their beaten path. They usually went up the San Pedro, and if they came into the Santa Catalinas at all it was to go through the pass between that range of mountains and the Rincons. Now and again they would steal a horse or kill a cow which strayed too close to the river.

When I tell them I was raised on an Arizona ranch, most people ask me one of two questions. Were we not afraid of Indians? or, How did I get my early education? We had a tutor on the ranch when we could get one, but usually we attended the public school in Tucson. Mabel was sent to stay with friends several times, but after I too got old enough to go to school Mother would rent a house in town and we all would spend the winter there. We would come in early in September while it was very hot, and I remember that the trip from the Rillito River into town on the second day of travel seemed endless. The Rillito is practically in town now. The trip back to the ranch in the spring was always a great joy.

My first schooling was in the first building erected in Tucson for that purpose—a long adobe on Congress Street between Sixth Avenue and Scott Street. After the first day I came home all elated and told Mother I had learned a new song. When she asked what it was, I said, "Columbia the jam in the *olla*." The second year I went to the Plaza School where Safford School now stands. It was a long walk across Military Plaza through the dirt and the brush to the school. I do not remember much of what I learned there; but I remember the *milcoche* man, a Mexican who carried a little table on his head and peddled cakes of raw sugar and long sticks of taffy candy called *milcoche*. And I can remember the play houses we made out on the plaza. We would pull over the branches of the scrub mesquites or the greasewood, put sticks up around them to make the walls, and then use bright pieces of broken glass for our "dishes."

Tucson in the 1880's was a small place with one-story mud houses that came flush with the sidewalk and narrow, dirty, unpaved streets. In summer some of the people who had no patios pulled their cots out on the sidewalks and went to bed. If you wanted to get from one place to another at night, you walked in the middle of the street. We lived on Stone Avenue out about at what is now Five Points, and in the evening all the children of the neighborhood would gather in the street and play Snap-the-Whip. I was small and usually was put on the end, and often I fell on my face. Sometimes we would play Hide-and-Seek. The bushes that grew in the street afforded good protection.

In those few years I think I contracted every child's disease ever given a name—measles, chicken pox, whooping cough, and even diphtheria. About the only thing I did not get was smallpox. Almost every year there was an epidemic of this dread disease. It was very prevalent among the Mexicans. From our front door one year we could count twelve yellow flags put up on their homes by the quarantine office, signifying smallpox within. I can still see the pathetic little Mexican funerals, the father walking down the street carrying the dead body of his child in a raisin or macaroni box all decorated with bright paper flowers and neatly scalloped white paper around the edge, and followed by his wife dragging one or more small child after her. But in a way the death of a Mexican child was not too sad, for the parents felt that God had called the child unto Himself while it was still young and innocent and therefore would always have its place in heaven.

*The narrative features interesting details concerning the appearance of the various places where the family lived in Arizona, and tells something of the difficulties the pioneers had in making a stable life there possible. Resourcefulness and ingenuity were necessary to create a semblance of a home in the Territory!*

The mother's trunk, whose contents impressed themselves so vividly upon the small girl's memory, stood there as a reminder of a more delicate and more refined way of life, which was not so bound by basic necessities and not so close to the hard core of reality. The child, however, had not experienced different conditions in the past, and was totally wrapped up in an enjoyment of the immediate present and all the wonders it offered. The narrative attests to the lasting influence of early impressions and the shaping power of the environment. Life was not totally unfettered for the small girl: she had to accomplish certain tasks, and her parents believed in discipline. Her mother, who never became "Westernized," tried to rear her in a "genteel" way: she was not allowed to mix with the cowboys, whom she admired so much, as they were not considered to be in the same class.

Edith Kitt was not particularly receptive to her mother's influence, however, and the masculine figures are dominant in her narrative, which stands in sharp contrast with Edith White's much more sensitive account. There was nothing of the traditionally "feminine" in her tastes: she preferred animals to flowers, had no eye for the picturesque but expressed a kind of rough appreciation of nature and a great closeness to it. Hers is a straightforward narration, which does not give much place to feelings or contemplation, but plunges us directly into life as it was experienced.

*Part 7*
LIFE IN THE WEST AS SEEN
THROUGH THE EYES OF TRAVELLERS

# Incidents on Land and Water; or, Four Years on the Pacific Coast

Mrs. D. B. Bates

(Boston: E. O. Libby & Co.) 1858.

*In her book, Mrs. Bates has set down a slice of her life which covers exactly four years. After a brief sentimental evocation of her childhood home in Kingston, Massachussets, she describes the circumstances of her departure with her husband on a ship bound for San Francisco in July, 1850, stressing their optimistic frame of mind and their high expectations. Many chapters are devoted to the journey and to the places visited; an additional dimension is gained by the inclusion of thoughts on human life, and the descriptions are always brisk and sprightly, which makes her account much more interesting and entertaining than most of the countless narratives left of similar trips by travellers.*

*The couple arrived in San Francisco in 1851 and opened a boardinghouse. But as prices were exorbitant, the profit they made was not sufficient to compensate for the work, so they decided to move nearer the mines. Mrs. Bates's narrative at this point features romantic descriptions of the landscape, and insights into conditions at Marysville and in California at that time. She had a keen interest in human nature, and her observations are always pungent. Information is also provided on the various attempts made by the couple to earn their living in the developing hotel business. Mrs. Bates insists on the financial problems involved, the constant toil, and the weight of cares and responsibilities. She fell ill, and it seems that at that particularly hard time her husband started going astray; here is how she presents the situation:*

*Sickness and trouble yes, such trouble as rankles deepest in the heart of a wife, compared with which, death would have been joy - was fast doing its work.*[1]

*From that point on in the narrative, allusions to the strain placed upon her by her husband's behavior appear every now and then. Mrs. Bates grew violent in her denunciations of prostitution and its pernicious effects; she gave her wholehearted support to the vigilance committees:*

> *May the blessing of God attend them, and prosper all their undertakings and endeavors to uproot and exterminate those hot-beds of vice, those quick-sands in the ocean of life, upon which the bark of many a promising youth, of many a young husband, and of many a middle-aged father, has been irrecoverably wrecked.*[2]

*Toward the end of the book, she devotes a whole chapter to the moral conditions in California, which centers around the story of a fallen woman. Such topics were usually only briefly alluded to in contemporary narratives; the lengthy treatment given to the theme of prostitution and the unusual reflection in depth upon it justifies its inclusion here:*

Before laying aside my pen, I am constrained to say a word regarding the moral tone of society as it existed in California as early as the years 1851 and 1852.

Recollect, kind reader, that the state of society in California at the present day is as unlike what it was at the time alluded to above as are the golden tints of the eastern sky ere the glorious orb of day bursts upon the view, and the dark, portentous gloom which overspreads the horizon, presaging a coming storm.

To what cause could be attributed this lack of morality, which seemed to pervade the greater portion of the community at that early day, and which necessarily dimmed the lustre of the brightest gem in God's magnificent footstool? Was it the atmospheric influence which surrounded them? or were the evil propensities of their natures more forcibly displayed for the very reason that they felt themselves beyond the reach of all those conventional forms of society which, in our puritanical country, serve to restrain, more or less, the inherent evil of our natures?

Travellers who have wandered in the sunny regions of a tropical clime, and have mingled with the inhabitants, can scarcely fail to perceive the effect of that balmy, blissful atmosphere upon the human passions. Their quick, impulsive natures, warm and generous hearts, overflowing with love and affection; the bewitching naiveté of manner so characteristic of the females has often proved a theme for the poet and historian.

California, although not situated within the tropics, many of its sunny vales possess all the characteristics of soil and climate, and afford to one all the delights pertaining to a residence in those genial climes, and, at the time to which I refer, many of those captivating females had found a home within its borders.

It is oftentimes the case that persons naturally pure, and possessed of good principles, by constant intercourse with those whose nationalities are less stringent with regard to morality, are almost unconsciously, as it were, led to adopt customs, and imbibe sentiments that at first were quite revolting to their natures.

Ever willing to place the best construction upon another's conduct, I would much rather infer that all of the evil which displays itself is the result of a vacillating mind, unable to withstand temptation, rather than of an innate desire to set at defiance the laws of God and man.

Persons from all classes were to be found in California,—the moral and the immoral, the tempter and the tempted. Well may it call a blush to the cheek of our own sex, when I assert that the immoral predominated, as far as the female portion of the community were concerned. I have been an unwilling observer of transactions, which, had they been related to me, would have shaken my opinion somewhat respecting the veracity of the narrator. Think of a town in California where the females numbered more than two hundred, and from that number the pure, high-minded, and virtuous could not have selected more than three or four with whom they could have associated, and have derived a sweet pleasure in the interchange of all those ennobling sentiments which shed such a halo of loveliness around fair woman's shrine.

Now, it is characteristic of my humble self to illustrate every subject by relating some event which has come under my personal observation, and which will, I think, serve to interest.

Among the first who emigrated from the city of Boston to the western El Dorado were a mother and daughter.

The daughter, yet scarcely fifteen years of age, gave promise of extreme loveliness. Carefully had that mother guarded her, lest a too early acquaintance with the chilling realities of life should rob her young and guileless heart of a portion of its pristine purity and undimmed faith.

Of that mother's early history but little was known; yet it was often whispered by the gossiping ones that the remembrance of her own sad, youthful experience had given that shade of melancholy, that tinge of sadness, which at times shaded so deeply her yet fair brow. Whatever had been her bitter trials and disappointments, it was evident to a casual observer that the whole wealth of her affections, the deep, unfathomable love of a mother's heart were centred on the well-being of her only child.

The better to acquire a competency, wherewith to surround the loved ones with all those appliances of comfort so desirable to a young and beautiful girl, the mother determined to seek a home within the precincts of the "Golden State." Better, far better, had she immured herself and child in the catacombs of Rome than thus to have launched their frail bark upon the golden wave of a California sea.

The most ambitious votary of admiration there at that time must have been satisfied, and even satiated, with the amount of homage, adulation, and heartless flattery, which was poured into their too willing ears. One can realize the danger likely to be incurred by placing a young, lovely, and attractive female in a country where virtue was regarded by the mass only as name, and while she was yet too young to discriminate between the respectful homage of sensible gentlemen and the soul-sickening, hypocritical, despicable flatteries which often flow so smoothly from under the moustache of the soulless, "vanity-puffed, shallow-brained apology" for a man. One saw many of those specimens in a day's walk through the city of San Francisco, and also in her sister cities.

Nightly they would convene in those gilded halls of iniquity, and pursue their soul-killing avocation. To be sure, they nightly won their thousands, little caring for the mental agony of their victims, whom they had robbed of the last ounce of dust, which they had been months, perhaps, accumulating, and which they had intended to have transmitted to their families in their far distant homes. Wait patiently, wife and little ones,—wait patiently for the father and husband to learn the best and most effective lesson ever taught by that inexorable schoolmaster, experience! If his first lesson is severe indeed, as a general thing, he is not over anxious to risk a second recital, and the absent wife may hope again to welcome his loved image to the now sorrowful home.

These professed gamblers are never content with ruining those of their own sex, but are ever on the alert and the watch for victims from among the youthful, unsophisticated, and beautiful of the opposite sex; and Lillie Lee was far too captivating to remain long in obscurity.

Notwithstanding the vigilance of her mother she had formed an acquaintance with one of the most enticing of the gambling brotherhood. For weeks and months he had been gradually gaining a strong foothold upon her affections, by practising all those insidious arts which too often successfully entrap the uninitiated. He knew he was beloved, and, knowing that, felt secure of his victim.

The affection bestowed upon that dissolute gamester was deserving a better object. Upon the promise of a speedy marriage, she left her mother's roof; and together they fled to one of the interior towns.

Who can graphically describe that mother's anguish, upon learning the flight of her darling? Within a few hours of their departure, the bereaved, heart-broken, and nearly frantic woman was on the track of the seducer and his victim. She arrived about midnight at the town where the fugitives had taken up their abode. After travelling nearly thirty-six hours without once tasting food, or taking any rest, this grief-stricken woman procured a suitable disguise, and, arming herself with a "Colt's revolver," started on her mission of death.

Grief had rendered her frantic, and, in the desperation of the moment, she had made a vow, and registered it on the tablet of a broken heart, that she would avenge her daughter's ruin by taking the life of her seducer; forgetting, in the frenzy of excitement, that she was assuming a power never intended to be usurped by the sinful children of earth.

She threaded her lonely way through the nearly deserted streets of that inland city, never wavering in her murderous intentions, until she paused at the entrance of one of those brilliantly lighted gambling-saloons which spread their contaminating influence on all around. She entered, expecting and hoping to find the object of pursuit engaged in his nefarious vocation. She saw, however, only the usual appurtenances of these houses of sin. Elegantly attired women, within whose natures long since had expired the last flickering spark of feminine modesty, were seated, dealing cards at a game of Faro or Lansquenet, and, by their winning smile and enticing manner, inducing hundreds of men to stake their all upon their tables. The stricken mother passed through the crowd, but could nowhere see the object of her search.

In this manner she visited all the houses of like reputation, with similar success. By some means or other, she obtained a clue to their whereabouts, reached the door of their room, and, in a disguised voice, demanded admittance. After a long delay, the door was opened, and the despoiled and despoiler met face to face. Quicker than thought, the revolver was levelled at his breast, when a piercing shriek broke on the stillness of the night, and the words, "Mother! oh, mother! in Heaven's name, desist!" burst, in tones of concentrated anguish, from the affrighted girl. In an instant she had thrown herself between the parties, and was imploring her mother to spare the life of him she loved.

What power had changed that mother's anger to grief too deep for utterance? Was it the vivid recollection of a similar scene, enacted long, long ago, in which she had participated? Did the form of her kind and sainted mother rise before her? Yes; she beheld again, in fancy, that calm, sad face, the memory of which had often disturbed her midnight slumbers. These harrowing recollections of the would-be-forgotten past were quite too overpowering. It was long before she was restored to consciousness; and not until repeatedly assured by that deeply dyed villain, that he would make ample restitution by marrying her daughter, could she be persuaded to return to her hotel. The earnest pleadings of the mother could not induce the infatuated girl to separate from her lover. The mother returned to San Francisco.

Months flew by, scarcely heeded by the happy child. The long-deferred marriage proved no source of grief to her. She *loved,* and was happy. She had so much confidence in his honor, that she felt certain he would marry her. Honor! what a desecration of the word, when used in connection with such a fiend in human shape!

Perhaps he would have married her,—for he seemed happy only when in her presence,—if he had not been indissolubly bound to another. Lillie had yet to learn that stunning truth. It must be so; yet how he trembled, and shrank from making a disclosure, which, he well knew, would chill the very life-blood in her veins!

The wife of his youth, tired of living alone in her distant home, had formed the determination to join her husband, and follow his fortunes in the "Golden Empire." Her decision was irrevocable. Even the time was appointed when he should meet her at the bay. He felt, at times, like flying with Lillie to parts unknown; for, depraved as he was, she, by her artless, winning ways, and rich wealth of affection, had stirred the long-dormant fountain of love in his bosom. Yes, now was coming his hour of retribution; for he loved Lillie, and must leave her to the fate that almost always attends the deeply erring. Time was pressing; he must reveal all. It was done; and for hours she sat like one petrified. She could only articulate, "Mother! mother! receive again your heart-broken child!"

They left, that day, for San Francisco,—he, to meet his injured, unloved wife; she, to be received in the arms of her wronged, but still loving mother. Under the influence of a powerful narcotic, which had been administered at her own option, she was conveyed to her mother's house; and there we will leave her for the present.

Behold how majestically that mammoth ocean steamer cuts her way through the sparkling waters of the bay! Now she gracefully turns her prow towards one of the piers, that is crowded with people. What varied emotions fill the bosoms of those there assembled! Some are eagerly, anxiously, expecting the loved wife, from whom they have been separated, perhaps for years; others, dreading, fearing, to meet those whom they have ceased to love, and wish they may never behold again. There were many who had formed connections there that were hard to sever; and among the last named we find Lillie's lover. On the steamer's deck stood his wife, all eagerness to greet her husband after a two years' separation.

The meeting once over, he felt he could sustain his part no longer. Pitiable wife! Henceforth she must be content with a bountiful supply of pocket money. She may revel in luxury, be surrounded with splendor, have every wish gratified but the one yearning desire to possess her husband's love. That was denied to her. She felt the estrangement keenly. What a miserable life was hers! Night after night, as her aching head pressed her lonely pillow, she prayed that death might end her sufferings.

Early morn, perhaps, would bring her husband home. Perchance his only word of salutation would be, "Well, wife, last night I won two, three, or four thousand dollars," just as the case might be; for he was one of those successful gamblers who are well versed in all the tricks used to defraud the unwary. Yes, his coffers were heaped high with his ill-gotten treasures! What cared the wife for riches, if she must ever be treated with that cold, studied politeness, always so freezing to the loving recipient?

Daily I was an unwilling witness to the inward struggles, the pent-up grief, of the proud woman, for we both resided under one roof. She had learned all, everything. Whispered rumors were borne to her ears; and from some source she had learned where was bestowed the affection which of right belonged to her.

In the interim, what had become of Lillie? Had she repented of her sin; and chosen purity's white robe, with which to deck her faultless figure? Ah, no! She did not possess moral courage sufficient to brave the heartless sarcasm, the keen reproach, of that class who are ever ready to judge their fellow-mortals, and who ever forget that divine precept which teaches us that "to err is human; to forgive, divine." And then, after taking the first step in wickedness, it is much easier to follow on in the downward track, than it is to turn, and tread the flowery path of purity, which leads to the mansion of happiness.

After the lapse of a few months, she returned to the inland city; "for," she remarked, "it is some pleasure to breathe the same atmosphere, to traverse the same streets, and frequent the same places of resort as the dearly loved." She rushed recklessly into dissipation. Her extreme beauty, and her adventurous, fearless course of conduct, won for her a widely extended reputation.

One day she would appear in splendid Turkish costume, which admirably displayed her tiny little foot encased in richly embroidered satin slippers. Thus would she promenade the thronged thoroughfares of the city, the observed of all observers. Again she might be seen, superbly dressed after the fashion of that class of people denominated "fast men." How gracefully she held the ribbons, and with what dexterity she managed her spirited horse, as she dashed madly on over the broad plains which surrounded the city. In the use of the cigarita she equalled, in point of fascination, the dark-eyed Spanish women.

I have seen her mounted on a glossy, lithe-limbed race-horse,—one that had won for her many thousands on the course,— habited in a closely-fitting riding-dress of black velvet, orna-mented with a hundred and fifty gold buttons, a hat from which depended magnificent sable plumes, and, over her face, a short white lace veil of the richest texture, so gossamer-like, one could almost see the fire of passion flashing from the depths of her dark, lustrous eyes. She took all captive. Gold and diamonds were showered upon her. Her ringing, musical laugh seemed the signal at which trouble, care, and sorrow fled away and hid themselves. Lillie was not soulless, or heartless either; but yet the hilarity of despair seemed to have fast possession of her. Many a tear has fallen at the thought of her sad future.

The unloved wife, finding that all efforts to reclaim her husband's love proved futile, decided to return to the home of her youth. She took passage from San Francisco in a steamer upon which Lillie's mother had also secured her passage; for, despairing of ever reclaiming her daughter, she was hastening to leave a country where so much existed to remind her of her fallen child. Thus were these two sorrowing females thrown together on ship-board; yet neither by word or look did they recognize each other. The mother still cherished the same revengeful feelings towards the seducer; and the proud wife rejected the idea of allowing, even for a moment, the mother of one who unconsciously had been instrumental in causing the sky of her existence to be shrouded in dark, impenetrable gloom, to suspect that she was suffering from unrequited affection.

The husband was happy again with Lillie, until about two years after his wife's departure, when he was unceremoniously hurried into the presence of his Maker. He met his death by the glittering knife of one whom he had defrauded of his last ounce of dust. The one to whom he had done the greatest injury, the most irreparable wrong, wept bitter tears of anguish over his unhonored grave.

There were many beautiful, depraved women in California who, previous to leaving their homes in the Atlantic States, had lived virtuous lives; many who had been the light and the life of the home circle—who had, indeed, been an ornament to the society in which they moved. Some of them were desirous of acquiring riches; and, hearing such glowing accounts of fortunes so speedily amassed in California, and also being possessed of an adventurous spirit, started, as they termed it, to seek their fortunes. Some went with their husbands, some with their fathers, some with their brothers, and too many went alone.

To such as had felt and known all the inconvenience arising from a limited purse, and thought that if they were blessed with riches, or a competency even, their happiness would be complete,—to such, I assert, it was a dangerous country to go to, unless their principles were as firm as the rocks of their native hills.

One beautiful young girl, in company with her brother, left a pleasant home, situated in the heart of the "Old Granite State," and together they reached the El Dorado of the West. He repaired to the mines, after having procured a lucrative situation for his sister as governess in a wealthy Spanish family. Previous to leaving the States, she had been a music teacher.

After awhile, she became tired of her rather monotonous life, and conceived the idea of going to one of the interior cities, to see if she could find something better to do. An offer was made of forty dollars an evening, if she would sit at a Lansquenet table, and deal the cards. At first she shrank with horror at the idea of thus appearing in a gambling-house. Then she thought of her widowed mother at home, deprived of all the comforts and luxuries so acceptable to the middle-aged and feeble. Said she, "What an amount of money I can earn in this way, wherewith to surround mother with every comfort, and yet not compromise my honor in the least!" Mistaken girl! No woman could long remain virtuous in one of those gilded saloons of vice, surrounded, as she must necessarily be, by men who looked upon the opposite sex very much in the same light as does the fishhawk, which soars above the surface of some clear lake, ever ready to pounce upon, and bear off in its talons, any one of the shining piscatory tribe that, more venturesome than another, approaches too near to the boundaries of its native element.

The night approached on which Jennie was to make her début in the sporting world. With a palpitating heart, she repaired, in company with her employer, to one of the most magnificent gambling establishments in the city. Upon entering, the dazzling brilliancy of the surrounding appurtenances, the delicious strains of magical music which burst upon her ear, were perfectly enchanting; but, as she raised her eyes to the walls, (from which depended numerous pictures, all calculated to excite the grosser passions of man, and which were inclosed in magnificently gilded frames,) she drank in at a glance her position, and fainted. She was taken to her hotel, and left, for that night, to her own gloomy reflections.

Oh, Jennie, if you had but listened to, and been guided by, the spirit-influence of your Guardian Angel, who is ever near and ready, unless obstinately resisted, to soothe the agitated, wavering heart, and, by sweet, whispered breathings of divine counsel, is able to lead the troubled soul to drink of the sweet waters of eternal happiness!

Next morning came the tempter; and, by increasing in amount the already liberal sum proffered for her services, he gained from her a promise to make a second attempt the ensuing evening. She went, and this time succeeded in reaching the seat provided for her; but her head swam, her step faltered; and well it might, for the licentious gaze of hundreds rested admiringly upon her superb figure. Her transcendently beautiful countenance was suffused with the blush of maidenly modesty; and that, having been an unseen and unheard-of feature in such a place, was all the more refreshing for its scarcity.

For some time she retained all her original purity; and then the angels in heaven might have wept, when they saw the tempter secure of his victim. She had launched her skiff upon the sea of immorality, freighted with that priceless treasure, virtue; and, in exchange for which, it had returned to her laden with gold, wherewith she could supply her dearly loved mother's every want. Thus she lived for months; not quite so daring as Lillie, yet drinking sufficiently deep at the Lethean fount to hush all the whisperings of conscience. She finally terminated her profitable career of vice by marrying a wealthy, popular man in one of the mountain towns,—one with whom she had lived on terms of the greatest intimacy for months before their marriage.

She now moves in good society in one of our Eastern cities, surrounded with all the appliances of wealth, in possession of the love of a popular and respected husband. Who, among her numerous friends, would stop to make inquiries of her past life? And, even if her fashionable acquaintances knew of her past follies, I am rather inclined to think they would "wink" at them rather than lose a *wealthy friend*. Such was life as I saw it in California.

*Mrs. Bates changed her residences many times during her four years in California, and never felt at home there. She finally returned East alone, a "sadder and a wiser woman," who had seen her bright hopes "blasted and blighted in the bud" and who had "drunk deep draughts of sorrow."[3] A distance is maintained between herself and the various objects she describes, except for the passages which are devoted to her personal problems. Her way of presenting her impressions is arresting, for she tried to see beyond the surface and liked to speculate about what she noticed. Her style is lively and metaphorical, showing Biblical and poetical influences. Among the huge amount of rather boring travel literature to which the events in California gave rise, Mrs. Bates's stands out sharply; it elicits a variety of responses from the reader, appealing sometimes to his reflection, sometimes to his emotions, sometimes to his sense of humor.*

1. Mrs. Bates, p. 149.
2. Ibid, p. 202.
3. Ibid, p. 272.
4. Another writer who was much concerned with the moral tone in California was Eliza Farnsham, *California In-Doors and Out; or how we farm, mine and live generally in the Golden State*. (New York: Dix. Edwards & Co.), 1856.

# California: A Pleasure Trip from Gotham to the Golden Gate

Myriam F. Leslie

April, May, June 1877. (New York: G.W. Carleton & Co., Publishers) 1877.

*Mrs. Leslie's book was published shortly after the trip it relates. In her Preface, she presents it in the following way:*

> *. . . this work of mine is a vehicle, through which, with feminine longing for sympathy, I convey to you my pleasures, annoyances, and experiences in the journey it narrates; or, if you like better, it is a casket, enshrining the memory of many a pleasant hour. . . .* [1]

*She expressed a particular concern with preserving her good memories and sharing them with congenial people, and insisted that to assess a woman's writings one must "have learned to read between the lines and find there the pith and meaning of the whole".[2]*

*Her book, which features many illustrations, starts with her departure on a train and includes descriptions of both the scenery and the other passengers, as well as a report on contemporary travelling conditions. What makes her narrative interesting are the sharp comments she offers from time to time. She was not impressed at all by the appearance Salt Lake City presented. Her account of her stay there includes lengthy discussions of polygamy and of the position of women in Utah, and also an interview with Brigham Young. She then goes on to describe the American desert and the tribes that lived there. Her description of San Francisco tries to embrace the many aspects of life, in addition to accounts of meetings with prominent figures such as Senator Sharon and Mayor Bryant. The following passage attempts to recapture the atmosphere in the streets of the city and to provide observations on the inhabitants' way of life:*

The most fashionable shops are on Kearney and Montgomery streets, the Broadway and favorite promenades of the city. The windows of these shops are large, and showily furnished, but the interiors are of limited extent, owing to the high price of land in these localities. Every imaginable object is to be bought in San Francisco, generally at very high prices; for, like most places of sudden growth, it is an extravagant place in dress, equipage, and general tone of living, the fortunes of the East becoming a modest competence here, and what would be comfort in Philadelphia or Baltimore dwindling to penury in San Francisco.

Many of the smaller shops are open to the street like booths, especially the cigar and liquor establishments, in one of which we saw a man throwing dice for a drink. Most of the sidewalks are of wood, and the street-car tracks are paved with that material, although we were told that none but the Nicholson pavement has proved a success here, as the long, dry heat of certain portions of the year, and the persistent dampness of others, shrink and swell, out of proportion, the blocks of all other kinds of wooden pavement.

The climate of San Francisco seems a point as difficult to settle as the standard of feminine beauty, or the intrinsic value of Wagner's music. Every one agrees that it is an exhilarating climate, that the air is more highly charged with ozone than in most localities, that the brain-worker can accomplish more here in a given time than anywhere else, and wear himself out faster; for dear Starr King died of exhaustion, of old age, in fact, after doing the work of a generation for his adopted State; and such a career as that of W. A. Ralston would scarcely have been possible in any city other than high-pressure San Francisco. But this ozone, this fourth-proof oxygen, is borne upon the wings of high, cold winds, piercing the very marrow of a sensitive form, and alternating with fogs and dampness, fatal to any rheumatic or neuralgic tendencies, and unfavorable to pulmonary complaints. A few hours of nearly every morning are charming out of doors, and the rest of the day a fire or a bow-window full of sunshine is still more charming. One person says, "The climate of San Francisco is all that keeps me alive"; and the next one shudders, "The climate is killing me; I must get out of town to warm my blood, or it will congeal altogether." All confess, however, that this is the chilliest and breeziest point upon the whole coast, for it stands in a gap of the hills, guarding the shore for miles above and below, and once in the sheltered valleys lying between this coast line and the Sierras, one comes into a tropical and paradisaical climate as enervating to the brain as the breezy air of San Francisco is exciting. Let us conclude that the climate, like the society, like the morals, and like the social habits of San Francisco, is a little mixed, and that a wise eclecticism is desirable in choosing a residence therein.

One feature of the street scenery in this city is the large proportion of foreign physiognomy and the accents of almost every language under the sun, which meet one's ear in all the crowded thoroughfares. The easy access of the Pacific coast from the other side of the globe has led thither a class of Oriental strangers who are seldom seen even in New York, and not only the Chinaman, but his neighbors of Asia and Africa—"Mede, Parthian and Scythian"—here find a home, a field of labor, and a share, however small, of the almighty dollar, which has proved more lovely in their eyes than the lands of the bul-bul and the rose.

To accommodate these various tastes, various amusements, shops, theatres, and especially restaurants, are established at every corner, and the Frenchman, scanning the *menu* of the Maison Dorée, may fancy himself at the Trois Frères, in Paris; while the German finds his sauerkraut, the Italian his maccaroni, the Spaniard his picadillo, and the Welshman his leek, each at his own house of refreshment; and the Chinese eating-houses are a feature of their especial quarter, to be mentioned hereafter. To live in lodgings and to eat in a restaurant is San Franciscan as much as it is Parisian, and even families possessing houses and domestic conveniences are often to be found at one or the other of these establishments, dining or lunching, "just for variety"; and also, perhaps, to see and to be seen a little.

A fashionable restaurant for gentlemen is "The Poodle Dog"; "Campi's" is as Italian as Naples, and the "Maison Dorée" is Delmonican in every respect. The code of social law in San Francisco permits young ladies to freely visit these establishments, even at the risk of occasionally encountering a male acquaintance, and a cynical observer may find more refreshment in quiet observation of the scenes around him than in meat or drink. Perhaps, on the whole, we would not advise the widowed mother of a family of lads and lassies to carry them to San Francisco for social training; the Prunes, Prisms, and Propriety system is not universal, and although there is a large class of charming, unexceptional, and rigidly moral society, there are several other classes shading into it by almost imperceptible degrees; and the bygone days, when every man was a law unto himself in this city, have left their impress in a certain recklessness and willfulness of feeling pervading every circle.

The style of street dress is more gay and showy than is consistent with the severest taste, and an afternoon promenade upon Kearney or Montgomery streets reminds one of a fashionable "Opening," when the lay figures have suddenly received life and the power of locomotion. It has been said that in other cities the *demi-monde* imitates the fashions of the *beau-monde*, but that in San Francisco the case is reversed, and the caprices of the former class are meekly copied by the latter. It may be a libel; but we certainly saw very elegant toilets, and very fine jewels, both in carriages and upon pedestrians to whom we had no letters of introduction.

Noticing a goodly proportion of churches among the handsome buildings of San Francisco, we inquired if anybody ever visited them, and were indignantly informed that religion was one of the most flourishing imports of the City of the Golden Gate. Everybody knows, of course, that it was originally founded as a mission by the Franciscan Fathers, the first of whom, the Padre Junipero Serra, scandalized that no station had as yet been dedicated to his patron saint, prayed to him for a fortunate harbor in his next voyage of exploration; and being led or driven through the Golden Gate, considered that the Saint thus indicated the spot where he would have his altar erected, and so named the waters upon which the mission vessel floated, "The Bay of San Francisco." The Mission House and Church were more elaborately styled "Los Dolores de nuestro Padre, San Francisco de Assissi," and is still called the Mission Dolores; while the presidio and fort erected to protect the good monks in their holy work was called San Francisco, and the town that languidly grew around them took the name of Yerba Buena, from a medicinal plant growing abundantly in the vicinity. It was not until 1847 that the name of San Francisco was formally given to the little town, then just upon the eve of its marvelous upward bound to the rank of a great city. The Romish faith thus planted has kept its ascendancy in the city of San Francisco d'Assissi, and claims to-day about one-half of the population. St. Mary's Cathedral, St. Francis's, St. Patrick's and St. Ignatius's, are all with large and wealthy congregations, and there are ten more Roman churches in the city. The Presbyterians are most numerous among the Protestant denominations, and Calvary Church is one of the handsomest in the city. Grace and Trinity are the most prominent of the Episcopal Churches, and both claim large and fashionable congregations; and the Congregationalists, Methodists, Baptists, and other denominations are in a hopeful condition. Attendance at all of these churches for morning service is quite general, but the afternoon and evening of Sunday are devoted to amusement by the San Franciscan, and each in his degree seeks some place of public or private entertainment, or the day is spent in ruralizing, or in driving and visiting.

*Chinatown is described in great detail and occasions some rather censorious comments. The fate of the Chinese prostitutes, which is so often alluded to in writings of the time but rarely looked at very closely, is presented in the following words:*

"This is pretty rough," said the guide, stopping at the entrance of a dark and dismal court, whose odors seemed even more sickening and deadly than those we had breathed before; "but say the word and I will take you in."

The word was said, and stumbling up some crazy stairs we found ourselves at last in a narrow balcony overhanging the reeking court. Some Chinese women clustered at the end of this balcony staring at us, behind them was a shrine containing the Goddess of Love, with gilt paper and Joss-sticks burning in the tray before her. From this gallery we passed into the house and became involved in a perfect honeycomb of little rooms, dimly lighted, or not lighted at all; no doors were visible, the doorways being shaded by long, pink calico curtains, and as they blew or were drawn aside we saw every room crowded with men and a few women, smoking, drinking tea, or playing at dominoes or cards. Every room we entered was exceedingly clean, and the inmates looked remarkably neat and tidy. Some effort at decoration was visible in the way of gilt and red paper, bright-colored scarves and peacocks' feathers upon the walls, and pretty little Chinese tea-pots and other pottery upon the tables and shelves. Everyone was smiling and bland as possible, and seemed overjoyed to receive a call; in one room especially, where a man and woman and some boys were all squeezed up together in a space of six feet square or so, they all chatted and laughed and stared as if we were long lost brothers at least, asking "What you wantee? Where you comee from?" and saying "Glad to see you, come again velly soon!" at parting, in the most sociable manner possible.

In another room was a fat, good-looking woman of thirty or so, with her hair elaborately coiled, puffed and ornamented with bright gold pins, making tea at a little table set out with queer cups and saucers which excited our ceramic covetousness; the room was very small and very neat, with a bed in one corner enclosed with white curtains tied with scarves at the corners, and upon the bed a little tray holding two vases of lilacs and other common flowers, besides a lamp, pipe, and opium box; curled up beside this festive preparation lay a man who arose and welcomed us with great enthusiasm and seemed so much at home that we concluded he must be the host, and after complimenting him upon the flowers decking his opium tray, the neatness of the room and the pretty tea-service, we inquired if the woman were his wife; but at this he seemed very much amused, laughed a great deal and said: "No, no, me no mally, no wife; no mally at all!" and the woman seemed as much delighted as himself at the absurd mistake.

In another room we found a dozen men or more and one woman crowded around a table playing cards; the woman was by no means unattractive and wore beautiful earrings and had a large diamond ring, and on her fat and pretty arms bracelets which our guide said were twenty-carat-fine gold. She showed us these ornaments with much pride, and on our admiring them paid us the Spanish compliment of saying they would better become us than herself. When asked if they were gifts from some of these gentlemen she answered with a sudden assumption of dignity: "Me got velly good husband, me mallied woman!" We assured her that we were delighted to hear such favorable accounts of her condition, and so passed on, peeping into a dozen or more little rooms, all crowded with men and a few women, but no babies, no little children, nothing to relieve the brazen face of the whole establishment. The women were mostly without beauty or grace, and usually dressed in dingy blue sacks with huge sleeves, their hair drawn back and curiously puffed, coiled or plaited behind. They all wore the mechanical smile which seems part of the national character; but their faces were thin and haggard, and the paint did not disguise the wan weariness which was eating away their lives. These poor creatures are most of them bred to evil from infancy by parents who make merchandise of them in early girlhood. Sometimes the wretched creature sacrifices herself, signing a contract and receiving a certain sum in advance for services during a term of years or for life; the larger part of which sum goes to the broker or intermediary. These slaves—for they are so considered, and, as a general thing, are very harshly and penuriously treated—receive only a maintenance and coarse clothing during their brief period of health, and when overtaken by sickness are turned out to die in any hole they can creep into.

Great discontent exists among the better class of San Franciscans at the constant importation of these slaves from China, the open and revolting traffic forming a terrible satire upon the hecatomb of the best lives of our own country sacrificed in the late war to abolish Negro Slavery!

Coming out of this house, we passed a row of tiny windows, breast-high to a man, looking out upon the narrow sidewalk of the court, at each of which appeared the face of a woman, the little room behind her as bright and attractive as she knew how to make it; one in especial was quite illuminated and decked with flowers and draperies, and the inmate, a rather pretty young girl, was singing in a sort of cooing little voice.

These unfortunates are seldom reclaimed; they feel no sense of sin or shame in their lives, and if well treated are quite content. Occasionally the Christian Missionaries who wage an unequal and all but hopeless warfare against heathendom in San Francisco succeed in persuading one of them to escape and accept such refuge as charity provides for them; but as a general thing their masters succeed in tracing them and show willingness to expend more money and time in repossessing themselves of them than the victim can possibly be worth, and the last state of these reclaimed slaves is worse than the first.

There are said to be about fifteen hundred Chinese women of this class in San Francisco; seven-tenths of all who come to this country belonging to its dismal ranks, and it is surmised that not more than a hundred reputable Chinese married women are to be found in the city, the inducements to the better class of men to bring their families to these shores being small indeed, for the free and noble principles of our government suffer insult and wrong, not only at the hands of slave-dealers but at those of our own people, who permit the ruffians infesting San Francisco to rob, insult and maltreat the Chinaman at every turn, revenging upon him, as is the habit of degraded natures, the galling sense of their own baseness and inferiority.

Let us close this painful subject, with a confession of its most repulsive phase. We were informed that the most beautiful and accomplished imported Traviatas in China Town were intended for and maintained by white gentlemen exclusively. Let us subscribe liberally to the mission to Borrioboola Gha, and send flannel waistcoats to Afghanistan, and then let us devote what is left of our money and energy and Christian zeal to the conversion of these "gentlemen," and the Hoodlum who maims and insults and robs the honest Chinese laborer!

*Mrs. Leslie's narrative then offers descriptions of the scenery around San Francisco, and moves on to conditions in Los Angeles and southern California.[3] One of the last places which is depicted in detail is Virginia City; Mrs. Leslie had a poor impression of the town, and her scathing comments prompted one of the leading local newspapers,* The Territorial Enterprise, *to undertake a mud-slinging campaign against her: a special issue which came out in 1878 expressed the strongest doubts concerning her character and that of her husband. Here is the gist of the controversial passage:*

To call a place dreary, desolate, homeless, uncomfortable, and wicked is a good deal, but to call it God-forsaken is a good deal more, and in a tolerably large experience of this world's wonders, we never found a place better deserving the title than Virginia City.

To commence with, the conditions of its being are highly disagreeable, for it is a town hooked on, as it were, to the precipitous side of a barren and rocky mountain, and one is always apprehensive that the adhesive power may become exhausted, and the whole place go sliding down to the depths of the valley below.

The streets are mere narrow terraces built along the face of this precipice, like the vineyards along the Rhine, or the steps of the Pyramids, whose arid and dusty desolation they also imitate, without the grandeur and mystery which make one forget the rest.

Leaving the station we climbed a steep and long flight of wooden steps to the street above, where stood the hotel, a very good one, by the way, and flanked by some substantial stone and brick buildings, but this block is the exception in the way of architecture, the rule being frame houses, as loosely and carelessly put together as a child's card house. The style may be inferred perhaps from the fact that about two years ago the whole town burned down one night, and was rebuilt as good as ever in six days.

Nowhere does one find a level, the streets are all parallel, with the exception of one, leading up the mountain from the depot, and standing in any of them, one looks off as if from a belfry, across the tops of the houses below, and over the chimneys of quartz mills and mining works still lower down, until vision loses itself among the crowding brown peaks and waving mountain ranges, never coming to any resting point of level or of greenery, before the horizon line closes the dreary scene.

The Prince of the Power of Air reigns supreme in this region, and the fierce cold wind sweeps through the narrow streets with force enough to take one off one's feet. Very little rain falls here, but plenty of snow, coming early and remaining late, indeed possible in any month of the year, and sometimes lying there three feet deep in May, in which jocund month we were there.

Virginia City boasts of forty-nine gambling saloons and one church, open the day we were there for a funeral, an event of frequent occurrence in the lawless little city. The population is largely masculine, very few women, except of the worst class, and as few children.

Chinese are rare, not being in favor with the miners, who have a horror of their cheap labor, and show their dislike in very vigorous fashion when the opportunity occurs.

The hotel has been running only a few months, but is very comfortable, with a pretty parlor and handsome dining-room, where we enjoyed one of the best breakfasts since leaving San Francisco. A carriage was in waiting as we came out of the dining hall and took us to the Bonanza Mines, zigzagging from one steep and narrow street to another, like a magnified Yosemite trail with all the attractiveness left out, until at length we dismounted at the great building over the shaft of the California or Bonanza Mine.

Postponing any farther investigations until the morrow, we left the mills and drove about the city, seeing little more, however, than has already been described, returned to the hotel for dinner, and after a while strolled out to see what changes might have been wrought by night and moonlight.

The changes were noticeable but not beautifying, and the two policemen, who followed close at our heels, were by no means a guard of ceremony but a most necessary protection. Every other house was a drinking or gambling saloon, and we passed a great many brilliantly lighted windows, where sat audacious looking women who freely chatted with passers-by or entertained guests within.

Cheyenne did not seem to us to deserve its mournful sobriquet, and Virginia City equally did seem to deserve, although it has not received it.

The next morning we walked to the assaying office, to see the gold and silver taken from the crucibles in which they are finally purified, and we subsequently returned to the Bonanza or California Mine, the chief and some others of the party having resolved to explore its depths.

This mine is principally owned by Messrs. Flood & O'Brien, and Mr. Fair. The two former kept a small drinking saloon in San Francisco, and were on intimate terms with some of their miner customers, one of whom, waxing confidential and good-humored in his cups, informed them of a wonderful "lode" just discovered and not yet known. With wise audacity they sold all that they possessed and invested every cent in the quarter indicated, managed to get control of the whole mine, worked it wisely and fortunately, and to-day are said to be worth fifteen millions each.

Mr. Fair, although equally rich, resides on the spot, and passes three hours daily down in the mine, personally superintending its operations. The receipts for this mine during fifteen months, were $24,850,524.85—and for over a year it has divided a million monthly, with no signs of exhaustion.

Mr. Fair took us first to the large long room where the miners change their clothes, and which was hung closely all around from the roof with miners' shirts and trousers, while on a long frame down the middle of the place stood their big, heavy shoes or brogans.

The men are divided into gangs, each working eight hours, and each gang having its division of this room, and every man his own especial hook, where he keeps his mining suit not in wear, it being necessary to change thoroughly every time they come out of the mine.

The men are mostly Cornish—no Irish and no Chinese allowed. The owners would like to employ the latter, but the Miners' Union is too strong for them, dictating eight hours a day as the period for labor, wages of four dollars per diem, and no competition.

The miners embrace every class of men, socially speaking, from the lowest grade of laborer to the ex-United States Senator, or man of title, obliged to resort to manual labor, and too proud to perform it in open daylight, preferring to pass his existence in digging living graves 1,700 feet below the surface of the earth.

Returning to the shaft, we encountered a party of miners just dressed to go down, having changed their clothes in the little office near the mouth of the pit. They looked very wild and strange in their great solid hats, like roofs, stiff enough to protect the head from falling bits of rock, their uncouth clothes and great brogans, each man carrying a lantern in his hand.

Nine men crowd upon the elevator at once, and at a given signal go dashing down into the hot, white steam, disappearing in a moment, absolutely swallowed up in the earth. The place swarmed with miners waiting their turn to go down, the elevator making its trip in about fifteen minutes.

A set came up while we stood looking after those who had gone down the other shaft, and such a set of ghosts one never saw: pale, exhausted, dripping with water and perspiration, some with their shirts torn off and naked to the waist, all of them haggard and dazed with the long darkness and toil. The heat in the shaft is fearful, and although the galleries are cooler, it is still so warm that the men are obliged to work half naked, sometimes wholly so, and word is always sent down when ladies are about to visit the mine.

Presently the chief, with the "forlorn hope," who had volunteered to accompany him underground, retired to the dressing-room, and soon returned so queerly metamorphosed that it was hard to recognize them, and various complimentary remarks and quizzical comparisons accompanied them as they somewhat gingerly stepped upon the elevator and began their descent.

A sudden thrill of vague horror, however, superseded all disposition to laughter as the car swiftly and suddenly took our friends from our very midst, leaving only the black shaft with its ghostly clouds of hot, white steam to show where they had been. It was too much like that other dark and mysterious pit into which most of us have watched our friends go down to return no more, and I for one turned away shuddering and afeard.

The party remained below two hours, and returned tired, excited, delighted, and loquacious, to find us comfortably settled in Mr. Taylor's room, dispelling our anxiety as best we might by selections from our host's numberless volumes of our favorite poets.

So soon as our friends had bathed—for the directors have a private bath and dressing-room, which had been placed at the disposal of our party—and resumed their usual attire, and we had bidden good-by to our courteous hosts of the Big Bonanza Mine, we returned to the hotel, dined, and then drove to our car in the midst of a drenching rain, almost an unknown phenomenon in Virginia City, and looked our last upon the bare, brown hills and the city in the air through vertical sheets of drifting waters.

*Mrs. Leslie's book provides original and provocative views on the places she visited and the people she met in the course of her trip out West. They are valuable especially as a basis for comparisons with other writings. Clearly, she was in quest of the sensational, and enjoyed discussing controversial issues such as polygamy and prostitution. Her manner of writing is often vivid, and she had a fine gift for recreating atmosphere.*

1. Mrs. Leslie, p. 5.
2. Ibid, p. 6.
3. Her comments on southern California have been reproduced in an article edited by Richard Reinhardt: "On the Brink of the Boom: Southern California in 1877 as Witnessed by Mrs. Frank Leslie," *California Historical Society Quarterly*, 52 (1973), 64-79.

# To and Fro, Up and Down in Southern California, Oregon, and Washington Territory, with sketches in Arizona, New Mexico and British Columbia

Emma Hildreth Adams

(Cincinnati, Chicago, St. Louis: Cranston & Stowe) 1888.

*In her preface, Emma Adams explains that she was a correspondent of several leading dailies from 1883 to 1886 and occasionally contributed to prominent religious journals. Her articles were favorably received, and this prompted her to put them into book form. Here is a statement of her aims and method:*

> *The title of this book aptly expresses the character of its contents. Its chapters form a series of sketches, picturing such only of the scenes, events, incidents, industries, enterprises, institutions, and people of the coast as came within the writer's observation or knowledge, and as, it is believed, will contribute most to the service and enjoyment of the reader.*[1]

*Many illustrations are added to the text. The first part of the book is entitled "To and Fro in Southern California." It provides detailed information on the population, history and resources of New Mexico and is at pains to provide figures and specific data. Geographical details, descriptions of mining and a historical sketch of Tucson are part of the chapters on Arizona. Life in southern California is presented, with a particular emphasis on the vegetation and resources. Several pages are devoted to Hubert H.*

Bancroft, whom the author met, and to his great historical
undertaking. Mrs. Adams also provides some information on the
native Californians, their way of life and their customs. She talks at
length about such prominent figures as Don Pio Pico, and was
especially interested in colonization schemes and the agricultural
development of southern California. In one chapter, she stresses
women's participation in it and points out the success some of
them met with in their enterprises:

One day in June last the writer was one of a dozen passengers
in the "morning stage" from Los Angeles to Pasadena. The vehicle
was not one of those oval-shaped, springy, swaying coaches
which, as I fancied in my childhood, insure the very perfection of
carriage riding, and which the traveler of the present day may test,
should he ever cross the rugged Siskiyou Mountains in one of the
coaches of the Oregon and California stage-line, but was a long,
four-seated conveyance, with high, square top and open sides.
From it we could obtain a fine view of the picturesque country for
miles around.

The passengers were all in their seats only one-half hour after
the time, and presently the four-in-hand dashed off from the *cigar-
store* in Temple Block, claiming to be the head-quarters of the
stage company. The little seven-by-nine room is by no means a
pleasant waiting point for ladies, and I being usually ahead of time
when setting out on such a jaunt, had the pleasure of seeing no end
of money set fire to, in little slender rolls of tobacco, during the
hour I watched for the stage.

The morning was cloudy. The atmosphere was laden with
chilling moisture, which the breeze drove sharply into our faces.
Anywhere in the East, under such circumstances, an all-day rain
might confidently have been predicted; but in Southern California
it "never rains when it does," so we were not disappointed to see
the mist drift away long before noon. Then down came the genial
sunlight, making the earth and ourselves rejoice.

Our road twice crossed the Arroyo Secco, a chatty stream
flowing from the Sierra Madre. All around, the country was
covered with wrinkles, like an aged face furrowed by years of
care. Now we sped across a pretty valley, decked with venerable

live-oaks, ever green, and singularly effective in the landscape, but some of them painfully distorted in shape. Now we were borne up a long hill, from whose top we had a view of scenes quite worthy the brush which put the Yo-Semite on canvas.

Upon the seat beside me sat an intelligent lady from some town in Iowa. She had been on a visit to Elsinore, a new colony springing up, with fair prospects, not far from Riverside. Her husband, as I soon learned, was one of its projectors, and, as was entirely proper, she appeared to be much interested in the sale of Elsinore lots. She quietly advised a young man, forming the third party on our seat, and evidently just catching the real-estate fever, to "see Elsinore before investing elsewhere in Southern California." That was kind of her. The new town occupies a location as charming as is its name, on the border of Elsinore Lake, where it would be delightful to dwell. The place has advantages all its own, and might exactly meet the wants and means of this stranger. If so, two men had been helped.

It is very noticeable how quickly bright-minded women from other parts of the country become interested, and then engaged, in real-estate transactions on this coast. It is worthy of remark, too, what ability they display in the business, and what success they achieve. Some one has said that as large a proportion of women as men, increase their fortunes by this sort of trade. They are quick to discern the favorable or unfavorable points in a piece of property, and seem to know when they have received a good offer from a purchaser.

A friend recently informed me that of a certain large tract of land near the city, which was put on the market lately in small lots, nearly one-half the buyers were women; and also, that it is not a rare thing for numbers of feminine speculators to attend the auction sales of land frequently taking place, and to bid quietly but intelligently for the property.

Of the sixty-five or more women employed as teachers in the public schools of Los Angeles, there is scarcely one who is not the owner of land somewhere in the State. Numbers of women on the coast—in California, in Oregon—personally superintend considerable farms, the titles to which are in their own name. They themselves make the sales of the crops. In some instances they have brought their land up to a high figure by putting it under fine cultivation. Of the five women who happen to be at this moment in the house where I write, all possess land in or near the city.

Much has been said about an educated and sensible young woman who, with her invalid father, resides in one of the colonies not very distant from Los Angeles. She is the owner of a raisin vineyard of ten or more acres, every vine in which was planted by her own hands. The vineyard is now in full bearing. Every year she superintends the picking, curing, and packing of her crop, and makes her own terms with the dealers. I think she is the possessor also of ten acres of orange trees, in thrifty condition. The story goes that when the little cottage in which they live was in process of erection, the roof being unfinished, a severe storm threatened. This made it necessary for the father—his own carpenter, I presume—to have aid in the shingling. None being obtainable in the small town, the indomitable girl climbed to the roof, and laid shingles until the work was complete, acquitting herself as creditably at carpentry as she does at raisin-making.

I am now obliged to add that, no sooner had this brave, energetic girl acquired her pretty home, and become well advanced toward competency, than there chanced that way a Methodist minister, who, admiring her noble qualities, invited her to become his wife. And she, pleased with the idea, accepted the invitation, and is about to be married.

In the same village live two sisters, young women from Wisconsin, who, with a widowed mother, came to the place but a few years ago. With their slender means they purchased a few acres of land near, and soon had growing upon it a raisin vineyard and an orange grove, much of the labor of planting them being performed with their own hands. While their vines and trees were growing, one of them, a girl rarely endowed, applied for the position of postmaster in the community, and received the appointment, "her application being indorsed by nearly every voter in the town."

About this time the Southern Pacific Railway, learning that she was an accomplished telegrapher, gave her important employment in that occupation, her sister becoming her efficient deputy in the post-office. These young women are the daughters of a Congregational clergyman who died some years ago, and are, of course, cultured, Christian girls. Their womanly ways, promptness, and conscientious discharge of duty, as daughters, in the Church, in society, in business, have won them the good will and respect of all parties. As a result of economy and judicious investments in real estate, their combined fortune now, at the close of about five years, amounts to some sixteen thousand dollars.

We are now well on the way to Pasadena. Suddenly the four-in-hand wheel into a flower-bordered drive-way on our right. Then comes to view a trim little cottage crowning one of the "wrinkles." Now out of the front door-way bound two or three young children, shouting "Mamma!" After them comes a babe in somebody's arms. The place was the home, these were the children, of the lady from Elsinore. Ourselves happy over the welcome she received, we bade her adieu, turned back to the main road, and began climbing Hermosa Vista Hill, one of the sightliest eminences in all this picturesque region, and, as has been said in a previous chapter, the seat of a college for young men.

The summit gained, a short time brought us into Orange Grove Avenue, the finest street in Pasadena. Throughout its entire length vineyards, orange groves, inviting grounds, and comfortable abodes grace both sides. Speeding on a couple of miles, we at last turned into the broad, arched gateway at Carmelita, the beautiful home of Dr. Ezra S. Carr and his family. Here the stage left the writer for a twenty-four hours' sojourn. As we wound through the drive-way to the house, we noticed among the great variety of choice trees in the grounds, cedars from Lebanon, India, Norway, Oregon, and the Norfolk Islands; also, the maple, butternut, mulberry, palm, bamboo, several species of eucalypti—natives of Australia—and the sturdy sequoia, of Calaveras stock, with other home and foreign trees.

Carmelita is intended to suggest not only the name of its proprietor, but also Mount Carmel, in Syria. Naturally it calls up the days of Elijah, and the scenes of the august miracle which took place on that summit, with its attendant human slaughter. The cottage, framed in with flowers and vines, occupies the crown of a long descent toward the east. In the foreground, on that side, stands an apricot orchard in splendid condition. Beyond that, a part of the lovely village comes into the picture. Farther away, stretches the rich San Gabriel Valley. On the left, three miles distant, rise the stately Sierra Madre Mountains. Thus are brought into the beautiful panorama the extremes of scenery. Walking about the perfect grounds at Carmelita today, noting the scope of the improvements on every hand, it is difficult to persuade one's self that seven years have sufficed to produce fruit and forest trees of such magnitude; and still more difficult to believe the whole is the result of one little woman's effort.

Seven years ago—this account was penned in 1884—Doctor Carr and his family were living in the city of Sacramento, himself being the State Superintendent of Public Instruction. With health impaired by forty years of arduous labor in educational fields, he was admonished that a retreat where rest could be assured, would soon become a necessity. This led to the purchase of the forty acres now constituting Carmelita. They were then a mere barren waste. Not a furrow had ever been turned upon them. Soon after they were acquired Mrs. Carr left her home in Sacramento, came to Pasadena, set men to breaking up the soil on this place, built a temporary habitation for her family, laid out these now beautiful grounds, and from that time, with great energy, carried forward her improvements. At that time Mrs. Carr was the Assistant State Superintendent of the Public Schools of California. For years she had been associated with her husband in educational work

On many occasions during this period had women of culture and ability sought her advice, with reference to earning a livelihood for themselves. In reply she had often urged the obtaining a support from the soil, in some one of the many pleasant departments of horticulture possible in California. Most, if not all of them, had lacked the courage to make the attempt. In the development of her forty acres, therefore, she determined to furnish them a practical illustration of the views she had advocated And, to day, Carmelita, with its many different lines of production, is her noble, self-denying answer to a multitude of women desirous of learning how they may support themselves, and provide something for the future.

Mrs. Carr has endeavored to exemplify what a woman may accomplish on a few acres of land in one, two, three, and four years, with much or with little capital. The particulars of her effort are as interesting as useful, but must be excluded from this volume. Suffice it to say that Carmelita is, in many of its departments, a splendid object-lesson for women having families of children to support. It is a favorite project in the mind of Mrs.

Carr to some day convert Carmelita into a State school of horticulture for women. May she live to do it!

Of Pasadena itself all the world has heard; how attractive it is; how delighfully situated, at the head of the fair San Gabriel Valley; and how, in the space of a few swift years, it sprang from a desert state into square miles of vineyards and orchards of all kinds. It is the gem of Southern California towns, and will long remain such. Tourists can find no lovelier place to winter in. But the man of limited means, seeking a home there for his family, would be shut out by the high price of land.

A little farther away down the valley stands the notable Sierra Madre Villa, a view of which adorns a preceding page. The praise of its situation, and of its delights as a resort, have been heralded all over the Union. Very seldom does a tourist to Los Angeles omit this villa, or Pasadena, from his trip. Immediately back of the premises rise the frowning summits of the Sierra Madre Mountains. Gracing the long broad slope in front of the building are shining orange-groves and thrifty vineyards. From its tower are to be seen leagues of the charming vale of San Gabriel, a spot more or less highly cultivated for a century past.

*Another undertaking by women which drew her attention was the flower festival in Los Angeles, which was organized to gather money for charitable purposes.*

*The second part of her book is entitled "Up and Down in Oregon and Washington." It is organized in much the same way as the first section and provides the same kind of material.*

*Her book as a whole is informative, and she sometimes points out unusual features of the regions she visited. Her descriptions, however, are often too brief and only present sketchy evidence. They raise interesting questions and suggest directions for research.*[2]

1. Emma Adams, p. 1.
2. For a woman's account of her experience in farming life in California, see Eliza Farnsham, *op. cit.*

# References

Billington, Ray Allen. *America's Frontier Heritage* (Hinsdale, Illinois: the Dryden Press), 1966.

Cleland, Robert Glass ed. *Apron Full of Gold: the Letters of Mary Jane Mecquier from San Francisco; 1849-1856.* (San Marino: The Huntington Library), 1949.

Cott, Nancy ed. *Roots of Bitterness; Documents of the Social History of American Women.* (New York: E. P. Dutton & Co., Inc., a Dutton Paperback), 1972.

Faragher, John and Christine Stansell. "Women and their Families on the Overland Trail to California and Oregon, 1842-1867", *Feminist Studies* vol. II (1975), 150-166.

Farnsham, Eliza. *California In-Doors and Out; or, how we farm, mine and live generally in the Golden State.* (New York: Dix, Edwards and Co.), 1856.

Cressley, Gene M. and Howard R. Lamar. "A Shrinking Frontier?" in *The American Issues Forum: a National Bicentennial Discussion.* Voice of America, 1976.

Jacobs, Victoria. *Diary of a San Francisco Girl.* (Santa Monica: Norton B. Stern, Publisher), 1974.

Palmer, Louise. "How we Live in Nevada." *Overland Monthly,* II (May 1969), 457-462.

Paul, Rodman. *Mining Frontiers of the Far West, 1848-1880.* (New York, Chicago, Toronto, London: Holt, Rinehart and Winston), 1963.

Reinhardt, Richard. "On the Brink of the Boom: Southern California in 1877 as witnessed by Mrs. Frank Leslie." *California Historical Society Quarterly,* vol. 52 (1973), 64-79.

Richie, Elinor. *Eminent Women of the West.* (Berkeley: Howell North Books), 1975.

Royce, Sarah. *A Frontier Lady; Recollections of the Gold Rush and Early California.* Ed. R. H. Gabriel. (New Haven: Yale University Press), 1932.

Shepperson, Wilbur S. *Restless Strangers: Nevada's Immigrants and their Interpreters.* (Reno: University of Nevada Press), 1970.

*Territorial Enterprise Extra,* containing a full account of "Frank Leslie" and wife. Virginia City, July 14, 1878.

Wheat, Carl ed. *The Shirley Letters from the California Mines, 1851-1852.* (New York: Ballantine Books, a Comstock edition), 1971.

# Further Reading

Writings on Women and on Conditions in California,
Nevada and Arizona, 1849-1900.

Abbott, Carslisle. *Recollections of a California Pioneer.* (New
York: the Neale Publishing Company), 1917.

Adams, Ward R. *History of Arizona,* 4 vol., under the supervision
of Richard Sloan. (Phoenix: Record Publishing Company),
1930.

Aikman, Duncan. *Calamity Jane and the Lady Wildcats.* (New
York: Ballantine Books, a Comstock edition), 1973.

Arnold, Oren. "Arizona's Aunt Adaline", *Arizona Quarterly,* vol. 2
no. 3 (1946), 5-15.

Asbury, Herbert. *The Barbary Coast.* (New York: Ballantine
Books, a Comstock edition), 1973.

Athearn, Robert. *Westward the Briton.* (Lincoln: University of
Nebraska Press), 1971.

Atherton, Gertrude. *California; an Intimate History.* (New York
and London: Harpers and Brothers Publishers), 1914.

Bancroft, Hubert. *The Works of Hubert H. Bancroft:*
vol 23: *History of California,* vol. vi: *1848-1859*
vol 24: *History of California,* vol. vii: *1860-1890*
vol 25: *History of Nevada, Colorado and Wyoming*
vol 27: *History of Arizona and New Mexico, 1530-1888.*
(San Francisco: the History Company Publishers),
1888-1890.

Barr, Pat. *A Curious Life for a Lady.* (New York: Ballantine Books,
a Comstock edition), 1972.

[335]

Bartlett, Richard A. *The New Country. A Social History of the American Frontier, 1776-1890.* (London, Oxford, New York: Oxford University Press), 1976.

Beadle, J.H *Western Wilds, and the Men who Redeem them.* (Houston: T.N. James and Company), 1879.

Bean, Walter. *California: an Interpretive History* (New York: McGraw-Hill Book Company), 1968.

Beard, Mary. *Woman as Force in History.* A Study in Tradition and Realities. (New York: Collier Book), 1973.

Beasley, Delilah. *The Negro Trail Blazers of California* (Los Angeles) 1919.

Bedunnah, Gary. *A History of the Chinese in Nevada, 1855-1904.* A thesis. (Reno: University of Nevada Press), 1966.

Bell, Horace. *On the Old West Coast; being the Reminiscences of a Ranger* ed. Lanier Bartlett. (New York: William Morrow & Co), 1930.

Bell, Major Horace. *Reminiscences of a Ranger, or Early Times in Southern California* (Los Angeles, Mathes, Printers), 1881.

Berry, Edna. *The Bushes and the Berrys.* (Los Angeles), 1941.

Bettelmann, Otto. *The Good Old Days—They Were Terrible!* (New York: Random House), 1974.

Billington, Ray Allen. *The Far Western Frontier (1830-1860).* (New York: Harper & Row, a Harper Torchbook), 1962.

Billington, Ray Allen. *Westward Expansion: a History of the American Frontier,* (New York: the Macmillan Co), 1967.

Boehringer, Louise. "Josephine Brawley Hughes—Crusader, State Builder", *Arizona Historical Review,* vol. 2 no. 4 (January 1930), 98-107.

Boehringer, Louise. "Mary Elizabeth Post: High Priestess of Americanization",*Arizona Historical Review,* vol. 2, no. 2 (July 1929), 92-100.

Borthwick, J.L.B. *Three Years in California* (Edinburgh and London: William Blackwood & Son), 1857.

Bosqui, Edward. *Memoirs of Edward Bosqui.* (Oakland: the Holmes Book Company) 1952.

Bowman, J.M. "Prominent Women of Provincial California", *The Historical Society of Southern California Quarterly,* vol. xxxi, no. 2 (June 1957), 152-165.

Braly, John Hyde. *Memory Pictures: an Autobiography.* (Los Angeles: the Neuner Company), 1912.

# Further Reading

Brown, Dee. *Women of the Wild West.* (London and Sydney: Pan Books), 1975.

Bullough, Vern L. *The History of Prostitution.* (New Hyde Park, New York: University Books), 1964.

Calhoun, Arthur W. *A Social History of the American Family from Colonial Times to the Present,* 3 vol. (Cleveland: the Arthur H. Clark Company), 1918.

*California as it is.* Written by 70 of the leading editors and authors of the Golden Gate for the *Weekly Call.* (San Francisco Call Company), 1882.

Carr, John. *Pioneer Days in California*—History and Personal Sketches. (Eureka, California: Times Publishing Company, Book and Job Printers), 1891.

Christman, Enos. *One Man's Gold. The Letters and Journals of a Forty-Niner.* (New York: Mc Graw-Hill Book Company Inc.), 1930.

Clark, Henry. "Their Pride, their Manners and their Voices: Sources of the Traditional Portrait of the Early Californians", *California Historical Society Quarterly,* 53(1974), 71-82.

Cleland, Robert Glass. *From Wilderness to Empire*—a History of California, 1542-1900 (New York: Alfred A. Knopf), 1944.

Clum, John P. "Nellie Cashman", *Arizona Historical Review,* vol. 3 no. 4 (January 1931), 9-35.

Cole, William. *California: its Scenery and Climate, Productions and Inhabitants* (New York: Irish-American Office), 1871.

Cone, Mary. *Two Years in California.* (Chicago: S.L. Griggs and Company), 1876.

Coolidge, Mary R. "Jane Fourr, a Pioneer Mother, 1854-1942", *Arizona Quarterly* vol. 1, no. 3 (1945), 27-33.

Cotton, Chas S. *Early Days in Nevada* (Cowansville: Cotton's Cooperative Publishing Co., Inc.), 1912.

Davie, John L. *My Own Story.* (Oakland: the Post Enquirer Publishing Company) 1931.

Davis, H.P. *Gold Rush Days in Nevada City.* (Nevada City, California: Berliner and McGinnis), 1948.

Davis, Reda. *California Women: a Guide to their Politics, 1885-1914.* (San Francisco: California Scene), 1957.

Davis, Sam ed. *The History of Nevada,* 2 vol. (Reno and Los Angeles: the Elms Publishing Company), 1913.

Debouzy, Marianne. "La femme americaine" dans *Histoire Mondiale de la Femme* ed. Pierre Grimal, 4 vol. (Paris: Nouvelle Librairie de France), 1966.

Dexter, E. Hersey. *Early Days in California* (Denver: Tribune Republican Press), 1866.

Dick, Everett ed. *Tales of the Frontier*. (Lincoln: University of Nebraska Press, a Bison Book), 1963.

Dornin, George. *Thirty Years Ago, 1849-1879*. (Berkeley), 1879.

Drago, Harry. *Notorious Ladies of the Frontier*. (New York: Dodd, Mead and Company), 1969.

Dunlop, Richard. *Doctors on the American Frontier*. (New York: Ballantine Books, a Comstock edition), 1975.

Duniway, Abigail Scott. *Path Breaking. An Autobiographical History of the Equal Suffrage Movement in the Pacific Coast States*. (New York: Schocken Books), 1971.

Eaton, W. Clement. "Frontier Life in Southern Arizona, 1858-1861", *The Southwestern Historical Quarterly*, vol. xxxvi, no. 3 (January 1933), 173-192.

Eblen, Jack W. "An Analysis of Nineteenth Century Frontier Populations", *Demography*, vol. 2 (1965), 399-413.

Elliott, Russell ed. "Letters from a Nevada Doctor to his Daughter in Connecticut, 1881-1891", *Nevada Historical Society Quarterly* vol. 1, no. 1 (September 1957), 15-31.

Elliott, Russell. *History of Nevada*. (Lincoln: University of Nebraska Press), 1972.

Ferguson, Charles. *The Experiences of a Forty-Niner during Thirty-Four Years' Residence in California and Australia* (Cleveland: the Williams Publishing Company), 1888.

Fitzgerald, O.P. *California Sketches*. (Nashville: Southern Methodist Publishing House), 1887.

Flexner, Eleanor. *Century of Struggle. The Woman's Rights Movement in the Unived States* (Cambridge, Massachusetts: the Belknap Press of Harvard University Press), 1968.

Fohlen, Claude. *La vie Quotidienno au Far West, 1860-1870*. (Paris: Hachette Litterature ), 1974.

Forbes, Robert H. *The Penningtons, Pioneers of Early Arizona* (the Arizona Archeological and Historical Society), 1919.

Fowler, William. *Woman on the American Frontier*. (Hartford: S.S. Scranton and Company), 1879.

## Further Reading

Frazier, Mrs. *Reminiscences of Travel from 1855 to 1867.* (San Francisco), 1868.

Gallego, Hilario. "Reminiscences of an Arizona Pioneer", *Arizona Historical Review*, vol. 6 no. 1 (January 1935), 68-84.

Gardiner, Howard. *In Pursuit of the Golden Dream; Reminiscences of San Francisco and the Northern and Southern Mines, 1849-1857.* ed. Dale Morgan. (Stoughton, Massachusetts: Western Hemisphere Inc.), 1970.

Gentry, Curt. *The Madams of San Francisco.* (New York: Ballantine Books, a Comstock edition), 1973.

Gilmore, Ray and Gladys Gilmore. *Readings in California History (New York: Thomas Y. Crowell Company), 1966.*

Goldman, Marion, "Prostitution and Virtue in Nevada", *Society* (November-December 1972), 32-38.

Goode, Kenneth. *California's Black Pioneers—A Brief Historical Survey* (Santa Barbara, California: MacNally and Loft Publishers), 1974.

Gray, James H. *Red Lights on the Prairies.* (New York: New American Library, a Signet Book), 1973.

Greener, William S. *The Bonanza West. The Story of Western Mining Rushes, 1849-1900.* (Norman: University of Oklahoma Press), 1963.

Grey, William. *A Picture of Pioneer Times in California* (San Francisco: W.M. Hinton & Company), 1881.

Hafen, Leroy, W. Eugene Hollon, Carl Cole Rister. *Western America: the Exploration, Settlement and Development of the Region beyond the Mississippi.* (Englewood Cliffs: Prentice Hall Inc.), 1970.

Hahn, Emily. *Once upon a Pedestal.* (New York: New American Library, a Mentor Book), 1975.

Hall, Dr. J. *Travels and Adventures in Sonora* (Chicago: the J.M.W. Jones Stationery and Printing Company), 1881.

Hall, Sharlot M. "Story of Early Arizona" in *Women Tell the Story of the Southwest,* ed. Mattie Woten. (San Antonio: the Naylor Company), 1940.

Hall, Thomas Wakeman, *Recollections of a Grandfather.* Beinecke Library, Yale University.

Hamilton, Patrick. *The Resources of Arizona* (San Francisco: A.L. Bancroft and Company, Printers), 1884.

Hartman, Mary and Lois Banner. *Clio's Consciousness Raised. New Perspectives on the History of Women.* (New York: Harper & Row; a Harper Torchbook), 1974.

Hayes, B. *Pioneer Notes from the Diaries of Judge Benjamin Hayes, 1849-1875.* (Privately Printed at Los Angeles), 1929.

Hazzlett, Fanny G. "Historical Sketches and Reminiscences of Dayton, Nevada" *Nevada Historical Society Papers,* 1921-1922, 3-93.

Hill, Myles and John Goff. *Arizona past and Present.* (Cave Creek, Arizona: Black Mountains Press), 1970.

Hiltzinger, John. *Treasure Land; A Story.* (Tucson: published by the Arizona Advancement Company), 1897.

Hine, Robert. *The American West. An Interpretive History.* (Boston: Little, Brown and Company), 1973.

Hislop, Herbert. "An English Pioneer in Arizona: the Letters of Herbert R. Hislop", *The Kiva,* vol. 25, no. 2 (December 1959, 1-23 (February 1960), 23-26, 4 (April 1960), 33-49.

Hittell, F. *History of California.* (San Francisco: N.J. Stone and Company), 1897.

Hogeland, Ronald W. ed. *Women and Womanhood in America.* (Lexington, Massachusetts: Heath & Co), 1973.

Hollingsworth, Harold H. and Sandra Myles ed. *Essays on the American West.* (Austin and London: University of Texas Press), 1969.

Hollon, W. Eugene. *The Southwest, Old and New.* (New York: Alfred A. Knopf), 1961.

Hulse, James W. *The Nevada Adventure—A History.* (Reno: University of Nevada Press), 1965.

Humphrey, Grace. *Women in American History.* (Freeport, New York: Books for Libraries Publishers), 1968.

Hunt, Rockwell. *California in the Making.* (Caldwell, Idaho: the Caxton Printers ), 1953.

Hunt, Rockwell, and Nellie Sanchez. *A Short History of California* (New York: Thomas Y Crowell Company), 1929.

Irvine, Leigh ed. *A History of the New California: its resources and people* 2 vol. (New York, Chicago: the Lewis Publishing Company), 1905.

Johnson, Dorothy M. *Some Went West.* (New York: Dodd, Mead and Company), 1965.

## Further Reading

Keen, Effie R. "Lola Oury Smith", *Arizona Historical Review*, vol. iv, no. 4 (January 1932), 20-22.

Kelly, Geo M. ed. *Legislative History, Arizona, 1864-1912*. 1926.

Kelly, G. Wells ed. *First Directory of Nevada Territory* (Los Gatos, California: the Talisman Press), 1962.

Kenderdine, T.S. *California Revisited, 1858-1897*. (Newton, Pennsylvania), 1898.

Klose, Nelson. *A Concise Study Guide to the American Frontier*. (Lincoln: University of Nebraska Press), 1964.

Kraditor, Aileen S. *Up from the Pedestal* (Chicago: Quadrangle Books), 1968.

Kuelthau, Margaret. "Arizona's Mollie Monroe—Calamity's Counterpart", *Tucson Daily Citizen*, 16 October 1973, p. 48.

Lacour-Gayet, Robert. *La Vie Quotidienne aux Etats-Unis, 1830-1860*. (Paris: Hachette), 1958.

Lamar, Howard. *The Far Southwest, 1846-1912; a Territorial History*. (New Haven and London: Yale University Press), 1966.

Lavender, David. *California: Land of New Beginnings*. (New York: Harper & Row Publishers), 1972.

Lecouvreur, Frank. *From East Prussia to the Golden Gate*. (New York and Los Angeles; Angelina Book Concern), 1906.

Lerner, Gerda. *The Woman in American History*. (Menlo Parks, California; Don Mills Ontario, London: Addison-Wesley Publishing Company), 1971.

Lewis, Flannery. *Suns go down*. (New York: the Macmillan Company), 1937.

Lewis, Oscar. *The Big Four: the Story of Huntington, Standford, Hopkins, and Crocker, and of the Building of the Central Pacific*. (New York: Alfred A. Knopf), 1951.

Lewis, Oscar. *Bonanza Inn*. (New York: Ballantine Books, a Comstock edition), 1971.

Lillard, Richard. *Desert Challenge; an Interpretation of Nevada* (Lincoln: University of Nebraska Press), 1942.

Lyman, George D. *John Marsh Pioneer - the Life Story of a Trail Blazer on Six Frontiers* (New York: Charles Scribner's Sons), 1930.

Lyman, George. *The Saga of the Comstock Lode*. (New York: Ballantine Books, a Comstock edition), 1971.

[341]

Lockwood, Frank C. *Pioneer Days in Arizona*. (New York: the Macmillan Company), 1932.

Mack, Effie Mona. *Nevada: a History of the State from the Earliest Times through the Civil War*. (Glendale, California: the Arthur Clarke Company), 1936.

Mac Kee, Irving ed. *Alonzo Delano's California Correspondence*. (Sacramento: Book Collectors Club), 1952.

Major, Mabel, and T.H. Pearce, *Southwest Heritage*. (Albuquerque, New Mexico Press), 1972.

Margo, Elizabeth. *Taming the Forty-Niner*. (New York and Toronto: Rinehart and Company, Inc.), 1955.

Marshall, Mrs. A.J. *The Autobiography of Mrs. A.J. Marshall* (Pine Bluffs, Arkansas Adams Wilson Printing Company), 1897.

Marston, Anna Lee ed. *Records of a California Family* - Journals and Letters of Lewis C. Gunn and Elizabeth Le Breton Gunn. (San Diego, 1928).

McClellan, Guy. *The Golden State. A History of the Region West of the Rocky Mountains*. (Philadelphia: William Flint and Company), 1876.

Mc Clintock, James. *Arizona: Prehistoric-Aboriginal-Pioneer-Modern* (Chicago: the S.J. Clarke Publishing Company), 1916.

Mc Dermott, John Francis ed. *Travelers on the Western Frontier*. (Urbana,: Chicago, London: University of Illinois Press), 1970.

McWilliams, Carey. *North from Mexico: the Spanish-speaking People of the United States* (New York: Greenwood Press Publishers), 1968.

Miller, Ronald. *Shady Ladies of the West*. (Los Angeles: Westernlore Press), 1964.

Morgan, T. *California Sketches*. (D. Edward & Co, Towyn), 1898.

Mowry, Silvester. *Arizona and Sonora. The Geography, History and Resources of the Silver Region of North America*. (New York: the Mowry Mines Co), 1904.

Newton, John. *Memoirs of John Marsh all Newton*, 1913. Beinecke Library, Yale University.

Nunis, Doyce B. Jr. "Kate Douglas Wiggin: Pioneer in California Kindergarten Education", *California Historical Society Quarterly*, vol. 41 (1962), 291-307.

# Further Reading

Nye-Starr, Kate. *A Self-sustaining Woman, or the Experience of Seventy-two Years*. (Chicago: Illinois Printing and Binding Company), 1888.

Olmsted, John. *A Trip to California in 1868*. (New York: Trow's Publishing and Bookbinding Company), 1880.

Ostrander, Gilman. *Nevada: the Great Rotten Borogh, 1859-1864*. (New York: Alfred A. Knopf), 1966.

Pare, Madeline. *A Students' Guide to Localized History*. (Columbia University: Teachers College Press), 1969.

Paul, Rodman. *California Gold*. (Lincoln: University of Nebraska Press, a Bison Book), 1969.

Paul, Rodman ed. *A Victorian Gentlewoman in the Far West: Reminiscences of Mary Hallock Foote*. (San Marino: the Huntington Library), 1972.

Paxton, Frederick. *History of the American Frontier, 1763-1893*. (Boston: Houghton Mifflin Company), 1934.

Peck, Anne. *The March of Arizona History*. (Tucson: Arizona Silhouettes) 1962.

Pennoyer, Sheldon ed. *This Was California*. (New York: G.P. Putnam's Sons), 1938.

Phillips, D.C. *Letters from California*. (Springfield: Illinois State Journal Company), 1877.

Ray, Grace Ernestine. *Wily Women of the West*. (San Antonio: the Naylor Company), 1972.

Pitt, Leonard. *The Decline of the Californios*. (Berkeley: University of California Press), 1971.

Powell, John. *The Land of Silver*. 1876 Beinecke Library, Yale University.

Quille, Dan de. *The Big Bonanza*. (New York: Alfred A. Knopf), 1964.

Rice, Harvey. *Letters from the Pacific Slope*. (New York: D. Appleton & Co), 1870.

Rieupeyrout, Jean-Louis. *Histoire du Far West*. (Paris: Tchou), 1967.

Ringgold, Jennie. *Frontier Days in the Southwest - Pioneer Days in Old Arizona* (San Antonio: the Naylor Company), 1952.

Rolle, Andrew. *California — a History*. (New York: Thomas Y. Crowell Company), 1969.

Roske, Ralph J. *Everyman's Eden; a History of California*. (New York: the Macmillan Company), 1968.

Ross, Nancy Wilson. *Westward the Women.* (New York: Ballantine Books, a Comstock edition), 1972.

Sargent, Grace Tompkins. "Forgotten Mother of the Sierra: Letters of Julia Tyler Shinn", *California Historical Society Quarterly,* vol. 38 (1959), 157-228.

Sands, Frank. *A Pastoral Prince; the History and Reminiscences of J.W. Cooper* (Santa Barbara), 1893.

Sargent, Shirley. *Pioneers in Petticoats: Yosemite's Early Women, 1856-1900* (Los Angeles: Trans-Anglo Books), 1966.

Schafer, Joseph ed. *California Letters from Lucius Fairchild* (Madison: State Historical Society of Wisconsin), 1931.

Schmitt, Martin, and Dee Brown. *The Settlers' West.* (New York: Ballantine Books) 1974.

Scott, Anne F. *The American Woman: who was she?* (Englewoods Cliffs, New Jersey, Prentice Hall Inc., a Spectrum Book), 1971.

Scrugham, James ed. *Nevada — a Narrative of the Conquest of a Frontier Land,* 3 vol., (Chicago and New York: the American Historical Society Inc.), 1935.

Shaw, Hon. D.A. *Eldorado, or California as seen by a Pioneer, 1850-1900.* (Los Angeles: B.R. Baumgardt & Co), 1900.

Sinclair, Andrew. *The Emancipation of the American Woman.* (New York: Harper & Row, Harper Colophon Books), 1965.

Skinner, Emory Fiske. *Reminiscences.* (Chicago: Vestal Printing Company), 1908.

Smith, Mrs. Gregory. *Notes of Travel in Mexico and California* (St Albans, Vermont: printed at the Messenger and Advertiser office), 1886.

Smith, Page. *Daughters of the Promised Land — Women in American History* (Boston: Little, Brown & Co), 1970.

Smuts, Robert. *Women and Work in America.* (New York: Schocken Books), 1974.

Sprague, William. *Women and the West: a Short Social History* (Boston; the Christopher Publishing House), 1940.

Stafford, Mollie. *The March of Empire through three decades,* embracing sketches of California History. (Geo Spaulding & Company, General Printers), 1884.

## Further Reading

Staples, Mary Pratt. *Reminiscences, 1850-1862.* (circa 1886) Bancroft Library, the University of California at Berkeley.

Starr, Levin. *Americans and the California Dream, 1858-1915.* (New York: Oxford University Press), 1973.

Stewart, Patricia. "Sarah Winnemucca", *Nevada Historical Society Quarterly* vol. xiv (Winter 1971), 23-38.

Still, Bayard ed. *The West - Contemporary Records of America's Experience across the Continent,* 1607-1890 (New York: Capricorn Books); 1961.

Townley, Carrie Miller. "Helen J. Stewart: First Lady Of Las Vegas", *Nevada Historical Society Quarterly,* vol. xvi, no. 4 (Winter 1973), vol. xvii, (Spring 1974), 3-32.

Twain, Mark. *Roughing It.* (New York: New American Library, a Signet Book), 1962.

Wagoner, Jay J. *Arizona Territory, 1863-1912: a Political History* (Tucson: the University of Arizona Press), 1970.

Walker, Franklin. *San Francisco's Literary Frontier.* (New York: Alfred A. Knopf), 1939.

Wallace, Andrew ed. *Pumpelly's Arizona* (Tucson: the Palo Verde Press), 1965.

Wallace, Andrew ed. *Sources and Readings in Arizona History* (Tucson: Pioneers' Historical Society), 1965.

Weed, Joseph. *A View of California as it is.* (San Francisco: Byron & Wright Publishers), 1874.

Wells, C.M. *Three Years' Wanderings of a Connecticut Yankee in South America Africa, Australia and California* (New York: American Subscription Publishing House), 1859.

Whipple-Haslam, Mrs Lee. *Early Days in California - Scenes and Events of the '50s as I remember them.* (Jamestown, California), 1925.

Willey, S.H. *Thirty Years in California* (San Francisco: A.L. Bancroft and Company Printers), 1879.

Wills, Mary. *A Winter in California.* (Norristown, Pennsylvania), 1889.

Wilson, C.E. "From Variety Theater to Coffee Shoppe", *Arizona Historical Review,* vol. vi, no. 2 (April 1935), 3-13.

Wren, Thomas. *A History of the State of Nevada: its Resources and its People* (New York and Chicago: the Lewis Publishing Company), 1904.

Wright, Doris. "The Making of Cosmopolitan California, 1848-1870", *California Historical Society Quarterly*, 19 (1940), 323-341, 20 (1941), 65-79.

Wright, Louis. *Culture on the Moving Frontier*. (New York: Harper & Row, a Harper Torchbook), 1961.

York, Sarah Butler. "Experiences of a Pioneer Arizona Woman", *Arizona Historical Review*, vol. 1 no. 2 (July 1928), 69-75.